LADY ALMINA
AND THE REAL
DOWNTON ABBEY
THE LOST LEGACY OF
HIGHCLERE CASTLE

Lady Fiona Carnarvon married the current Earl of Carnarvon in 1999, and they took over Highclere eight years ago.

LADY ALMINA
AND THE REAL
DOWNTON ABBEY
THE LOST LEGACY OF
HIGHCLERE CASTLE

BY

THE COUNTESS OF CARNARVON

HODDER

First published in Great Britain in 2011 by Hodder & Stoughton
An Hachette UK company

First published in paperback in 2012

I

Copyright © The 8th Countess of Carnarvon 2011

A CIP catalogue record for this title is available from the British Library

ISBN 978 1 444 73084 5

Printed and bound in Great Britain by Clays Ltd, St Ives plc

Hodder & Stoughton policy is to use papers that are natural, renewable
and recyclable products and made from wood grown in sustainable forests.
The logging and manufacturing processes are expected to conform to the
environmental regulations of the country of origin.

Hodder & Stoughton Ltd
338 Euston Road
London NW1 3BH

www.hodder.co.uk

For my husband and son, who I adore,
and my beloved sisters

Contents

Prologue

This is a book about an extraordinary woman called Almina Carnarvon, the family into which she married, the Castle that became her home, the people who worked there, and the transformation of the Castle when it became a hospital for wounded soldiers during the First World War.

It is not a history, although it is set against the exuberance of the Edwardian period, the sombre gravity of the Great War and the early years of recovery after the conflict.

It is neither a biography nor a work of fiction, but places characters in historical settings, as identified from letters, diaries, visitor books and household accounts written at the time.

Almina Carnarvon was an enormously wealthy heiress, the illegitimate daughter of Alfred de Rothschild. She was contracted in marriage to the 5th Earl of Carnarvon, a key player in Edwardian society in Britain. His interests were many and eclectic. He loved books and travel and pursued every opportunity to explore the technologies that were transforming his age. Most famously he discovered the tomb of Tutankhamun with Howard Carter.

Almina was an unbelievably generous woman in spirit and with her money. She was a guest at some of the greatest royal pageants, until – as it did for so many people – the

First World War transformed her life, involving her in running hospitals instead of great house parties and showing her to be an adept nurse and skilled healer.

Highclere Castle is still home to the Earls of Carnarvon. Via its television alter ego, Downton Abbey, it is known to millions of people as the setting for a drama that has thrilled viewers in more than a hundred countries around the world.

Living here for the past twelve years, I have come to know the bones and stones of the Castle. My research has revealed some of the stories of the fascinating people who lived here, but there is so much more. My journey has just started.

The Countess of Carnarvon

I

Pomp and Circumstance

On Wednesday 26 June 1895, Miss Almina Victoria Marie Alexandra Wombwell, a startlingly pretty nineteen-year-old of somewhat dubious social standing, married George Edward Stanhope Molyneux Herbert, the 5th Earl of Carnarvon, at St Margaret's, Westminster.

It was a lovely day, and the thousand-year-old white stone church was crowded with people and overflowing with gorgeous flowers. Some of the congregation on the groom's side might perhaps have remarked that the decorations were a little ostentatious. The nave had been filled with tall potted palm trees whilst ferns spilled from the recesses. The chancel and sanctuary were adorned with white lilies, orchids, peonies and roses. There was a distinct touch of the exotic, combined with the heady scents of English summer flowers. It was an unusual spectacle, but then everything about this wedding was unusual. Almina's name, the circumstances of her birth and most of all her exceptional wealth, all contributed to the fact that this was no typical Society wedding.

The Earl was getting married on his twenty-ninth birthday. His family and title were distinguished and he was slim and charming, if somewhat reserved. He owned houses in London, Hampshire, Somerset, Nottinghamshire and Derbyshire. His estates were grand; the houses were filled with paintings by the Old Masters, objects brought back from trips to the East and beautiful French furniture. Naturally he was received in every drawing room in the country and invited to every party in London, especially where there was an eligible daughter or niece for him to meet. Though they would doubtless have been gracious on such a special occasion, there must have been some inwardly disappointed ladies in the congregation that day.

He arrived with his best man, Prince Victor Duleep Singh, a friend from Eton and then Cambridge. The Prince was the son of the ex-Maharaja of Punjab, who had owned the Koh-i-Noor diamond before it was confiscated by the British for inclusion in the Crown Jewels of Queen Victoria, Empress of India.

The sun poured through the new stained-glass windows, which depicted English heroes across the centuries. The ancient church, which stands next to Westminster Abbey, had recently been refurbished by Sir George Gilbert Scott, the pre-eminent Victorian architect. The church was, in fact, a quintessentially Victorian blend of the traditional and the modern. It was the perfect setting for this marriage of people who came from such different sections of society, but who were each in possession of something the other needed.

As the organist, Mr Baines, struck up the opening chords of the hymn 'The Voice That Breathed o'er Eden', Almina, who had been waiting in the entrance porch, took her first steps. She walked slowly and with as much calm and dignity as she could muster with all those eyes upon her, her gloved hand resting lightly on that of her uncle, Sir George Wombwell. There must have been nerves, but she was excited, too. Her soon-to-be-husband's brother-in-law, Lord Burghclere, had remarked that she was something of a 'naïve damsel', but also that she appeared to be 'head over ears in love' and could barely contain herself in the weeks and days leading up to her wedding day.

Perhaps she took some comfort from the knowledge that she looked exquisite. She was tiny, just over five foot tall, with blue eyes and a straight nose framed by glossy brown hair elegantly styled high on her head. Her future sister-in-law, Winifred Burghclere, described her as 'very pretty, with an immaculate figure and tiny waist.' In the language of the time, she was a veritable 'Pocket Venus'.

She wore a small wreath of orange blossoms under a veil of fine silk tulle. Her dress was by the House of Worth, of Paris. Charles Worth was the most fashionable couturier of the age and was known for his use of lavish fabrics and trimmings. Almina's dress was made of the richest *duchesse* satin with a full court train and draped in a veil of lace caught up on one shoulder. The skirts were threaded with real orange flowers and Almina was wearing a gift from the bridegroom: a piece of very old and extremely rare French lace that had been incorporated into the dress.

The whole ensemble announced Almina's show-stopping arrival on the public stage. She had in fact been presented at Court by her aunt, Lady Julia Wombwell, in May 1893, so she had made her debut, but she had not been invited to the highly exclusive, carefully policed social occasions that followed. Almina's paternity was the subject of a great deal of rumour, and no amount of fine clothes or immaculate manners could gain her access to the salons of the grand ladies who quietly ruled Society. So Almina had not attended all the crucial balls of her debut season, occasions that were designed to allow a young lady to attract the attentions of an eligible gentleman. Despite this, Almina had nonetheless secured a husband-to-be of the highest order, and she was dressed as befitted a woman who was making her ascent into the highest ranks of the aristocracy.

Eight bridesmaids and two pages followed Almina: her cousin, Miss Wombwell, her fiancé's two younger sisters, Lady Margaret and Lady Victoria Herbert, Lady Kathleen Cuffe, Princess Kathleen Singh and Princess Sophie Singh, Miss Evelyn Jenkins and Miss Davies. All the bridesmaids wore cream silk muslin over white satin skirts trimmed with pale blue ribbons. The large cream straw hats trimmed with silk muslin, feathers and ribbons completed a charming picture. The Hon. Mervyn Herbert and Lord Arthur Hay followed, dressed in Louis XV court costumes of white and silver, with hats to match.

Almina had known her bridegroom for nearly a year and a half. They had never spent any time alone, but had met on half a dozen occasions at social gatherings. It was almost certainly not enough time for Almina to realise that the frock coat the Earl had been persuaded to wear on his wedding day was quite different from his usual casual style.

As the young couple stood in front of the altar, the massed family and friends behind them represented a glittering cross-section of the great and the powerful, as well as a smattering of the rather suspect. On the right-hand side sat the bridegroom's family: his stepmother, the Dowager Countess of Carnarvon and his half-brother the Hon. Aubrey Herbert, the Howards, the Earl of Pembroke, the Earls and Countesses of Portsmouth, Bathurst and Cadogan; friends such as Lord Ashburton, Lord de Grey, the Marquess and Marchioness of Bristol. The Duchesses of Marlborough and Devonshire were in attendance, as were Lord and Lady Charteris and the greater part of London Society.

Lord Rosebery, the ex-Prime Minister, was a guest. He had travelled to Windsor Castle just four days previously to give his resignation to the Queen, who then asked Lord Salisbury to form a government. Queen Victoria, who had been a recluse for many years, was not present, but she sent greetings to the young couple. Her connection with the Carnarvons was long-standing: she was godmother to the Earl's youngest sister.

The bride's family and friends were rather different. Almina's French mother, Marie Wombwell, was born Marie Boyer, the daughter of a Parisian banker. It would have been easy to conclude, observing the two, that Almina had inherited her vivacity and style from Marie. Sir George Wombwell, brother of Marie's late husband, had stepped in to give Almina away. The Wombwells were seated next to many representatives of the most influential and fabulously wealthy of the newly ennobled mercantile classes. Here were Sir Alfred de Rothschild, Baron and Baroness de Worms, Baron Ferdinand de Rothschild, Baron Adolphe de Rothschild, Lady de Rothschild, Mr Reuben Sassoon, four other Sassoon cousins, Mr Wertheimer, Mr and Mrs Ephrusi, Baron and Baroness de Hirsch. Both Marie and Sir Alfred had a great many friends in the theatre and the celebrated prima donna, Adelina Patti, now Madame Nicolini was also a guest.

As Almina contemplated her destiny, standing in front of the group of illustrious churchmen who had been drafted in to officiate at her marriage, her hand in that of her new husband's, she might well have felt overawed or nervous at the thought of married life. Perhaps she caught her mother's eye and was reminded of just how far she had come. But then again, she must also have been conscious of the fact that with the marriage contract the Earl of Carnarvon had signed with Alfred de Rothschild, she was protected by a level of wealth so stupendous that it could buy respectability, social acceptance and access to one of the grandest and best-connected families in late-Victorian England. Almina went into St Margaret's the illegitimate daughter of a Jewish banker and his French kept woman, but she emerged, to the strains of Wagner's bridal march from *Lohengrin*, the 5th Countess of Carnarvon. Her transformation was complete.

This remarkable ascent up the social ladder had not been entirely trouble-free. Even Rothschild money couldn't atone for the fact that Mrs Marie Wombwell – widow of the heavy drinker and reckless gambler, Frederick Wombwell and, more importantly, the long-standing confidante of Sir Alfred – was not received in Society.

Almina's childhood was spent between Paris and London, her teenage years in 20 Bruton Street, W1, in the heart of Mayfair. There were also occasional visits to the Wombwells in Yorkshire. Sir George and Lady Julia remained very kind to Marie and her children even after her husband died. The address in Mayfair was excellent, but Marie Wombwell's credentials were not.

She had been a married woman, though estranged from her husband when she met Sir Alfred. Sir Alfred was a leading figure in public life; he had been a director of the Bank of England for twenty years, and was also a bachelor, an aesthete, and a confirmed man about town. He delighted in spending the vast family fortune on a lavish lifestyle that included 'adoration dinners', soirées for the pleasure of his gentlemen friends, at which they could meet the leading ladies of the day.

Marie may have been introduced to Sir Alfred by her father, who knew him through connections in the banking world, or by Sir George and Lady Julia, who spent weekends as his guests at Halton House in Buckinghamshire. Alfred and Marie shared a passion for the theatre and the opera and became close friends, and then lovers. Alfred was a generous companion who provided handsomely for Marie and her daughter. Since Alfred was prepared to settle a vast sum of money on her, Almina was a serious contender in the marriage market. But even Marie could surely never in her wildest dreams have imagined that her daughter would make the leap to the heart of the Establishment.

Apparently, this success rather went to Marie's head. She was quite insistent that the venue for the wedding breakfast should be sufficiently grand to do justice to the occasion, but this presented considerable problems of etiquette. It was traditional for the celebrations to be given at the bride's family home, but that was impossible, since her mother was beyond the pale and her father was, for form's sake, referred to as her godfather. It was Rothschild money that was paying for the magnificent festivities, but they could not be held in a Rothschild house.

Elsie, the 5th Earl's stepmother and prime mover behind the wedding planning, had been fretting over this conundrum for weeks. As she wrote to the Countess of Portsmouth, the Earl's devoted aunt, 'We have a family difficulty. We have neither called upon her [Mrs Wombwell] nor received her, tho' Almina of course has been with us constantly.' With great delicacy, Elsie, who had an instinctive sweetness and had taken Almina under her wing, had been making enquiries amongst such family friends as Lord and Lady Stanhope, hoping to secure the use of a neutral but impressive venue for the wedding breakfast. Various houses were offered but not accepted before, in the end, Mr Astor offered the loan of Lansdowne House on the south side of Berkeley Square, and Marie agreed that this would do very well.

So, after the church service, the guests made their way to the Mayfair mansion. It was a stately house, designed by Robert Adam and built in 1763, with many elegant reception rooms. The entrance hall was filled with hydrangeas; then each room was themed with different flowers. As in St Margaret's, palms and ferns featured prominently in the saloon, where Gottlieb's celebrated orchestra, which had been brought over from Vienna, was playing the latest fashionable waltzes. Drinks were served in one room, the wedding breakfast, complete with a three-tiered cake, in another. Mrs Wombwell greeted guests wearing a dark purple dress, while Elsie, the Dowager Countess of Carnarvon, whose rank naturally dictated that she be first in the receiving line, wore a dress of green and pink shot silk.

The wedding gifts to both bride and groom were carefully catalogued and displayed at the party. From Sir Alfred, Almina had received a magnificent emerald necklace and tiara, jewels befitting her new rank, to be worn when entertaining at Highclere or in town. She was given a vast quantity of beautiful things, from crystal vases to gold scent bottles and endless *objets de virtu*. The bridegroom was presented with equally charming bejewelled ornaments and adornments, from rings to cigarette cases.

After all the worries beforehand, the day passed off without a hitch. If there were mutterings at the elevation of Miss Wombwell, they were muted. Mrs Wombwell behaved impeccably and everyone maintained a discreet silence over the part played by Alfred de Rothschild. In fact, the spectacular wedding was judged to have been one of the most successful events of the Season.

Perhaps the real moment of anxiety for Almina came not when she stepped into the church or Lansdowne House, where she was after all surrounded by familiar faces, but when she was driven away from her old life, her girlhood, and began her journey to Highclere. She must have received some words of encouragement from her mother, surely a kiss and a blessing from her father. But now she was embarking on her first steps as a wife, in the company of a virtual stranger who had so far shown no real inclination to get to know her.

Leaving their guests during the afternoon, the newly married couple were driven by Lord Carnarvon's head coachman, Henry Brickell, across London to Paddington to catch a special train for the country. They were to spend the first part of their honeymoon at Highclere Castle in Hampshire, the grandest of the Carnarvon estates. They had both changed their clothes. The Earl shrugged off his long, formal coat at the earliest opportunity and was now wearing his favourite, much-darned blue jacket. Once out of town, he added a straw hat. Almina was wearing a charming pompadour gauze dress, diamonds and a hat by Verrot of Paris.

The train from Paddington was due to arrive at Highclere Station at 6.30 p.m. Lord and Lady Carnarvon alighted and took their seats in an open landau drawn by a pair of bay horses and driven by the under-coachman. A mile later, the carriage turned in to the lodge gates, winding through arching trees and dark rhododendron bushes. As they passed the Temple of Diana above Dunsmere Lake, a gun was fired from the tower of the Castle. Ten minutes later, the landau arrived at the crossroads in the park and the couple got down from the carriage. A processional arch studded with flowers had been set up over the driveway. The horses were unharnessed by heads of departments from the estate: Mr Hall, Mr Storie, Mr Lawrence and Mr Weigall. Ropes were attached by the farm foreman and the forester foreman, and the couple took their places once again. Twenty men then picked up the ropes to pull the landau beneath the archway and up the hill to the main door of the Castle, accompanied by a lively march from the Newbury Town Band, which had been paid seven guineas for its services.

The Mayor of Newbury was in attendance and would

shortly present His Lordship with a wedding gift on behalf of the people of the local town: an album containing their good wishes on the occasion of his marriage, exquisitely illuminated in the style of a medieval manuscript. It was illustrated with views of Newbury Corn Exchange and Highclere itself, and bound in cream calf's leather with the linked Carnarvon initial C's stamped on the front.

Some of the estate tenants were in the gardens to watch proceedings. They had all been entertained in a marquee by the band and there had also been a tea party given for 330 of the local children. The event had been threatened by thunderstorms, but luckily the weather had cleared in time for both the tea party and the arrival of the bride and groom. It was almost the longest day of the year, and the sun was still strong.

As well as the fee for the band, £1 11s 6d was paid for the attendance of five constables and a donation of £2 was made to the Burghclere bell-ringers, who had been sending out peals of bells from the local church spire ever since the Earl and Countess disembarked from the train.

The red and blue flag proudly displaying the colours of the family's coat of arms flew from the top of the tower, whose delicate turrets and stonework were interspersed with all manner of heraldic symbols and beasts, that seemed to survey the scene.

Drawing up at the heavy wooden door of the Castle, the Earl and his new Countess alighted once again from the carriage and were greeted by Mr Albert Streatfield, the house steward (a position more commonly referred to as that of butler) and Major James Rutherford (the agent who ran the estate) and his wife.

11

What must Almina have thought as she watched the men of Highclere labouring to haul her to her destination? What ran through her mind when she gazed upon this house as its new chatelaine? It was not her first sight of it. She had visited twice before, for the weekend, with her mother. But now she was the Countess of Carnarvon, expected to manage the running of the household and to perform her numerous duties. Everyone at Highclere, whether they worked above or below stairs, on the farm or in the kitchen, had a role to fulfil, and Almina was no different.

It must have felt exhilarating. Almina was an energetic and high-spirited girl, and marriage, motherhood and now service to the Carnarvon dynasty would have looked like a very agreeable destiny to most girls able to imagine themselves in her shoes. She was accustomed to living an indulged life, and had no reason to suspect that she would ever want for anything she desired. She was already very much in love with her new husband. But surely there must have been feelings of trepidation, too.

If she had been in any doubt beforehand, she needed only to glance at the press on the Saturday after her wedding to see that her life would henceforth be lived in public. Then, as now, the weddings of the aristocracy and the rich and famous were eagerly covered by the press. The 'World of Women' column in the *Penny Illustrated* paper carried a full-length portrait of Almina (although in a slip-up she was described as Miss Alice Wombwell in the caption) and described her gown in detail. Almina had passed from almost total obscurity to object of media scrutiny in a moment. With her new status came all sorts of pressures.

Almina wasn't given very long to wonder what lay in

store for her. Lord Carnarvon spent the next few days taking his bride around the park and neighbouring villages to meet the local families, in order that Almina could begin to explore alone and become familiar with her new home. They went to Highclere Church for morning service on the Sunday after they were married. Sir Gilbert Scott had been at work here, as in Westminster. He'd designed and built the church some twenty years previously, at the request of Lord Carnarvon's father, the 4th Earl. And then, business concluded, the couple left for the Continent and the second part of their honeymoon. It was a chance to get to know each other properly, in private, at last. They spent two weeks away before returning to Highclere, when normal life resumed. Except that, for Almina, nothing would ever be the same again.

2

Welcome to Highclere

When Almina stepped from the carriage outside her new home on that early summer day, her arrival had been much anticipated for months. A web of rumour and gossip had circulated all sorts of information and speculation about the Earl's young bride amongst the people living at Highclere.

The life of the great houses at the end of the nineteenth century was still marked by structures and patterns unchanged for centuries. Families served for generations. Highclere Castle was the family home of the Earls of Carnarvon, but the Castle was also the servants' Castle, and the family their family. Highclere was a tight ship, captained by Streatfield, the house steward. The reality, as everyone knew, was that Countesses come and Countesses go. It wasn't that Almina was without influence or importance, but she did need to grasp, quickly, that she was only one part of a machine that would long survive her. Part of her initial task on arrival was to understand the history and community that she was becoming a part of.

Highclere Castle lies at a crossroads between Winchester and Oxford, London and Bristol, built on a chalk ridge of high land and guarded by an ancient route between Beacon Hill and Ladle Hill. Just to the south of Highclere is Siddown Hill, topped by an eighteenth-century folly, Heaven's Gate. The views to the north extend beyond Newbury towards the spires of Oxford.

It is an area long praised for its natural beauty. In 1792, just over a hundred years before Almina arrived at Highclere, Archibald Robertson wrote in his topographical survey, 'High Clere Park stands in Hampshire; and for extent, boldness of feature, softened by a mixture of easy swelling lawns, shelving into pleasant vallies, diversified by wood and water, claims the admiration of the traveller, and may be considered as one of the most elegant seats in the country.'

There has been a settlement at Highclere for thousands of years. There is an Iron Age hill fort at Beacon Hill and the land was owned by the bishops of Winchester for 800 years before passing into secular hands and eventually, in the late seventeenth century, to the Herbert family, Earls of Pembroke and ancestors of the Earls of Carnarvon.

The park is a harmonious mix of natural and landscaped features, designed for the 1st Earl of Carnarvon in the eighteenth century by Capability Brown. The different drives wind amongst the contours of the land to hide and reveal the first views of the Castle. Long and short views have been created by skilful planting; everywhere you look there are exotic imported trees, gracious avenues and ornamental follies that direct your eye along some particularly glorious line. It is its own world and, even now, visitors are struck by the strong sense of place, the unity between the land, the Castle and the people who live and work there.

The house in its current incarnation was built for the 3rd Earl by Sir Charles Barry, the architect of the Houses of Parliament. It was a major undertaking. The old Elizabethan brick manor had been remodelled into a Georgian mansion in the late eighteenth and early nineteenth centuries, but all that was to be transformed entirely. The first stone of the new house was laid in 1842. The work took twelve years to complete and, by the end, Highclere Castle, as it was now called, dominated its surroundings completely. It is a statement house, purposeful and confident; it doesn't feel like a place that has grown up over time, been added to and tinkered with. It is much more the product of a single architect's vision. Gothic turrets were absolutely the pinnacle of fashion as early Victorian architecture turned to medieval influences in a backlash against the classical designs of the eighteenth century. The house was intended to impress visitors with the status and good taste of its builders. It has a peculiarly masculine feel about it, an aesthetic that prizes solid style and soaring immensity over prettiness.

Almina and her mother had often visited Alfred de Rothschild's country estate, Halton House in Buckinghamshire, which was completed in 1888. Halton was a different style again: all Baroque fantasy, and so over the top that it embodied what was called, slightly disparagingly, 'le style Rothschild'. She must have been conscious when she looked at Highclere that, although it was only fifty years older than Halton House, its lands and its setting, its gorgeous honey-coloured tower in Bath stone, represented an idea of English tradition that was totally different to anything she had previously known.

Back in October 1866, one particularly illustrious visitor was overcome with delight as he was driven through the park, crying out, 'How scenical, how scenical,' as he approached the Castle.

Benjamin Disraeli, who at the time of this visit was Chancellor of the Exchequer, but who went on to be Prime Minister twice, had caught a specially laid-on train from Paddington to Highclere. He was met and driven by carriage past London Lodge, its gateway arch upheld by classical pillars and surmounted by the Carnarvon coat of arms.

Through groves of rhododendrons and past spreading Lebanon cedars, now 150 years old, Disraeli, who was comfortably wrapped in carriage rugs against the autumn chill, could look around him, full of admiration. Every vista proved enchanting. As the road wound past the Temple of Diana, built over Dunsmere Lake, the highest tops of the Castle's turrets, still more than a mile away, could be glimpsed above the trees. Disraeli noted the curving medieval embankment of the deer park before sweeping around towards the Castle drive. Capability Brown had taken tremendous trouble to construct the last approach. The Castle emerges obliquely in front of the visitor, thereby appearing even larger and more impressive than it actually is. The whole landscape so romantically lent itself to creative thought that the following day, Disraeli and his host, the 4th Earl of Carnarvon, took a very agreeable walk in brilliant sunshine through the grounds, and talked affairs of state.

The 4th Earl, father of Almina's husband, served in politics for some forty years. At the time of Disraeli's visit he was Colonial Secretary, a position that satisfied his great love of travel and took him to Australia, South Africa, Canada, Egypt and New Guinea. Much of the time he travelled on his own yacht, but there were also numerous shorter missions on government business across Europe. He possessed considerable intellectual curiosity and was one of the foremost classical scholars of his generation, translating Homer and Aeschylus as well as Dante. In all, he served in three Conservative cabinets. He was appointed Secretary of State for the Colonies first by Lord Derby, then by Disraeli, and then made Lord Lieutenant of Ireland by Lord Salisbury. He was renowned for his hard work and thoroughness and for being a man of principle, who twice resigned his position, once over Disraeli's handling of the Eastern Question, and later over the thorny issue of Home Rule for Ireland.

The 4th Earl and his Countess pioneered the practice, which soon became a fashionable trend, of giving weekend house parties at the great houses. These were not only social gatherings but also networking opportunities and, thanks to the Earl's prominent part in public life, Highclere was a hub of power.

He was fortunate to have married a woman who turned out to be the perfect political wife. Lady Evelyn was the daughter of the Earl of Chesterfield and the couple married in Westminster Abbey in September 1861, the first time that honour had been extended to a non-royal partnership in many centuries. Sincere, kind, and possessed of quick wits and an instinctive understanding, Lady Evelyn was an asset to her husband. Invitations to Highclere were freely given to men of politics, public officials, intellectuals and travellers. Expertise could be pooled and congenial solutions to difficult problems found more easily whilst strolling in the park or over some excellent brandy and cigars in the Smoking Room, than in the febrile atmosphere of Westminster.

The couple had four children: Winifred, who was born in 1864, George Edward, the son and heir who would go on to marry Almina, who had been born four months before Disraeli's 1866 visit, and two more daughters. Margaret was born in 1870 and, on 30 December 1874, the baby who would be christened Victoria.

Lady Carnarvon never recovered from giving birth to her last child. She lingered for a few days, during which time Queen Victoria made constant enquiries about her health and that of the baby. Victoria had been living in almost total seclusion ever since the death of her beloved Prince Albert fourteen years previously, but she kept herself informed about her friends' lives and, when she heard the news that Lady Carnarvon was unlikely to survive, she expressed a desire to be the child's godmother.

Evelyn rallied briefly but died on 25 January 1875. Her husband was devastated, as was her mother, who had been at her bedside throughout her illness. The diaries of her sister-in-law, Lady Portsmouth, contain a grief-stricken account of the courage and calmness that Evelyn showed as she slipped away. 'How sore my heart is,' she wrote. Lady Carnarvon lay in state in the Library at Highclere and was buried at the family chapel in a beautiful corner of the park.

It was a cruel loss for the whole family. Childbirth was a perilous business, and no one was immune to risk, no matter if they had access to the best medical care available. Winifred was ten, George (who was always known as Porchy, a nickname derived from his courtesy title, Lord Porchester) was eight, Margaret four and little Victoria just three weeks old when their mother died. Although in aristocratic families the children were cared for primarily by a nanny, Lady Carnarvon had been much loved and her children were heartbroken. After her death they were passed between the households of two doting but elderly aunts, a slightly chaotic arrangement that fostered a particularly strong bond between the two eldest children. The loss of his mother at such a very young age may well have contributed to the 5th Earl's sense of emotional self-containment, something that his own son later remarked upon.

For a while the weekend house parties were no more, and Highclere and the Carnarvons went into formal mourning. There was strict etiquette governing mourning in nineteenth-century England, especially in the wake of the Queen's decision to withdraw from public life after Prince Albert's death in December 1861. Special clothes had to be worn and the bereaved were expected to seclude themselves from social life. A widower would wear a black frock coat for up to a year and children wore black for at least six months to mark the death of a parent. Even servants wore black armbands. No lady or gentleman could attend – much less give – a ball for at least a year after the death of a close family member.

But, eventually, the 4th Earl decided that it was time to move on. In 1878 he visited relatives at Greystoke Castle in the Lake District and found a house full of laughter and conversation. It must have felt like a return to life, and it led to a proposal of marriage to his cousin Elizabeth (Elsie) Howard who, at twenty-two, was twenty-five years his junior. They had two sons, Aubrey and Mervyn, during twelve years of very happy marriage. Lord Carnarvon's friend Lady Phillimore wrote to her husband, 'They are happy together, those two, and make sunshine around them.'

There's no doubt that the children's childhood and adolescence were made considerably easier by the arrival of their stepmother, to whom they were close for the rest of her life. Elsie was a motherly figure, and her presence at Highclere meant that Porchy, who had always been a sickly child, once again had somewhere stable to call home. The house could also resume its role as a social and political centre of power.

If Elsie could be indulgent, Porchy's father was quite clear that discipline and diligence were highly desirable qualities in a young gentleman who was bound to inherit significant duties. The 4th Earl loved practical jokes, but he was also driven by a powerful sense of public service, both at Highclere and in office. He expected his son to apply himself. 'A good education is the best heritage we can give our children,' he declared.

But although Porchy discovered a love of books and reading, his 'greatest solace', he did not inherit his father's academic diligence. He opted out of Eton early and briefly considered a career in the Army but, after failing the medical, he set off around the world on his travels. He was fortunate that his father was generous, broadminded and understood his restless spirit perfectly, since he was himself an avid traveller. The 4th Earl was on occasion frustrated by his son's reckless streak, but he appreciated his heir's native intelligence and curious mind; in any case, Porchy continued to receive an education since a tutor travelled with him constantly. He was reasonably fluent in both French and German as well as the classical languages, and also studied mathematics, music and history.

Two years later he went to Trinity College, Cambridge, where the first thing he did was offer to scrape the paint in his room to reveal the original wooden panelling beneath. He loved the town's curiosity shops and was more often found at Newmarket racecourse than in the library. He managed two years of study before buying a 110-foot yacht, the *Aphrodite*, and sailing from Vigo to the Cape Verde islands, from the West Indies to Rio. He heard Italian opera in Buenos Aires and was persuaded not to return through the Magellan Straits, since it was far too perilous at that time of year. His next journey was to South Africa, where he went elephant hunting and got a terrible shock when the elephant turned the tables and chased him up a tree.

He read a vast amount about the countries he visited and learned on his feet, nurturing patience, self-reliance and calm. The practicalities of life at sea meant he had to be one of the team, whether taking the helm when the captain was delirious or helping with surgical operations on board. He usually spent summers in town going to the opera, then went for some shooting at Bretby in Nottinghamshire, another of the Carnarvon estates, or Highclere, where he stayed on into the autumn before dashing off on his travels again. He collected books, paintings and acquaintances in equal measure. He was, despite his family's concern that he should begin to apply himself, thoroughly indulged.

This delightful routine had been interrupted by the 4th Earl's death in June 1890, at his house in Portman Square in London. Porchy had been able to get back from his voyage to Australia and Japan in time to be at his father's bedside. The Earl's health had been failing since 1889, and his friends from all walks of life were moved by his patience. He was said to possess a genius for friendship. General Sir Arthur Hardinge, an old friend and veteran of the Crimean War, wrote of him, 'He was one of the greatest gentlemen I have ever met, and whilst he did not give his confidence easily, when he did, he gave it in full measure.'

His coffin was brought down from London to lie in state in the Library as his first wife's had done. Lady Portsmouth recalled that 'there was a special train from and to London bringing the Queen [Victoria] and Prince [of Wales] to the mortuary chapel. It was a beautiful service by Canon Lydonn . . . I feel sometimes I must have been dreaming, but his last words were "very happy".'

When he died he left six children. His heir, George, Lord Porchester, was now the 5th Earl of Carnarvon.

Succeeding to the title didn't actually mean any immediate change in lifestyle. After his father's funeral and the reading of the will, the new Lord Carnarvon went travelling again, leaving Elsie with Aubrey, Mervyn and his two younger sisters, Margaret and Victoria (who was known as Vera). They all lived between Highclere, Bretby in Nottingham-shire, London, Elsie's own estate, Teversal and a villa in Portofino, Italy, that the 4th Earl had left to his widow.

Winifred, Lord Carnarvon's older sister, had just married the future Lord Burghclere. Lady Portsmouth wrote in her diary, 'dear Winifred has engaged herself to Mr Herbert Gardner – worse luck – a natural son of the late Ld Gardner, but if he cares for her and is well principled and good tempered what more can you wish – she is a sweet dear child and I wish her happy.'

Lord Carnarvon's father had been a prudent as well as a successful man and had safeguarded the financial fortunes of the family. The estates were well managed by trusted staff; there was nothing to keep the new Earl at home against his tastes and inclinations.

Lord Carnarvon was undoubtedly fond of his father – he spoke of him with warmth and respect all his life – but once the arrangements had been made and niceties observed, he was ready to take his inheritance and upgrade an already lavish lifestyle – even more travels, more antiquities purchased, more of everything. His trip to Egypt in 1889 was a particularly significant jaunt since it sparked a lifelong obsession that was going to prove very costly.

Three years later he was, if not broke, then very heavily in debt. Yachts, rare books and art treasures do not come cheap, and the running costs of maintaining a household at Highclere, a London house at Berkeley Square, plus his other estates, was considerable. He owed £150,000: a vast sum, but by no means an unusual one for young men of his class at that time. The Prince of Wales was the most impecunious but extravagant of them all, making it entirely normal for the upper classes to live utterly beyond their means. Lord Carnarvon was careless but he wasn't reckless. He was his father's son, after all, and he knew he had an obligation to protect the patriarchal

– basically feudal – way of life that still existed at Highclere. Whole families depended upon him; and in any case, he didn't want to lose his beloved home. It was time to look for a way to secure his financial future.

3

Almina, Debutante

In August 1893, three months after Almina's presentation at Court, she encountered Lord Carnarvon when they were both guests at one of Alfred de Rothschild's weekend house parties at Halton House. Sir Alfred was very much in the habit of entertaining in spectacular style. He would doubtless have been only too delighted to welcome Lord Carnarvon, who was an excellent shot and had a great collection of anecdotes from his travels, as well as being in possession of one of the grandest titles and estates in the country.

Given that the 5th Earl was also languishing beneath a significant burden of debt, he had seemingly arrived at the conclusion that it would be imprudent to marry without money. And Almina, with her rumoured connections to the Rothschilds, had caught his eye.

They probably met for the first time at the State Ball at Buckingham Palace on 10 July, which Almina attended with her aunt, Lady Julia, and cousin. This was the opening event of the debutantes' Season, and everyone who had been presented went, as well as virtually every Duke, marquess and Earl in the land. Given that Almina was highly unlikely to be invited to any other big social occasions by any of the grander sort of people, this was probably her only chance to attract the attention of a suitor from the upper echelons of Society. She didn't squander it.

Her wardrobe for the Season had been carefully selected after close consultation with her mother and aunt. Almina loved fashion and was lucky enough to have the means to purchase the finest clothes, hats and jewels. There were strict rules about what was appropriate attire at each occasion and her dress for the ball would have been white and relatively unadorned, with minimal jewels and shoulder-length white gloves. Consuelo Vanderbilt, an American heiress who went on to marry the Duke of Marlborough six months after Almina's wedding, was shocked when she came to London as a debutante, having first been presented in Paris. In France the girls wore very demure dresses, but in England it seemed it was the done thing to use a lower neckline so that the girls' shoulders were more exposed.

There were hundreds of debutantes at the palace, all of them nervously aware that they were on display and longing to meet a lovely and eligible man. They sat with their chaperones and their dance cards, a little booklet in which a young man could mark his name against a waltz or a polka. It was a subtly but highly competitive business that could be the making of a girl for life.

Almina was very pretty with beautiful posture, a little Dresden doll of a girl. And she had all the vivacious charm that came from growing up in Paris, the acknowledged capital of refined elegance and luxurious decadence. Lord Carnarvon must have spotted her, perhaps as she was dancing, and made a beeline. Almina would go on to prove herself made of stern stuff, not at all inclined to fits of the vapours, but her heart must have been pounding as she curtseyed to the Earl. There would have been a short conversation, an engagement to dance once, perhaps twice, but no more. It was enough for the two young people to charm each other. When she left Buckingham Palace that night, Almina was excited about the young man she had just met. There was of course nothing she could do except wait to see what might transpire. She might never hear from the Earl of Carnarvon again. But the Earl was taken with this lovely girl, and would have known that — as well as being charming, pretty and fun — Almina had friends in the wealthiest circles in London.

If a young man of good credentials were looking to acquire significant sums, it was natural that his attention should be drawn to some of the fabulously wealthy financiers who had amassed spectacular fortunes during the years of speculation of the 1860s. The Victorian period is sometimes thought of as being one of strict morals and prim behaviour, in all aspects of life, but it was also an age of materialism and wild confidence. The Empire was expanding, and British commercial interests with it. Dizzying amounts of money were made in the City of London by men who were prepared to step in and offer loans to the government or to the East India Company or even to individual entrepreneurs. Sir Alfred de Rothschild was one such man, and he came from a family who had been at the heart of funding the British imperial project for two generations.

Alfred's father was Baron Lionel de Rothschild, who inherited a fortune accumulated in an extraordinarily short time by *his* father, Nathan Mayer de Rothschild. Nathan had arrived in Britain from Germany in 1798; over the next thirty years he established the Rothschilds as the pre-eminent investment bankers in Europe. Baron Lionel continued his father's work and was instrumental in loans of approximately £160 million to the British government over the course of his lifetime, including, in 1876, the £4 million advanced for the purchase of 44 per cent of the Suez Canal shares from the Khedive of Egypt. He cleared a profit on this deal alone of £100,000. His legacy bears tribute to his brilliant judgement and tremendous influence: he was the first Jew to be admitted to the House of Commons, without having to renounce his faith, in 1858.

Alfred was the second of Lionel's three sons. His older brother, Natty, was elevated to the peerage by Queen Victoria in 1885, the first Jewish member of the House of Lords, his younger brother Leopold was more interested in the Turf and was a prominent member of the Jockey Club. Alfred was industrious, but loved the high life as well. He worked at the family bank throughout his life, although he rarely arrived much before lunchtime on any given day. He became a director of the Bank of England at the age of twenty-six, a post he held for the next twenty years. When sent to an international monetary conference by the

British government in 1892, he was the only financier to turn up with four valets, vast quantities of luggage and an impeccable buttonhole.

So by the time Lord Carnarvon went to Halton House for the first time in December 1892, probably to shoot, the Rothschilds were by no means marginal figures. Their willingness to put their vast amounts of money at the service of the Crown, coupled with the family's very generous interest in philanthropic causes, meant that they were accepted figures in Society. Sir Alfred epitomised the social mobility of the Victorian Age.

Alfred's final stamp of approval had been provided by his friendship with His Royal Highness, the Prince of Wales. Alfred had received the education of an English gentleman and had become firm friends with the Prince of Wales at Trinity College, Cambridge. They had a surprising amount in common. They were both of recent German descent, spoke that language as well as French, and yet were part of the English Establishment. They also shared a love of fine food and wine, and a life of pleasure. The difference was that Alfred, unlike the Prince of Wales, could afford it.

Bertie, as he was known to his mother even when he was in his fifties, was kept on a very tight budget by the reclusive and pious Victoria. Periodically he applied to the House of Commons to supply an increase in his living expenses, in return for his assuming some of the tasks that Victoria no longer cared to fulfil. He was always thwarted by his mother, who distrusted him intensely, despite support from various prime ministers, including Gladstone. So the Prince of Wales didn't have enough work to do, and didn't have enough money to pay for his leisure pursuits. He was always in dire need of very wealthy friends, and Alfred was not only very rich and very generous, he was also a scholar, an aesthete, a bachelor, a wit and a sartorialist. The friendship endured for the whole of the Prince of Wales' life.

In fact, Alfred was disparaged more by his own family than by wider society, in particular his older brother's wife, Emma, who thought him frivolous, self-indulgent and eccentric. When Alfred, who never married, began a relationship with Marie Wombwell, a woman who was not only married to another man, but to a man who had been arrested for poaching from his own in-laws, there was strong disapproval. The fact that he maintained Marie in lavish style at one of the most exclusive addresses in fashionable Mayfair, and went on to dote upon Marie's child Almina, was seen as further evidence of his disregard for the dignity of the family.

Whilst the question of Almina's paternity can't be conclusively determined with any certainty, Marie had been estranged from Fred Wombwell for years when Almina was born. He did turn up occasionally. She and Alfred were certainly confidants and lovers, but they were not by any means an established couple.

Marie's background was very respectable. Her father was a Parisian financier and her mother was from a wealthy Spanish family. She grew up in Paris but spent a lot of time in England. Her two sisters both made good marriages to titled English gentlemen, but Marie's marriage was less successful. Frederick Wombwell was the youngest son of a baronet and their wedding was attended by several prominent members of the aristocracy. But Frederick proved to be a bad lot, a drunkard and a thief; although the couple had one son, also called Fred, they were estranged after Fred senior's misdemeanours became too much for Marie to bear. (The hapless Wombwell eventually died, six years before Almina married, thus avoiding any further embarrassment and allowing his brother, Sir George Wombwell, to step in on her wedding day and give her away.)

Marie was a lonely woman when she met Alfred de Rothschild. Still young and attractive, she was marginalised by the fact that her husband was disgraced and she had very little money. Marie must have delighted in the companionship of a man who was happy to spoil her lavishly. Alfred and Marie appear to have enjoyed a good relationship throughout their lives, but there was never any chance of marriage, even after Fred Wombwell died, since Alfred had no desire to give up the freedom of his bachelor status or to marry a Roman Catholic. When Marie's daughter was born, Alfred doted upon her, and although he never formally acknowledged the child as his, Almina's unusual name, which was formed of a combination of her parents', was a reference, albeit a coded one, to the reality of her parentage. Her mother was always known as Mina, to which was simply added the first two letters of her father's name.

By the latter years of the nineteenth century, attitudes to affairs – at least amongst the upper classes – were generally tolerant, so long as discretion was maintained. Adultery was definitely a lesser evil than divorce. Disgrace came in exposure, not in the act, even for women. Although some of the Rothschilds were outraged (evidence, perhaps, of their less well-established status), and Marie was not received by the higher echelons of polite society (not just because of the affair but also, crucially, because of her husband's fall from grace), the relationship flourished in a grey area in which everyone turned a blind eye and politely agreed not to notice.

Almina was educated at home by a governess, as was the custom for girls from upper-middle- and upper-class households. The aim was to ensure she was well read and could fulfil the social skills required 'for the drawing room', which meant music, dancing, singing and sketching. Ordinarily there would also have been French lessons, but Almina already spoke the language fluently, having grown up speaking it with her French family.

Throughout her childhood, whether in Paris or London, Almina received a visit from her 'godfather', Sir Alfred, on her birthday. He always brought excessive presents. Almina got to know her benefactor well, especially when she was older, and was very fond of him. He adored her; and at some point, presumably, Almina must have been told the truth about her birth. It was, after all, an open secret.

By the time she was seventeen she was visiting Halton with her mother on a regular basis. Alfred being Alfred, the atmosphere was exuberant – the whole purpose of the gathering was to have fun. Everything was magnificently excessive. Alfred, who loved music, was fond of conducting the orchestras – which were brought in from Austria to play for his guests – with a diamond-encrusted baton. He had a private circus at which he was the ringmaster. He installed electric lighting so that his guests could properly appreciate his exquisite art collection. Alfred could be frivolous, but he was also a serious collector of artists such as Titian and Raphael. Typically, he was also a great benefactor and a founder trustee of the Wallace Collection. Highclere still has some beautiful Sèvres and Meissen porcelain almost certainly given by Alfred to Almina.

In an atmosphere in which no expense was spared in the pursuit of pleasure and the acquisition of beautiful things, Almina enjoyed herself immensely. She had been spoiled all her life, but now she had a space in which to show off. Good clothes would have been ordered, day dresses and evening wear, hats and gloves in colours to match. The fashion of the 1890s was for corseted waists laced down to almost nothing, shoulders bare in the evenings, masses of lace trims and feathered fans. They were opulent times for the upper classes, and Almina's wardrobe was her arsenal in the battle to attract a suitable husband. Doubtless the proprieties were observed in terms of her dress and her introduction to male company, but Almina certainly attended dances, dinners and concerts, all the regular entertainments in Alfred's weekend home, always chaperoned by her mother, but very much on display. Out of sight of the critical gaze of London Society, Almina could be introduced, under strict conditions, to people that she had no opportunity to meet in town. She flourished and, given that she was petite, beautiful and charming, she began to attract attention.

Sir Alfred let it be known, discreetly, that he was prepared to settle a fortune on his 'goddaughter' on her marriage. Lord Carnarvon had been charmed by Almina at the State Ball in July; on discovering the good news about her prospects, he secured an invitation to a house party she was attending at Halton House in August 1893. They spent the weekend getting to know each other a little better. They were never alone, but flirtation could be managed, discreetly, in the drawing room or strolling in the gardens. She must have been delighted with this handsome, amusing, eligible young noble. Lord Carnarvon could be reserved in big gatherings of people, but he was a man with a knack for making you want to know him better. Almina was, in any case, vivacious enough for both, and there was a definite attraction between them. The courtship took a long time to come to fruition, though. Carnarvon was asked to shoot at Halton in the December after he met Almina, but after that there appears to have been a hiatus. He took off on his travels and left England to winter in warmer climes, as usual, and there is no record of a further meeting until almost a year later, again at Halton, in November 1894. It would seem, however, that whatever the doubts on the Earl's part, or outstanding finer details of the arrangement, they had by then been resolved, because in December 1894, Almina was invited with her mother to spend the weekend at Highclere.

It was a small party: just Almina, Marie and three other friends. Almina must have known that she was on the brink of securing a future as the Countess of Carnarvon. The machinations behind the scenes had all been overseen by her father. The process sparked by Carnarvon's attraction to her person and prospects was drawing to a conclusion. She would have been on tenterhooks when she arrived at the Castle that weekend, aware that her destiny was hanging in the balance. If she was nervous, there is no trace of it in her signature in the Highclere guestbook. The letters flow in perfect copper-plate script, in faded sepia ink, looping gracefully. Almina's handwriting is almost a carbon copy of her mother's, whose name is signed a little further down the page.

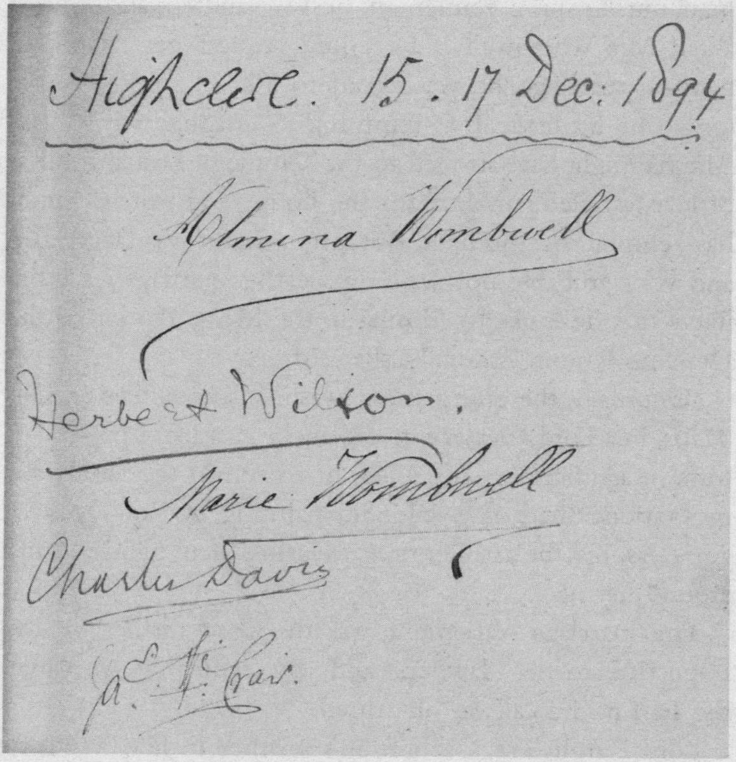
Highclere. 15. 17 Dec: 1894

Almina Wombwell

Herbert Wilton.

Marie Wombwell

Charles Davis

Miss and Mrs Wombwell clearly acquitted themselves perfectly, because that visit was enough to seal the deal. Sometime that weekend, the 5th Earl asked Almina to be his wife. Lord Carnarvon was not a demonstrably romantic man, but he was a gentleman, he was smitten, and, having asked Mrs Wombwell if he could request her daughter's hand in marriage, he was about to ask a beautiful young girl to be his bride. It is tempting to imagine that he and Almina might have strolled to the Temple of Diana, goddess of love, a mile's ramble from the house, and that he might have chosen that moment. But, given that it was December, and very probably not walking weather, perhaps it's more likely that he spoke to Almina in the Music Room, or the Drawing Room. Naturally, she said yes.

Unusually, the engagement was not announced in *The Times*, but Lord Carnarvon did make Almina a present of some magnificent pearls. They had been in the family for generations; there is a splendid painting by Van Dyck of Anne Sophia, the 1st Countess, wearing them lightly strung around her neck.

The marriage settlement was discussed further by the respective parties' lawyers and, on returning to town, the Earl paid a call on Sir Alfred.

Lord Burghclere, Carnarvon's brother-in-law, wrote to his wife Winifred to reassure her on the subject of her brother's marriage. 'Porchy had to see A. Rothschild and it is practically settled about Almina. I am really glad . . . P is not the sort of person to marry merely for money . . . he likes the girl and that being so the rest will follow. You will hear from him yourself no doubt and from the others so I will not enlarge on the topic but I think you may ease your mind on the subject and hope for the very best.'

With everything resolved to his satisfaction, Lord Carnarvon promptly chartered a steam yacht and took off for South America with his great friend Prince Victor Duleep Singh.

Marie and Almina came on a second visit to Highclere, in her fiancé's absence, to get to know her prospective family and home better. They made the acquaintance of Winifred, the Earl's elder sister, and Aubrey, his younger half-brother. They had already met Elsie, the Dowager Countess, who had been extremely kind to them both, and who was equally charming on this occasion. Plans began to be made for the wedding, and Almina was fizzy with excitement. Elsie invited Almina to call on her in town, although notably, Marie Wombwell, while most welcome in the country, was still not to be received in London.

Almina now spent a large proportion of her time in London with Elsie at the Carnarvon town house at 13 Berkeley Square and was apparently every bit as excited as an eighteen-year-old engaged to be married could be. Lord Burghclere, writing to his wife again, said, 'I have seen Elsie, who is very good and a dear about Porch – and A. who seems to live there. I do not think [she] can keep it secret any time – she was literally bursting with it . . . she seems to be head over ears in love and says why can't we be married and go on the yachting cruise together?'

But Almina was not merely excited. She was, unsurprisingly, almost needy in her clinginess and enthusiasm. After a lifetime spent living half in shadows, between worlds, she was clearly relishing the prospect of being more secure, not just socially, but emotionally. Marie and Almina seem to have been extremely close; the fact that Marie was a frequent visitor to Highclere all her life reflects the continued strength of the relationship. But, despite the relative tolerance afforded by her parents' domestic situation, the anxiety and frustration produced by her mother's *demi-mondaine* status and the antics of Marie's late husband, Frederick Wombwell, must have been considerable. Certainly it was obvious enough for Lord Burghclere to comment on. In the same letter he wrote, 'The poor little thing seems desperate . . . (as I told Elsie) for a decent family as well as a husband.' He added, rather sweetly, 'I hope Porch will get on with A 1/50th as much as we do.'

The settlement had been drawn up by the couple's wedding day, but it was not executed until one month later, safely after the happy event had taken place. The three parties were Alfred de Rothschild, Almina Wombwell – now the Countess of Carnarvon – and the 5th Earl. Carnarvon may have been struck by Almina's many lovely qualities and have already developed a fondness for her, but he had also sensed his opportunity to drive a bargain. The Earls of Carnarvon had married heiresses before, thereby acquiring various other estates, and he was fully aware that aristocratic lifestyles frequently needed injections of new money to maintain them.

The first clause stipulated that Alfred de Rothschild would pay £12,000 yearly to Lady Carnarvon, or Lord Carnarvon if she died before him, throughout his life. A Highclere footman was paid £22 a year at that time, so the multiplier would put the value of this annual income at £6.5 million in today's terms. This in addition to the fact that Lord

Carnarvon had asked Alfred to clear his substantial debts before the wedding took place so he could start married life with a clean sheet. Provision was also made for any children born to the couple. Alfred readily agreed to everything and the way was eased for these two young people to live in their gilded world, with every sort of extravagance and delight to amuse them.

4

A Triumph for Her Ladyship

Almina arrived at Highclere as an outsider, but with an enormous sense of excitement and self-confidence. How could she not, when recent events suggested that she had finally managed to combine the social prestige brought by her marriage with the fabulous wealth of her father? Now she was sure of her place and her role, for the first time in her life. She had a title that told her who she was: as of now, Almina Wombwell was the 5th Countess of Carnarvon.

But she was only nineteen and this role, this title, was so much bigger than she was. She was the Countess, but she was also a teenager, a high-spirited girl sure of herself one moment, nervy the next. Moving into Highclere was, if not humbling (Almina was never in her life humbled), definitely

43

overwhelming. Relics of Almina's desire to impress herself upon the place – literally – are still visible all over the Castle. She engraved and stamped her new initials and the Carnarvon coronet on innumerable household accessories, from visitor books and notebooks, to stationery, travelling trunks, linens, menu cards and calling cards.

She brought trunks full of clothes and set about installing her belongings in the bureaus and cupboards of Highclere. She also brought with her one trusted personal servant, Miss Mary Adams, her lady's maid, who helped her to unpack and to settle in. She, alone of all the servants, was allowed to sleep on the same storey as her mistress. Mary was an ally and a friend, the other stranger at Highclere who was her eyes and ears in the servants' hall, a bridge between the staff and their new mistress. In those first few weeks after her marriage, whilst touring the estate, meeting the local gentry and the tenants, finding her feet, Almina grew to rely completely on Mary.

Almina had always been the special child, doted upon; lavished with love by her mother and with money by her father. Her wedding had enshrined her own sense of her importance. But actually, now she had signed up for life as the Countess of Carnarvon, she had to adjust to living in a world in which she was not the centre of the universe. The furniture and the superb paintings didn't really belong to her, or even to her husband, but to the house, to Highclere as a presence in its own right. The Castle, layered with decorations reflecting the taste of its inhabitants over the years, had to be sustained across the generations. When Almina arrived, the Drawing Room was in need of refurbishment. Alfred de Rothschild had given her bolts of green silk as part of his wedding present and she used them to cover the walls. Following his taste, she redecorated in the style of the *ancien régime*, with gilded ceilings and doors. The green silk damask had been inspired by Marie Antoinette's sitting room at Versailles. Meissen porcelain was displayed on the eighteenth-century furniture that Almina loved.

Six weeks after their wedding, Lord Carnarvon left Highclere to go to Scotland to shoot, as was his custom once the grouse season opened on 12 August. Given his newly improved bank balance, he decided to take a month's shooting at a grouse moor near the Balmoral estate. Almina could go with him or not, as she pleased, but there was no possibility that he would alter his routines for her.

She was very keen to go to Scotland with Carnarvon on his shooting trip. It wasn't the custom for ladies to go out with the gentlemen, and nor in fact was Almina particularly interested in riding, but she enjoyed her time with her husband and began to get to know his friends. Lord Carnarvon, who was an excellent shot, took a party of close friends with him: their royal highnesses Prince Victor and Prince Freddie Duleep Singh and James Rutherford, his agent at Highclere, amongst others. It was a very male occasion, and Almina must have felt like an adornment rather than a participant, but it was a magnificent landscape, and a very popular and fashionable place, given the proximity to Balmoral, which was adored by Queen Victoria.

Alfred de Rothschild was elegantly networking behind the scenes in London. He hoped to engineer a visit by the Prince of Wales to Highclere Castle; it would testify to the success of Almina's arrival and give a royal seal of approval. Highclere was renowned as one of the most exciting shoots in England and the Prince knew the food would be exquisite and copious in quantity, the wines the best that Alfred de Rothschild could procure. His private secretary confirmed the dates for the visit.

The royal party had accepted an invitation for the middle of December and Almina threw herself into preparations. Carnarvon continued to travel from one estate to the next with the same band of friends. He went to Bretby, his house in Nottinghamshire, and to Shelford for more shooting. In fact, by 1 December, Lord Carnarvon had shot on more than sixty days since the season opened.

Back at Highclere, Almina set about spending an extraordinary amount of money on redecorating, hiring extra staff and laying in provisions. It is unlikely that she had met the Prince before since, despite the fact he was a great friend of Alfred's, he didn't visit Halton House at the same time as her. Alfred's advice on the delicate details that would ensure a successful visit was most welcome. The two men had been socialising together for years, either at Marlborough House, the Prince's London home, at Halton House or at Seamore Place, Alfred's London house, where the Prince enjoyed the intimate dinners that Alfred delighted in giving. The Prince of Wales was a gourmand and, as the next King and Emperor, tremendously grand. Almina wanted to make sure that every little comfort had been thought about, that all was opulent and perfectly delightful, just as it should be and just as he was used to. She threw money at the situation, spending £360,000 in today's terms on the three-day visit.

The first task was to redecorate a bedroom for the Prince

of Wales. A large bed was commissioned (the Prince was notoriously unable to curb the amount he ate and had a girth of some four foot), and new French furniture, vases and clocks filled the room, which was hung with red silk damask. The adjoining dressing room received the same treatment.

Almina spent £856 13s 9d with W. Turner Lord & Co., who were specialist decorative contractors based in Mount Street, Mayfair. Carpets were bought from Turbeville Smith & Co. for £312 13s 2d. China, lamps and curtains were bought and hired. The billiard table was re-covered; hundreds of the finest beeswax candles were bought.

Extra carriages and horses were hired and special railway carriages were commissioned to bring everything, and everyone, down to Highclere. Records of various gifts give an idea of the extent of the preparations. There were gifts in November to four inspectors at Paddington Station, and all the stationmasters from Reading to Whitchurch, Newbury, Highclere and Burghclere benefited from Almina's determination that no detail was too small and that nothing should go wrong. There were also gifts to postmasters, police superintendents and all the tenant farmers on the estate.

As for the food, which was to be a central part of the whole proceedings, no expense was spared either on the supplies or the kitchen staff. All the meals were rigorously planned in advance, and then Almina dispatched Streatfield to London to hire Savoy chefs and waiters, to order flowers by the armful from Veitch of Chelsea, and to purchase an incredible amount of provisions, wines and champagnes. Streatfield spent £215 4s 4d (approximately £22,000 today) on meat, chickens, eggs, fruit, and chocolates from Charbonnel.

The stoical Streatfield was a loyal retainer and well used to carrying out orders without so much as a raised eyebrow. In private, he might nonetheless have looked somewhat askance at all this expense. He had been the house steward at Highclere for eight years and had seen a fair few entertainments for the great and the good in his time, but the 4th Earl's taste in party-giving had not been on the scale of Almina's. And, of course, Streatfield's shopping bill for the weekend was more than four times his annual salary, a fact he surely cannot have failed to notice.

When the day of the visit finally arrived, Almina herself wrote the menus for that night, in French, as always. The placement of guests at dinner had taken some time to arrange and her clothes had been planned in advance with Adams. Five or six different outfits might be needed each day. The bare minimum at such an occasion was a dress for the morning, one for walking in the afternoon, a tea dress and then evening clothes.

Almina stood next to her husband, near the iron-studded walnut door of Highclere Castle, to greet the Prince of Wales as he alighted from the carriage. As she dropped into a deep curtsey, Almina hoped that she had done everything in her powers to provide amusement and entertainment for him. The Castle loomed up behind them in the low winter light. Inside, it was lit by over 150 oil lamps, and candles provided a warm glow around the galleries and in the new Drawing Room.

The Earl and Countess of Carnarvon had given a great

deal of thought to the question of their other guests. It was usual to invite both local friends of the Prince of Wales and some of his familiar Marlborough set, whose company he clearly enjoyed. In the end it was a large party that included family: Lord and Lady Burghclere and friends: among them the Earl and Countess of Westmoreland, Lord Ashburton, Lord and Lady Chelsea, the Nevilles and the Colebrookes. They also asked the Russian Ambassador, who was a friend of the Prince's. The crowd were there partly to enjoy themselves, of course, but they had also been asked in order to entertain the Prince and had been selected with his interests in mind.

Dinner that night was an Epicurean feast and the Prince was extremely appreciative. Almina had received numerous compliments already on her exquisite taste, on the beauty of the Drawing Room she had decorated and the charming and comfortable bedroom she had put at his disposal. The Prince was in a humour to be pleased with everything, and dinner was never going to disappoint. It began with a soup, a consommé, followed by the fish course: turbot *grillé* Duglèré (after Adolphe Duglèré, who was one of the most famous chefs in nineteenth-century Paris and had cooked for the Rothschild family for years). Then came the entrées: pâtés and a chicken dish. Next up were the roasts, a vast amount of game birds, stuffed with foie gras, all served with numerous vegetable side dishes. It was followed by *soufflé d'orange* and ices.

After the entertainments (on this occasion, accounts show that a band played for the assembled guests in the Music Room), there was a little light supper of cold meats such as pheasant and cold beef. Unsurprisingly, the Prince retired to bed satiated and in an excellent mood. Almina must have breathed a deep sigh of relief.

The shoot took place the following day, and this was Carnarvon's territory. It covered two drives on the Highclere estate: Biggs and Warren. The higher chalk downland was essentially a rabbit warren and wasn't farmed, so as to provide excellent shooting. There were eight guns – HRH the Prince of Wales, Lord Westmoreland, Lord Burghclere, Lord Chelsea, the Hon. Seymour Fortescue, Sir Edward Colebrooke, M. Boulatsell and Lord Carnarvon. Between them they shot a tremendous quantity of birds and rabbits – it was the era of quantity rather than quality in shooting circles.

The Castle's game book records the disposal of all the game shot at Highclere – nothing was ever wasted. It was compiled using figures given to the housekeeper by the head gamekeeper who, at the time of the Prince of Wales's visit, was a man called Cross, soon to be replaced by the long-serving Henry Maber. Flicking through the pages it is possible to track the social life of the Castle from year to year, and mostly there are relatively modest lists of game given to guests at house party weekends. But on the pages that record the Prince's shoot, the columns are full; the list goes on and on. Like everything else about that three-day stay, the extravagance is startling.

Ordinarily, guns were given six pheasants each, but the Prince was given twelve. The long list of recipients demonstrates the Prince's wide social network: birds were sent to the Russian Ambassador and Nellie Melba, as well as to Mr Horace Voules, editor of *Truth* magazine, a well-known investigative periodical. (It is tempting here to imagine a delicate bribe to a forerunner of the paparazzi – the Prince was frequently the subject of gossip in the media, unsurprisingly given that he was an enthusiastic playboy throughout his life.) Marie Wombwell, Almina's mother, was sent a brace of birds, some were sent to Newbury Hospital, and even the waiters, the band and the visiting valets were given pheasant. The lamp-men, however, were given rabbits.

The visit was a tremendous success. It could not have gone off more perfectly, and Carnarvon must have felt delighted that his new wife had orchestrated the event so well. She had dazzled her guests and overseen a series of exquisite dinners and entertainments. Clearly, Almina's 'education for the drawing room' had ensured she was an excellent administrator and talented hostess – she was already excelling in the role of the Countess of Carnarvon.

The little nineteen-year-old was no longer the naïve damsel that Lord Burghclere had observed six months ago, desperate for a decent family and giddy with excitement about her future. She was a wife, a Society hostess. She was a triumph.

5

Life Downstairs

The fact was, of course, that Almina's triumph was completely dependent on a small army of other people. She occupied centre stage when the eyes of the world were upon her, but actually it was Streatfield who ruled the Castle, and he continued to do so for the rest of his life. He knew perfectly well that he was more of a fixture than the new Countess. He had, after all, known Lord Carnarvon for rather longer than she had. The little kingdom of Highclere would carry on as before and the staff would simply do their jobs and wait to see how things turned out.

At the time of his expensive shopping expedition to London, Streatfield was thirty-nine years old. Since he was a single man, he lived in the Castle itself, rather than in one of the staff cottages, which were reserved for married couples and families. As house steward he had a large square sitting room in the basement, next to the identical house-keeper's sitting room. This was Streatfield's domain, where he spent his leisure time, such as it was, and from where he ran the downstairs life at Highclere. It was comfortably furnished with an Indian rug and an easy chair. In one corner stood an old English grandfather clock and the room was full of mahogany desks and tables. It felt businesslike, as befitted a man with a great deal of responsibility.

Streatfield did the household accounts, ordered provisions and was in charge of the wine cellars and the silver safe, where the family plate was kept under lock and key. The safe was vast, a walk-in room, and contained some famous pieces collected by the great connoisseur, the Earl of Chesterfield, as well as jewellery and other heirlooms. It was carefully wrapped and stored in muslins on baize-covered shelves.

Streatfield had mutton-chop whiskers and a habit of dropping his aitches where they needed to be and adding them where they didn't. He was remembered by the 6th Earl as unflappable, utterly devoted to Lord Carnarvon and even more devoted to Highclere, a man who never let his professional manner slip but who had a soft spot for children. He would ruffle Porchy's hair when he was a very little boy, a gesture of familiarity that Streatfield, with perfect timing, dropped when the young lord went off to Eton from prep school. It wasn't until 1897 that he married a teacher from Essex called Edith Andrews and moved into one of the grace-and-favour cottages in the park.

Streatfield's bedroom was one of the larger rooms on the

first floor of the staff wing. The footmen and the groom of the bedchambers, Roberts, had smaller rooms, all well within Streatfield's orbit so that he could keep an eye on them. The footmen's rooms looked out over the courtyard and the grooms and coachmen lived over the stables, which formed the other three sides of the yard.

Mr Roberts's position was a relatively unusual one; it was a mark of great luxury to have a groom of the bedchamber. Alfred had such a person in his household, and Almina, like Alfred, found having someone in the role extremely useful. Roberts was a sort of valet 'at large'. He was tasked with a host of little details, from ensuring that Lord and Lady Carnarvon never ran out of writing paper or ink in their bedrooms, to being in charge of calling cards from visitors, announcing guests and liaising with Fearnside, the Earl's fiercely loyal valet, and Miss Adams. His remit was extended to cover the house parties when there were guests. Roberts's overall responsibility was to ensure that everyone's stay was exquisite.

The housekeeper at the start of Almina's time at Highclere was Mrs Emily Bridgland. Her title was given as a courtesy, as she was in fact single. Mrs Bridgland had her sitting room next to Streatfield's, but whereas his was dark and full of heavy furniture, hers had a lighter touch and was more comfortable. She had two sofas covered in brocade and a large rosewood lounge chair, as well as a writing desk and sewing machine. She knew where all the keys to each room were and kept the key to the china cupboards, which lay not far from her sitting room, on a chain around her waist. As with Streatfield and his silver, she guarded the china fiercely.

Every day at 10.00 a.m., Mrs Bridgland made her way up the staff stairs to the ground floor of the Castle. Lady Carnarvon's sitting room was directly underneath her bedroom and could be quietly reached from various private stairs. Almina had just redecorated. It now had a thick, dusky pink carpet, and the delicate Georgian plasterwork was complemented by soft pink walls, against which hung a charming collection of paintings and miniatures. It was a peaceful room, full of light, in which she could discuss household matters in privacy with Mrs Bridgland. As in everything at Highclere, the structures below stairs mirrored life upstairs, so just as Mrs Bridgland and Streatfield had their sitting rooms next door to one another, so too did Lord and Lady Carnarvon. Mrs Bridgland could ask Lady Carnarvon for her instructions and discuss plans for the day: what time guests were arriving and departing, the entertainments planned for the afternoon, the menus for lunch and dinner. Once they had concluded their business, Mrs Bridgland retraced her steps and delegated the jobs through the head housemaid and the cook.

On the wall of the corridor that ran the length of the house, from the back door to the wine cellars, was the panel of bells that the family used to ring for attention. It was positioned between the house steward's and the housekeeper's sitting rooms and there were sixty-six bells in total, one for each of the State Rooms and the family and guest bedrooms. Streatfield employed a steward's room boy in order to run and alert a maid or a footman when a bell rang.

Particular staff answered each bell. Streatfield, Fearnside and the footmen ensured that the family and any guests were properly greeted, announced – and that they lacked for nothing. The more senior housemaids would be on hand to look after the female house guests. But many of the staff rarely met the guests as only the footmen were in attendance at each lunch or dinner. A kitchen maid might go for months without ever seeing a member of the family since there was no reason for her to go upstairs and Almina seldom came downstairs.

The unmarried female servants lived in the main Castle, on the second floor and in rooms in the tower reached by a winding staircase. Each single room had its own bed and fireplace where water could be heated up for washing, but some of the junior maids shared, two to a room. Bedrooms were strictly for sleeping in, since there was a servants' hall and sitting room for relaxing, and there was no such thing as truly private space. Bedrooms could be inspected at any time, and although Mrs Bridgland was no tyrant, she took her duties seriously, opening cupboards and looking under beds for evidence of any wrongdoing. Policing of morality and observance of the social codes were as much a part of the house steward and housekeeper's duties as organising the wine cellar, keeping the key to the silver safe, ordering provisions or supervising housemaids. The maids were usually seventeen or eighteen when they started in service, and were often living away from family for the first time. There was an element of pastoral care to the role of the senior staff, who had to spot upset of any kind since it might disrupt the smooth running of the household.

The girls were a good long way from the male staff, which was obviously the intention, but they were also a long way from the ground if there were a fire. The provisions for escape in such an event were pretty terrifying in themselves. Outside the bedrooms there are painted notices that announce, matter of factly, 'In case of fire, use chute.' The heavy canvas tunnels were on iron hooks that could be wedged in the window frames. The far end was held firmly by a couple of men standing far below on the lawn. They must have worked, because later generations remember being made to practise a fire drill with them. The housemaids knew the main thing was to wear thick sweaters and hold their arms close to their bodies so they didn't catch their elbows in the metal hoops of the tunnel.

There were rules governing interaction below stairs at least as elaborate as those that prevailed upstairs. Streatfield dined every day with Mrs Bridgland and Mr Fearnside, the valet, in the steward's room. They were served by a junior footman. Mr Roberts, the groom of the bedchambers, and Miss Adams presided over the housemaids and footmen in the servants' hall, women on one side of the table, men on the other. Precedence was carefully preserved, with the senior housemaid sitting to the right of Roberts whilst the butler and under-butler would be seated either side of Lady Carnarvon's maid. The chef's departments were quite separate. Visiting ladies' maids and valets would be placed according to precedence: the rank of their family's title and size of establishment would be as carefully studied by Mrs Bridgland, poring over *Debrett's* in her parlour, as by Almina doing a table plan upstairs in the State Dining Room.

In Almina's time there were at least eighteen members of male indoor staff reporting in a strict hierarchical structure to Mr Streatfield. Even their clothes reflected their status. Streatfield changed to white tie when Lord Carnarvon dressed for dinner, since he would be serving in the Dining Room. Footmen likewise had to change from their liveries into white breeches with dark blue jackets and powdered wigs. Female staff wore blue dresses with white aprons and little frilly caps: the more senior their role, the more elaborate the cap. At the very top of the scale, Mrs Bridgland could dispense with the apron, and at the very bottom, the scullery maid had just one work dress and a vast quantity of aprons that she had to change constantly.

The Castle household ran like clockwork, with new arrivals slotted in to junior jobs in order to learn how things were done. Each different employee at the Castle had tasks to perform at different times of the day. A scullery maid, who was the most junior of all the maids, was up at 6.00 a.m. to light the fire in the kitchen so the senior staff could have their cups of tea. She would be frantically busy doing the washing up during cooking hours and after meals, and therefore up to her elbows in suds and grease from breakfast time to long after the family had finished dinner. A housemaid might have an hour of relative leisure mid-afternoon. On the other hand, housemaids also got up at the crack of dawn to begin the enormous and crucial task of lighting dozens of fires throughout the house. A junior housemaid would begin by cleaning the housekeeper's grate, and do the job every day first thing, until she got the hang of it and could be relied upon not to dirty the carpets in the State Rooms.

The fires had to be cleaned of the previous day's ashes and then re-laid with fresh white paper before the footmen brought in the hot coals to light them. After breakfast, the maids would begin to clear the rooms and make the beds, a task that could take them until lunchtime if the family was in attendance with guests. The staff had their main meal at midday in the servants' hall, an hour before the family ate at 1.00 p.m. The late afternoons would bring another round of duties. Once the Carnarvons and their guests had taken their tea and retired to the Library for a game of bezique or gone out for a stroll in the park, the maids had to clear away any evidence of their occupation of the rooms they weren't using, plumping cushions, emptying ashtrays and sweeping carpets to remove footprints. The task of restoring an impression of pristine readiness in the State Rooms could be completed when the house party retired to dress for dinner, but of course that also meant a new round of work in the bedrooms. There were more fires to be lit and then endless pails of hot water to be taken up. Bathrooms were not installed at Highclere until 1897, so before then baths were taken in freestanding tubs in front of the fire in the bedrooms. If there were twenty-five guests staying, plus family, that meant thirty fires and thirty baths to fill. There would have been a great deal of running up and down the back stairs, trying not to spill the water as the doormen lugged it up. Even once the plumbing was installed, some jugs of hot water were still taken up. Old habits die hard, and many guests preferred to use a jug and a bowl than the marble inlaid basins.

The main kitchen at Highclere is a large, high-ceilinged room tiled up to beyond the height of a tall man. There is an enormous and elegant wooden-framed clock on one wall, so that everyone could keep to the rigorous schedules demanded by the cook, and a huge table in the middle of the room. Gwendolen Gray, who was a scullery and then a kitchen maid, remembered 'the huge Caron stove, it took five hods of coal in the morning and five in the afternoon, the long white scrubbed table, the shelves with gleaming coppers – and when I was scullery maid, how I took a pride in those coppers!'

The Earl and Countess ate four times a day: breakfast, lunch, tea and dinner; there were a tremendous number of 'removes' for each meal, but especially for a dinner party. When in residence, Lord and Lady Carnarvon were rarely without visitors, and even on a slow day the pace of activity must have been relentless. Occasionally, mistakes were made. Dorothy Wickes was a kitchen maid during Almina's time and years later she told a nephew about the day the Lady of the House complained of oak leaves in the cabbage. The following evening Almina prepared the cabbage herself but Dorothy was feeling mischievous and added a couple of leaves later. There was no further complaint.

The cook had her own sitting room, a sign of her high status, and food was taken very seriously at Highclere. She had three kitchen maids as well as a scullery maid, and in addition to the main kitchen and two sculleries, there was a still room for more storage space and activities like making preserves that were not directly connected to the day's cooking requirements. There was a lot of equipment to store, from stew pans to preserving pans – and not merely general fish kettles but salmon and turbot kettles, too. Moulds of various shapes and sizes were used for cold first courses such as jellies *mousselines*, as well as the fruit jellies and puddings, all of which were beautifully presented.

Dinner was announced at precisely 8.00 p.m. by Streatfield. Two footmen could serve dinner on a quiet evening, but if there were ten guests or more, four footmen were in attendance, and they would be required to powder their hair, a practice that only ceased in 1918. A scullery maid recalled 'what a long way the second footman had to go to take the courses to the Dining Room. If there was a soufflé on the menu, I can still hear Mrs Mackie standing at the serving hatch begging the footman to "run, run, run". The butler would sometimes bring a note on a silver salver from His Lordship commenting on something concerning the dinner. Mrs Mackie called these her "billy dos".'

Both the Earl and Countess ate sparingly. Lord Carnarvon thoroughly enjoyed Turkish cigarettes, to be smoked over brandy and cigars with the gentlemen guests in the Dining Room. The ladies took coffee, in the Drawing Room. Almina didn't like to spend too long over a dinner party as the staff would have to clear and wash up and prepare for the next day.

There were always quantities of dripping left over from the preparation of these meals, so local people would bring along basins and Minnie Wills, who arrived at Highclere as a kitchen maid in 1902, would let them have some nourishing dripping in return for a penny or two placed in the slot of a neatly-made wooden box; at Christmas the coins would be shared amongst the servants.

Eventually the staff had their hot supper in the servants' hall, which was directly beneath the State Dining Room. It was a large room dominated by a massive seventeenth-century refectory table made of oak. 'Our food was as good as in the Dining Room,' according to Mrs Hart, a long-term Highclere resident who began as the fourth housemaid. She remembered learning to dance in the servants' hall after supper and there was often singing around the piano. The maids finished their day with hot cocoa with the head housemaid in the servants' sitting room, a separate space from the main servants' hall, and much cosier – full of easy chairs and decorated with framed prints.

It would be foolish to pretend that the life of the domestic staff was idyllic, however. In some great houses, any female member of staff who had 'a follower', i.e. a boyfriend, would be instantly dismissed – a practice which seems barbaric today – although Highclere may have been more liberal in this respect as numerous marriages occurred between estate staff. The pay was not generous, but of course food and lodging were included, so wages could be saved and service in a household such as the Carnarvons' was generally seen as a good job with possibilities for advancement. By the 1890s, changes to legislation meant that servants got a week's paid holiday a year, as well as their half-days on Sundays and, sometimes, an evening off in the week. During house parties the routine was arduous and days were extremely long and busy, but when the family was away in London or abroad, there was more opportunity to relax.

The work might have been hard, but the rule at Highclere was not at all tyrannical. Minnie Wills always said that she had come from a home that was not happy and Highclere became more her home than that one. The piano in the servants' hall and the care implied by that cocoa at the end of the day attest to a benevolent regime. The staff enjoyed trips to Newbury and, later on, to the racecourse. There was also an annual dance, held in the Library, to which staff from all the other large houses in the neighbourhood were invited. Lord and Lady Carnarvon upheld a tradition that Highclere should be 'a household of kindness'. Winifred, Almina's sister-in-law, remarked on this approvingly. And as Nanny Moss, the 6th Earl's much-loved nurse put it, 'No one from Highclere Castle will ever go to Hell.'

Perhaps it was at one of these dances, or at the races, that Minnie and Arthur Hayter, the groom, first got chatting. It was the beginning of a long friendship that would eventually end in romance. Relationships between members of staff were of course relatively common, but they could only progress if the couple married, as, quite apart from any moral codes, their lives were so segregated. For a woman, marriage meant the end of her working life, so many servants delayed their wedding a number of years, until they were more financially secure. Some women also decided to prioritise moving up the household's structure to become housekeeper, or a lady's maid. That might well have been the motivating factor in Minnie and Arthur's extended courtship.

Highclere was a symbiotic system, and mutual respect was the key to its success. The 5th Earl prided himself on an Old World courtesy, and that set the tone for the entire household. He took an interest in the well-being of the staff and the cottagers on the estate; often a donation would be made towards a fund for a tenant whose livestock had died, and money was also made available for the staff to have medical treatment. This attitude was maintained by his successor. The 6th Earl wrote in his memoirs that he considered his staff the lynchpin of his establishment and freely admitted that he would not be able to run Highclere without the invaluable help of his butler (Robert Taylor) of forty-four years' standing.

The Castle was, of course, only one part of the domain. The estate was a self-contained community with its own forge, sawmills, carpenters, brickies, dairy farm and electricians' workshops. There were vegetable gardens, fruit orchards, greenhouses and a brewery, pigs and cattle. There were security staff and gatekeepers, plantsmen, gamekeepers and foresters.

The gardens were extensive and, as in all great houses, the quality of the flowers for cutting and produce to be used in the kitchens was a matter of great pride. The head gardener in 1895 was William Pope, a fierce man, protective of his territory. He had between twenty and twenty-five men working under him. The walled kitchen garden was a good five acres in size, with a charming orchard beyond it, framed by plum trees whose fruit was famously delicious.

Mr Pope had not only to produce food throughout the year but also to know how to maximise yields and to store it so that nothing should go to waste. Greenhouses lined the south-facing walls to extend the growing season. A vinery, peach house and orangery were heated by a boiler, whilst rainwater was collected from all the gutters. A north-facing fernery provided a collection of different flower species for the Castle and there were roses from the Rose House and more flowers in the designated cutting beds.

The dairy yard lay near the kitchen gardens, and when the family was in town rather than at Highclere, the milk and cheeses were sent up to the London house in small silver churns. These churns are still piled, somewhat haphazardly, in one of the dozens of storerooms in the basement of the Castle. All houses accumulate clutter, and the nooks and crannies of Highclere provide ample room for hundreds of years' worth.

Opposite the dairy was the hayrack for the dairy yard and, next to that, beneath the shelter of the walls of the great kitchen garden, were the chickens. The damp boggy field leading west from the kitchen garden was used to grow potatoes.

Every day, Pope would send his senior gardener, Samuel Ward, to enquire of the cook what was needed. There was an entire family of delightfully named Digweed boys working as Highclere gardeners, and one of them would run up to the kitchens with the fruit and vegetables required.

The sawmills lay across the cricket field near White Oak, the large sprawling house where James Rutherford, the agent, lived. They had been refitted by the 5th Earl with the latest steam-powered saw. The division of labour in terms of overseeing the house and estate was firmly along traditional lines: anything outside the Castle was the Earl's concern and, just as Almina had wasted no time in refurbishing the Drawing Room, Carnarvon had spent money on the latest equipment out at the sawmill. He was very much a gadget man, delighting in the advances in technology that were coming fast throughout the 1890s.

The yard outside the mill was stacked high with different types of wood. The estate carpenters had a stock of planks, boarding, joists or posts; everything they needed. There were thirty men working under head forester William Storie and, as in the gardens, one family in particular, the Annetts, worked for generations as foresters.

Henry Maber, who became head gamekeeper in 1896, was a large, solid man who had moved to Highclere from East Anglia. He rode a cob and was steeped in knowledge of the countryside. He lived with his family in a house called Broadspear, overlooking the sweeping, Capability Brown-designed lawns. The house was close to the rearing pens at Penwood, the neighbouring village. The young pheasants were raised there before being taken out to the estate's various woods in late spring and left to grow to maturity in time for the shooting season.

It was a very prestigious job because Highclere was regarded as one of the great Edwardian shoots. Lord Carnarvon was one of the finest shots in the country and his close friends Lord de Grey and Lord Ashburton rivalled him for the same accolade. They were unsparing in their comments if they thought Lord Carnarvon had mismanaged a drive or his keeper was not up to form. Maber was always worrying about the weather, where the birds were and whether he could meet His Lordship's desired bag. He had four under-keepers and another fifteen men working for him. They were all given cottages and lived at the furthest-flung corners of the estate so that they could patrol the limits for poachers. He reported to both Lord Carnarvon and to Major Rutherford.

Like other estate staff, Maber talked frankly. One morning he greeted Lord Carnarvon with, 'Excuse me milord; afore you goes any further I'd like you to get to the lee side of me as Mrs Maber told me my breath didn't smell very sweet this morning.'

Some of the gardeners would earn extra money as beaters on the shoots in winter. One of the Digweeds was acting as a stop on a drive for Maber when the latter found him relieving himself against a tree. 'Now, Digweed you turnip-headed gardener, you stop that there dung spreading and get on with your job!'

His son was Charles Maber who grew up, learned the same countryside lore and served in turn as head keeper.

The U-shaped Georgian brick courtyard to the west of the Castle housed the small brewery and the riding and carriage horses in large cobbled stables. The carriages were also kept here. The grooms lived in a warren of rooms above, sleeping two to a bedroom, their trunks, full of possessions, at the ends of their beds. Arthur Hayter arrived to take up the position of most junior groom and coachman in 1895. His family were farmers and Arthur's new job was seen as a definite step up. He loved the horses in his care and could manage them brilliantly, whispering to them when they were upset. There were at least a dozen horses and one groom for each pair so the stables hummed with activity. Arthur reported to head coachman, Henry Brickell, who had driven the just-married couple on their wedding day. Brickell was a longstanding employee and a much trusted, steady man.

Nobody could possibly have known it, but Highclere was passing into a golden time. Everyone who lived and worked there was caught up in the last spectacular flourishing of a secure existence. The rules were understood by everybody: upstairs and downstairs worlds interacted only in very specific and controlled ways. A new Countess, even one with grand ideas and the cash to carry them out, was unlikely to provoke much lasting change. In 1895 the Empire was at its peak, Queen Victoria was two years away from her Diamond Jubilee, and Britain was, without question, the most prosperous and powerful country in the world. It was a time of peace and progress, of supreme self-belief. The threat to the old ways, as yet scarcely perceived, came not from any individual upstairs but from the new tech-nology and the bigger political forces reshaping society and the balance of power in Europe.

If you'd asked Henry Brickell how he felt about the future, though, he might not have been too cheery. His job was increasingly marginalised, in a sign of things to come, by Lord Carnarvon's passion for gadgets. The 5th Earl was exploring the exciting possibilities offered by the new horsepower – the motor car.

6

Dressing for Dinner

Lord and Lady Carnarvon set out for Christmas at Halton House a week after they had waved off their illustrious house guest, the Prince of Wales. Pleased with each other, themselves and the world, they had no reason to doubt that life would continue in its delightful round of balls, shoots and travels abroad, as far as they both could see. They were looking forward to being thoroughly spoiled by Alfred, who celebrated Christmas in style, despite being Jewish. It was an excuse for a party, and although he wasn't going to participate in the religious aspects, the secular trimmings were there to be enjoyed. It was a predictably jolly occasion, with Carnarvon's great friend Prince Victor Duleep Singh a fellow guest as well; a thoroughly multicultural and eclectic gathering of people, all bent on celebrating their own good fortune as much as anything more pious.

The Carnarvons were regular visitors to Halton House throughout the early years of their married life. There was a permanent whirl of moving between Highclere, London, Bretby in Derbyshire and Pixton in Somerset, as well as foreign travel. Given Almina's lifelong devotion to the city of her childhood, they went often to Paris, usually staying in the Ritz hotel, and popped out to the Bois de Boulogne for racing at Longchamps on a fine weekend.

For Lord Carnarvon it was a relatively sedate existence, compared to his long sailing missions to the other side of the globe. For Almina, though, the world was expanding faster and further than ever before. Young ladies simply did not travel as men did. They were kept indoors or close to home and groomed for the transition from their father's home to their husband's. Only now that she was Countess of Carnarvon could she diffuse some of her formidable energy in seeing a bit of the world. In the first ten years of her married life, Almina accompanied her husband to France, Italy, Germany, Egypt many times, America and the Far East.

When they were at Highclere or at their house in London, the Carnarvons were always entertaining. It was a curiously public existence compared to domestic life for most married couples today. They were hardly ever alone, and their house was always full of staff and guests. In the summer there were racing parties and tennis weekends; in the autumn there were shoots. All year long there were local fetes and garden parties and, to all of these functions, they invited the latest stars of the social scene, the newly married, the intriguing and the glamorous.

In May 1896, almost a year after their own marriage, they invited the newly wed Duke and Duchess of Marlborough to stay. Consuelo Vanderbilt was an American heiress of spectacular wealth, whom the 9th Duke had quite plainly married only for her money. She was a beautiful and charming woman, but the fact was that the couple loathed each other. They had both given up the people they really loved in order to marry each other, and Consuelo, who was only seventeen at the time, had been coerced into the marriage by her domineering mother. She later reported having cried behind her veil as she said her vows.

Consuelo spoke in almost hushed tones of her first London season, that summer of 1896. 'Those who knew the London of 1896 and 1897 will recall with something of a heartache the brilliant succession of festivities.' Part of those festivities, of course, were the inevitable weekend house parties, such as the one she attended at Highclere.

She and Almina were in oddly analogous positions. They were both beautiful young heiresses who had married into the aristocracy because of their family's fortune and despite its roots in trade. They were both outsiders. Almina had been sidelined by her illegitimate status, Consuelo was constantly sneered at for being American and therefore hardly worthy to be a Duchess. But there the similarity ended. Consuelo was miserable before and throughout her marriage, and separated from the Duke of Marlborough in 1906. Almina was giddily in love on her wedding day and the Carnarvons had a happy and companionable marriage for many years.

Did the girls recognise something in each other that weekend? Did they talk about the mishaps they'd had in the course of their apprenticeship in 'Being a Chatelaine'? Consuelo always recalled that she was totally unprepared for the rigid observance of precedence in her new world. A Duchess was higher ranking than a marchioness, who came higher up than a Countess, but there were endless distinctions between Duchesses, marchionesses and Countesses, the age of each title had to be taken into account, and older women took precedence over younger ones, all of which could reshuffle everything into a different order. Once, at a party at Blenheim Palace, her husband's seat, Consuelo was unsure of the sequence in which the ladies should be withdrawing from the dining room. Not wanting to appear rude, she dithered in the doorway, only to be shoved in the back by a furious Marchioness, who hissed at her, 'It is quite as vulgar to hang back as to jump ahead.'

Perhaps it was a relief to speak to someone who understood that alongside the luxury and privilege was the constant pressure not to do 'The Wrong Thing', since few people in that strictly codified world would have been prepared to laugh it off. And all the conventions only served to remind them that with the rank came the risk that all trace of their individuality would be swept away. Almina and Consuelo were adjusting to the fact that their personal wishes and desires were considerably less important than the main tasks in hand: producing an heir for the estate and enacting their roles as great ladies.

It would have been hard even to find a moment to have that conversation, since privacy was virtually impossible to come by when there could be up to eighty people in the house. But the impulse to share secrets and stories is strong and, in any case, new ways to get round the conventions were always being devised. It was considered improper to play games on the Lord's day, for example, so it became fashionable for the ladies to spend their Sunday afternoons walking in pairs, for *tête-à-tête* conversations. Social prestige could be measured by how many invitations to walk a lady received. Part of the appeal must surely have been that the strolls through the beautiful park afforded the opportunity to speak frankly, or at least more frankly than in the drawing room taking tea.

Hosting a weekend party was liable to produce endless opportunities to slip up, or to overlook a crucial detail. Almina had acquitted herself splendidly at her baptism of fire, the Prince of Wales's visit back in December, but the frantic activity and expense attest to a certain level of anxiety as well as exuberance. She might have tried to reassure the new Duchess, with the benefit of her extra six months' experience and her greater familiarity with English customs. Her advice would have come in handy a few months later, when the Duchess had to host her first shooting party at Blenheim, once again in honour of the Prince of Wales.

The marriage between Consuelo and Marlborough was already becoming a byword for loveless but lucrative arrangements at the time of the couple's visit to Highclere. Almina's curiosity and sympathy might have led to a few enquiries as the girls strolled. Unfettered gossip would not have been on the agenda, though. Everything about Almina suggests that she was deeply conscious of her own dignity. She had only just arrived at such an exalted position that she could be arm-in-arm with a Duchess, and neither girl would have wanted to be grouped together as the outsiders or to commit the cardinal sin of indiscretion. Almina was sensitive to any insinuation that she was letting herself down. Shame was a powerful inhibitor and could be experienced by proxy, as her son later attested.

But for now, Almina had no reason to worry about anything. She had been welcomed into the family with open arms, for the breezy energy she brought to the Earl's life, and of course for the immense amount of good that her wealth could do for the estate. A house such as Highclere, not to mention the other properties, was a responsibility as well as a privilege. The sense of custodianship that came with the inheritance meant that – to a large extent – the Castle owned the family, rather than the other way around. Almina was key to securing its future, and she knew it.

Quite apart from relieving everyone's anxiety about bills and maintenance, Almina's fortune allowed improvements on a scale that hadn't been seen since the 3rd Earl pulled down the old house. She didn't hesitate in calling again upon Sir Alfred's generosity to make Highclere one of the best-equipped and most comfortable private houses in the country.

It took the best part of six months, much of which Lord and Lady Carnarvon spent in London so as to be out of the way of the works, and cost Alfred de Rothschild many thousands of pounds, but in 1896, electric light arrived at the Castle. Almina took the opportunity to have more bathrooms installed as well. There were numerous water closets by the mid-1890s, not only adjoining the family's and guests' bedrooms, but also in the servants' working and sleeping quarters.

Highclere was transformed into a beacon of modernity: the shadows were banished and a huge amount of labour was saved. The whole house was wired, including the kitchens, sculleries, cellars and servants' hall and sitting rooms. Between the electric light and the running water in the bathrooms, there was a significant easing in the household's centuries-old work schedule. The lamp-men were saved the nightly ritual of lighting over a hundred oil lamps, and the housemaids no longer had to struggle upstairs with enough hot water for everyone to bathe in freestanding tubs.

Elsie, the Dowager Countess of Carnarvon, found the introduction of the lights and the water systems a huge practical improvement to the house she had once run. Elsie was a supremely good-natured and capable person, never in her life inclined to complain about anything. She had proved herself an ally back during Almina's engagement and continued to advise and help out on her occasional visits. On 10 June 1896, at Buckingham Palace, she presented her successor to the Princess of Wales, who was standing in for Queen Victoria. This occasion marked Almina's formal introduction to the Court in her new role as Countess of Carnarvon. It was three years since the last time Almina had curtseyed in front of a representative of her monarch and her life had been transformed in the interim.

By 23 June 1897, almost two years since their wedding day, Almina was feeling confident enough at event planning to invite 3,000 local schoolchildren and 300 of their teachers to spend the afternoon in the grounds of Highclere Castle. The occasion was Queen Victoria's Diamond Jubilee. The Queen had been on the throne for an unprecedented sixty years, and there were celebrations across the land. In the depths of her almost total seclusion from public life she had been unpopular, becoming a symbol of a stubborn refusal to move with the times. Britain's republican movement had its only moment of real public support. But her Golden and then her Diamond Jubilee increased the Queen's popularity again; and, in any case, popular or not, there was protocol to observe: the Earl and Countess would not be shown up through inadequate festivities. More specially-commissioned trains to Highclere were laid on to transport people, and a mile-long procession wound through the woods and park, accompanied by the marching bands from Newbury. Fortunately it was a beautiful day and Almina had organised swingboats and other entertainments, as well as a sumptuous tea, all laid out on trestle tables beneath the cedar trees on the lawns around the Castle.

Two weeks later on 2 July, the Earl and Countess attended a fabulously lavish celebration, the Duchess of Devonshire's Jubilee Costume Ball, given at Devonshire House on Piccadilly. The invitation stipulated that costumes should be allegorical or historical from a period pre-1820 and, judging by some of the surviving photos of guests, no opportunity to dazzle was passed up. Lady Wolverton, for example, was dressed as Britannia, complete with a breast-plate over her flowing white dress, plumed helmet, trident and shield emblazoned with the Union flag. Mrs Arthur Paget made a very fetching Cleopatra and Prince Victor Duleep Singh was much admired as the Moghul Emperor Akbar.

Lord and Lady Carnarvon spent Christmas at Alfred de Rothschild's house, as had become their custom, and then, in January 1898, they attended the wedding of Prince Victor Duleep Singh, who married Lady Anne, the daughter of the Earl of Coventry, in St Peter's Church, Eaton Square. The wedding caused something of a stir since it was the first time an Indian Prince had married an English noblewoman. The whole thing was typical of the contradictions of late-Victorian attitudes: at a time when patronising attitudes to England's colonial empire were endemic, wealthy Indians were nonetheless accepted into London Society and consorted with the best people. Marrying one of them proved to be just a step too far for some, though. The Prince of Wales was instrumental in calming chatter about the alliance's suitability and was also a guest at the ceremony. Prince Victor's brother was best man and Lord Carnarvon's youngest sister, Vera, was one of the bridesmaids.

Straight after the wedding, Lord and Lady Carnarvon left the country on what was to become the first of many voyages to escape the English winter. The destination was Egypt, which would prove so fateful for the couple. They arrived in Alexandria and were immediately immersed in a very different world from anything that Almina had ever known. Her travels until then had been confined to Europe, so the whitewashed walls and daily life of Alexandria provoked something of a culture shock. There were camels noisily kneeling to be loaded before swaying off, dragged along by small boys with sticks. The noises and smells were overwhelming; the streets full of donkeys and Arab horses pulling carts at barely controlled speeds. The bazaar was tremendously colourful, full of spices and leathers and antiquities of dubious provenance. However, although it felt exotic, the Carnarvons were in good company. Alexandria, Luxor and Cairo were all full of foreign tourists, and it wasn't unusual to see runners clearing the way before distinguished people. It was easy to spot the English on their thoroughbreds, riding between sporting engagements.

They enjoyed themselves in the luxurious surroundings of the Winter Palace Hotel in Luxor, and the Earl was keen to show Almina the mysterious temples and the glorious treasures that had captured his imagination back when he had visited as a solo traveller in 1889.

While they were on holiday in Egypt, Almina fell pregnant. It was what everyone had been waiting for, and Carnarvon in particular was naturally delighted. They returned to Highclere well rested and in high spirits and spent a quiet few months at home. For Almina the summer season that year was less rigorous than previous ones since, as a pregnant woman, there were a great many activities that were not considered appropriate for her. Almina spent more time in town, resting with her mother, and less time at Highclere organising weekend house parties.

In September she moved in with Elsie, the Dowager Countess of Carnarvon, so that she could give birth in London where the best doctors were available. Lord Carnarvon was touring the Continent in his beloved Panhard motor car at the time, which was probably another factor in Almina's decision to leave Highclere and head for London, where she would have congenial company and guidance as she prepared for motherhood.

The 5th Earl was known by the moniker Motor Carnarvon and had bought several of the first cars imported into Britain. In 1898 the choice of British cars was still very limited indeed, and the best marque for experienced drivers was considered to be the French Panhard-Levassor. Lord

Carnarvon travelled with George Fearnside, his valet, and his French chauffeur, Georges Eilersgaard. The car was left-hand drive, had four gears and could travel at the corresponding speeds of 4.5, 7, 10 and 13 miles per hour. Back in England later that month, he was summoned to appear in court in Newbury for driving at more than 12 miles per hour (the legal limit at the time). It was to be the first of numerous speeding fines for Lord Carnarvon.

Lord Carnarvon was at 13 Berkeley Square, though naturally not in the room with his wife, when on 7 November 1898, she fulfilled her primary task as the Countess of Carnarvon by giving birth to an heir. The safe arrival of a healthy baby boy meant an uncomplicated line of succession, and there was rejoicing both upstairs and down. Almina was still only twenty-two years old and, as usual, her life seemed charmed. She had a beautiful healthy baby boy – she was unassailable. Nothing ever looked too difficult for Almina. She had accomplished everything she'd ever put her mind to, had the good fortune to be pretty as well as rich, met a man whom she loved and who loved her, lived exactly as she pleased. She was a Countess, a wife and now a mother.

The baby was christened a little over a month later, after the traditional laying-in period. His sponsors were Alfred de Rothschild, Marie Wombwell, Prince Victor Duleep Singh and Francis, Lord Ashburton, another friend of Carnarvon's from Eton days. He was accordingly given a very long list of names: Henry George (for his father – both were good Carnarvon names) Alfred Marius Victor Francis. In practice he was most usually called Porchy, as his father had been before him and his son would be in due course.

The Carnarvons didn't stay long in town after the chris-tening. Porchy was to be brought up at Highclere, in the nursery on the second floor that Almina had prepared for the purpose. When Lord and Lady Carnarvon arrived at the Castle with their son they were met by the entire staff, who had lined up on the gravel drive outside the front door to welcome them. Almina stepped from the car with the baby in her arms, followed by the nurse she had engaged in London.

Later that afternoon all the staff assembled again, this time outside the Earl's study, and were summoned one by one to see him. The kitchen maids were twittery with nerves since they had never been upstairs; the grooms were just as bad but trying not to show it; everyone was dressed impeccably in clean aprons and caps. When a name was called, the person entered the study, curtseyed or bowed to His Lordship and received a gold sovereign in honour of his son and heir.

The photo taken at the Castle to mark Porchy's birth is heart-melting. The baby's crib is enormous and draped in muslin. Almina stands behind wearing a long loose gown and stares, rapt, into the face of her first child. The shot captures all the tenderness and amazement of a woman who has just become a mother.

Aristocratic childcare in 1898 was radically different from anything we would recognise today. Children lived not with their parents but in a separate realm, looked after first by a nanny and later by a governess, assisted by a couple of nursery maids. Almina arrived back at Highclere accom-panied by a nurse who was on hand during the first weeks to give her support and reassurance. The advice in those days was that the mother should feed the baby initially and then gradually introduce a mixture of diluted cows' milk. When Almina gave birth to her daughter, Evelyn Leonora Almina, who was always known as Eve, in August 1901, the baby joined Porchy in the nursery, under the care of Nanny Moss.

It is impossible to know what Almina felt about being a mother. It would be anachronistic to assume from the fact that she was often away from her children (as she was) that she did not love and care for them. Their day-to-day welfare was attended to by other people, but that was entirely normal in Almina's day.

Her son, Porchy, later the 6th Earl of Carnarvon, recalled in his memoirs that his parents' visits to the nursery, usually at tea-time on Sundays, could be excruciating occasions. There is a rather heart-breaking description of a family too awkward with each other to know what to say, the Earl blustering out questions about how the schooling was coming along just as his father had with him. Porchy heaved a sigh of relief when the adults turned on their heels and returned to their world. Almina doesn't appear to have been able to bridge the gulf between father and son, or to form a close bond with Henry herself.

Part of the problem must surely have been far bigger than any of the individuals concerned: Almina's children were born at a time when the maxim 'children should be seen and not heard' was not a laughably old-fashioned cliché but a statement of fact. Their status was quite simply lower than that of their parents, as was demonstrated by the fact that Porchy and Eve, for as long as they lived in the nursery, used the back stairs, with the servants.

There does seem to have been something else at work, though. In the same memoir, Porchy recounts the story of a childhood mishap. He was attending a garden party at Buckingham Palace, aged about nine, with his mother, and, in his over-excitement, not looking where he was going, he barged into King Edward VII's very ample stomach. His Highness hadn't lost any weight since the days of his visit to Highclere as Prince of Wales; grunting from the blow, he staggered to the ground. He was unhurt, and reassured the little boy that no harm had been done, but Porchy was mortified. Princess Mary saw that he was upset and took him off to feed him ice cream. Disaster struck again when Porchy fumbled his plate and spilled some of the pink raspberry confection all over the princess's white satin gown. As Mary was bustled away by her furious governess to change her dress, Almina arrived on the scene like some wrathful fury, grabbed his arm and hustled him home, where he was sent to bed with nothing but bread and milk. The words she used to express her anger were revealing. 'You disgraceful boy,' she told him, 'you shamed me today.' Perhaps, even after years of living at the heart of the Establishment, Almina still had flashes of anxiety. Exposure to disapproval or ridicule was anathema to her and there was no room for slip-ups, even schoolboy ones.

Maybe Almina just found it easier to get on with adults than children. Certainly, things seemed to get easier as her son got older. After he became the 6th Earl, he continued to rely on his mother for advice on the suitability of his second marriage, to ask her to stay at Highclere and to attend family occasions such as an engagement party for her beloved grandson. And Almina was extremely close to her daughter Eve all her life.

The year 1901 was of huge significance, not just on a personal level for the Carnarvons, but nationally. In January, when Almina was just pregnant with her second child, Queen Victoria finally passed away at Osborne House, her holiday home on the Isle of Wight. She was surrounded by her children and grandchildren. Her son, Bertie, Prince of Wales and soon-to-be Edward VII, was already sixty years old. Her eldest grandson, Kaiser Wilhelm II of Germany, who thirteen years later would lead Germany into war against his beloved grandmother's country, was also at her bedside. Queen Victoria had been on the throne for almost sixty-four years and presided over Britain's consolidation as the leading figure on the world stage. Her name is still synonymous with the era. For her subjects, all 440 million of them across the Empire, her death was an epochal event.

The Queen's body lay in state at Windsor Castle for two days. The whole country was in deep mourning: every adult wore black, and shops were festooned with black and purple banners. Even black iron railings were repainted to make them more appropriately gloomy.

The Carnarvons were present at the State Funeral at St George's Chapel in Windsor Castle on 2 February, which was attended by the crowned heads of all Europe and representatives of every British dominion. There was an outpouring of public affection for the dead queen and the new king, but also some anxiety. What would happen next? The British were still embroiled in the Boer War in South Africa. It was not popular, and the Army had learnt some sharp lessons about structure, tactics and the impact of disease on the ability of their men to fight. Lord Kitchener's 'scorched earth' policy and the Army's use of concentration camps were causing deep uneasiness. The campaign had also revealed the extent of the public health crisis amongst the nation's poor. Forty per cent of Army recruits were found to be unfit for military service.

Queen Victoria's reign coincided with a bustling period of progress, industrialisation, and the creation of extraordinary wealth in Britain. Her long lifespan led to a reassuring sense of continuity, and any unpopularity still lingering from when she was a reclusive widow was transformed at her death into a reverence for a time now lost.

The Prince of Wales, who was about to be crowned Edward VII, had very little experience of government matters, despite his age. He was without doubt genial, fond of processions and the trappings of kingship. His mother and courtiers, however, had always worried about his lack of reading and application, as well as his indiscretions with various mistresses. Those liaisons were facilitated by friends such as Alfred de Rothschild.

Nevertheless Edward VII was to prove a dignified, charming king and Emperor, and the Edwardian era, famous for its high glamour and easy elegance, was becoming the reality. The new King declared that the period of mourning for his mother, the late Queen and Empress, was to extend for only the following three months. Preparations could then begin for his coronation, at which no pomp was to be spared.

In the event, because of the King's appendicitis, the ceremony took place over a year later, on 9 August 1902, in Westminster Abbey. Alfred de Rothschild was invited to attend, as, of course, were Lord and Lady Carnarvon, the Dowager Countess of Carnarvon, and other members of the family.

The new century was under way and the modern world was fast approaching: not just Carnarvon's beloved motor cars, but also powered flight, the rise of the Labour movement and, on a distant horizon, socialism, revolution and war. But as the Carnarvons, dressed in their ermine robes, watched Edward being crowned King of the United Kingdom and the British Dominions, Emperor of India, they must have considered that their world looked as glitteringly splendid as ever.

7

Edwardian Egypt

The year 1901 opened with an outpouring of national grief, but by late spring the black banners had been folded away and there was a sense that the country needed to look to the future.

'Motor' Carnarvon was having a busy year. Births and deaths were important, but so was his obsessive love for his car. In July, a month before Evelyn's birth, he'd outraged a policeman in Epping, who described him as coming 'dashing down a hill at the terrific speed of what must have been 25 miles an hour.' To make matters worse, neither the Earl nor his mechanic, who was following in a second car, stopped when, blowing furiously on his whistle, the policeman put his hand up. Difficult for us to imagine a world in which 25 miles an hour was considered reckless driving, but the Earl was summoned to appear in court again for that offence, something that was becoming almost routine. Fortunately for him he had a barrister who already specialised in defending motorists, who was able to get the case dismissed. But a few months later, Lord Carnarvon's luck ran out when he suffered the first and most serious of his many car crashes.

It was late September, and Lord and Lady Carnarvon were both on the Continent, staying in Germany. They had travelled separately and were supposed to be meeting at Bad Schwalbach. The Earl and his chauffeur, Edward Trotman, were bowling along, enjoying testing the car's speed and handling when, as they crested a rise in the road, they came upon an unexpected dip and two bullock carts blocking their way. Carnarvon tried to steer the vehicle off the road, but the grass verge hid a scree of stones and he lost control of the car as it skidded, somersaulting to its resting place upside down across a muddy ditch. Trotman, who had been thrown clear, rushed to help Carnarvon and managed to drag him out, unconscious and unmoving, but still breathing. Some workers from a nearby field heard the desperate cries for help and went off in search of a horse and cart to transport the injured man to the nearest house to await the arrival of the local doctor. Carnarvon had a swollen face, concussion, burnt legs, a broken wrist and jaw and was covered in mud. He was lucky to be alive.

Almina had been sent for immediately and she rushed to join her husband. The first sight of him was terrifying, but Almina wasted no time in making arrangements for them to return to Britain so that Carnarvon could begin the long-term treatment he needed. On that voyage back, Almina discovered a talent that was to grow into her greatest passion: nursing. She looked after her husband tenderly, and found that she could bear the stress and the worry with calm and resilience. Once back in London, Almina summoned the finest surgeons and Carnarvon had a series of operations, but his health, always fragile, never fully recovered. The accident was to have a lasting effect on the dynamic between them, as well as changing both of their lives in ways neither could have predicted.

The first and most visible change was that the Earl, at the age of thirty-five, was no longer a vigorous man. He had to use a stick to walk and was even more prone to picking up any and every influenza or virus that was making the rounds. He suffered crippling migraines for the next five years, the result of his head injuries. Almina insisted that he needed a personal physician, and Dr Marcus Johnson joined the household as the family doctor. Over time he became a great friend, virtually a member of the family, and was always called Dr Johnnie.

Dr Johnnie initially advised the Earl to adopt a more sedate pace of life, but Lord Carnarvon had other ideas. He was determined not to lose his nerve after the accident, and had begun driving again as soon as he was able. Riding was now too much for him so he took up the newly fashionable pastime of golf, and decided to construct a nine-hole course on the estate. He was also a keen photographer. His lifelong love of gadgets and gizmos meant he was an early adopter of all the latest advances in technology. He proved to be talented and meticulous and built up a reputation as one of the most respected photographers of his time. But it was travel, his first love, specifically his trips to Egypt, which provided him with the hobby that would metamorphose into the obsession that guaranteed his lasting fame.

As winter settled in, Dr Johnnie suggested to the Earl that – given the state of his lungs – he should avoid the cold damp English winters and head for somewhere warm. This time Lord Carnarvon was entirely in agreement with his physician. The obvious choice was Egypt, where there is virtually no humidity and the air is always clear and dry. Carnarvon had visited for the first time in 1889 and loved it. Then in 1898 he had been holidaying there with Almina when she had fallen pregnant. Now Egypt was set to become a regular part of the Carnarvons' lives.

By the end of the nineteenth century, Egypt was very firmly on the tourist trail. Throughout the seventeenth and eighteenth centuries, travellers returned to their native lands laden with antiquities, and interest in all things Oriental provoked a craze of Egyptomania across Europe. The flood increased throughout the nineteenth century, and well-to-do British tourists astounded their friends back home with their watercolour sketches of the pyramids and stories of even greater wonders, just waiting to be discovered beneath the sands. By today's standards, though, the visitor numbers were pretty small. Travel was still the preserve of the very wealthy, and was not only expensive but arduous. The journey from Britain started with a train to Southampton, then a sea crossing to France, another train to the Riviera and a boat from Marseilles to Alexandria. The last leg of the trip was via another train to Cairo. But even in his enfeebled state, Lord Carnarvon was a man full of wanderlust and a need for distraction and diversion.

Virtually every year from 1902, just after Christmas, which once they had children they almost always spent at Highclere, Lord and Lady Carnarvon set out together for Egypt. There were exceptions to this choice of destination: in 1903 they thought they would try the United States, but although the *New York Times* described Almina as 'a very pretty young woman, small and *piquante*', it seems she didn't love America back, considering it too brash and too fast for her tastes. In the winter of 1906 they went to Colombo and Singapore. Porchy and Evelyn were left in the care of their grandmother, Marie, much to their delight since they were tremendously spoiled. There was a summer family holiday to Cromer in Norfolk when Almina joined the children and Nurse Moss on the beach. But mostly, the Carnarvons' trips were to Egypt.

Sometimes they stopped off in Paris en route. Almina had many friends there and perhaps her husband judged that a few days in the luxurious surroundings of the Ritz would be a delightful interlude before the discomforts that awaited her on site at the Earl's excavations.

In the early days, though, the trips to Cairo were leisured affairs. Lord and Lady Carnarvon stayed at Shepheard's Hotel on the banks of the Nile in Cairo, a magnificent building in classical French style that betrayed the influence of Napoleon's 1798 military campaign. It was the fashionable place to stay and was always full of artists, statesmen and sportsmen, as well as genteel invalids and collectors. Almina, who delighted in a good social scene, enjoyed herself, and Lord Carnarvon's health began to recover.

That first season in Egypt was so beneficial that on their return to Highclere Lord Carnarvon decided to focus on a long-cherished dream, and in 1902 he founded the stud that has been such a vital part of life at Highclere ever since. He had a lifelong obsession with racing and racehorses and had a lot of success as a breeder.

Almina also indulged her passion – in this instance, for clothes. The newspapers of her era were every bit as avid as any of today's glossy magazines for the details of trendsetters' wardrobes and Almina's taste was commended numerous times in the press. The descriptions of her dresses are mouthwatering. On one occasion 'her dress of all white orchids was much admired'. At a garden party at Kensington Palace she was 'very smart in white muslin with incrustations of fine lace'. After another function it was reported that 'Lady Carnarvon was gorgeous in terracotta satin with a pearl and diamond necklace.' Her combination of petite beauty and impeccable dress sense made her a cover star many times over. On 8 November 1902, a little over a year after Eve's birth, she appeared on the front cover of *Country Life* magazine, figure fully restored, waist laced down to nothing, looking radiant.

The routine of summer at home, winter in Egypt, improved the Earl's health immeasurably. In fact, he got so much better that within a couple of years, he was determined to apply for a concession and undertake some excavations himself. He had been reading about the cultures of Ancient Egypt ever since he was a boy and, as he wrote to his sister Winifred, had been seized with the 'wish and intention even as far back as 1889 to start excavating.' Now that he was spending more time out there, he struck up a close and enduring friendship with Sir William Garstin, who was director of the Ministry of Public Works. One of the departments within his ministry was that of Antiquities. It was run by a charming and gallant French Egyptologist called Professor Gaston Maspero.

Napoleon's campaign in Egypt had renewed interest and knowledge in all things ancient and curious, because his army had been accompanied by one hundred academics to record, sketch and investigate the lost culture. Thereafter, scholars, adventurers and bona fide Egyptologists had all set off to explore and return with histories of the architecture and works of art for public and private collections.

The fortunate discovery of the Rosetta Stone by the French, and its subsequent acquisition by the British, led to the decipherment of hieroglyphs. The tablet was engraved with a decree repeated in three different languages – demotic script, Ancient Greek and Ancient Egyptian hieroglyphs – which allowed Thomas Young and Jean-François Champollion to unlock the key to the ancient language.

Only at end of the nineteenth century was there any sort of requirement for a methodical approach towards excavation. Egyptian Exploration Societies, universities and private individuals could all apply for permission to excavate. Scholars were just beginning to appreciate how important it was to record the context of any discovery, and the British archaeologist Flinders Petrie set the standard for painstaking recording and study of artefacts.

The competition for concessions was intense, and private individuals such as Lord Carnarvon accepted that, to begin with, the sites they were granted would be the less exciting ones. Presumably Carnarvon was not sure about his own level of commitment either, given that the sums involved in mounting a serious excavation were absolutely vast. As Carnarvon wrote in the preface to his 1911 book *Five Years' Explorations at Thebes*, there could be anything up to 275 men and boys labouring on any team, and during one season he was running five teams. There were also overseers, mules and boats to be hired and digging and storage equipment to be bought. Lord Carnarvon had sold his two Somerset estates, Pixton and Tetton in 1901 to his stepmother, Elsie, who was to give one each to his brothers, Aubrey and Mervyn. Carnarvon was at this point well able to finance his excavation work, whilst Almina's fortune continued to fund the running of Highclere.

Back in 1906, when the Earl began his excavations, the first site he was assigned was an unprepossessing rubbish mound near Luxor. He was there for six weeks, enveloped in clouds of dust. Lord Carnarvon wrote to his sister Winifred, telling her that 'every day I go to my digging and command a small army of 100 men and boys.' A large screened cage had been constructed to provide a scrap of shade from the sun and protection from the flies. Carnarvon was poised, optimistically, to catalogue finds and draft maps of the site.

Almina loyally attended every day. Photos of Lord Carnarvon show him wearing a three-piece tweed suit, a wide-brimmed hat with a white band, and stout English shoes. Almina, on the other hand, was dressed for a garden party on a fine English summer's day, in a floaty tea dress and patent leather heels, complete with jewellery winking in the blinding sunshine.

It was gruelling and rather dull. Nothing much seemed to be happening. The couple would share a sandwich at lunchtime and struggle to keep each other's spirits high in the face of very little success. Almina always supported her husband in Egypt, and in the most concrete ways – with her money and with her presence – but she was interested in, rather than passionately intrigued by, his work.

After the travails of the dusty days, the Carnarvons retired to the Winter Palace Hotel, in time to watch the sun set over the rocky escarpments and temples on the west bank of the Nile. The hotel was by far the best place in town to stay: an elegant, dusky pink building with broad curved staircases sweeping up to the entrance, and magnificent gardens. It had a cool marble salon shaded with white blinds and decorated with aquarelles of the ancient sites. Outside there were lovingly watered lawns, hibiscus bushes and palms.

It was extremely luxurious but, naturally, the Carnarvons were adding even more extravagant pleasures to their stay. They took the central rooms, with balconies looking out over the river and towards the cliffs around Hatshepsut's temple. Their view at Highclere was over the lush rolling hills of a landscape that symbolised the permanence of power. When they looked out in Luxor, they saw the desert that had engulfed the palaces of kings.

If they were inclined to worry about the impermanence of things as they took their aperitifs on the balcony, they could always distract themselves with an excellent dinner. They dined in a private room and had brought with them supplies of food and wines, brandies and Madeira from the Rothschild cellars were also shipped in. As always, they were generous with all this abundance. Almina enjoyed the social life more than the day's activities, and the hotel was full of interesting people to invite to join them.

Domestic concerns and the small tensions of married life lurked in the background. Carnarvon was pleased to hear from Highclere that Henry [Porchy] had a new tutor who was 'very satisfied with him, says he has exceptional quickness and a remarkable memory.' The parental pride is touching, especially from a man who struggled to be at ease with or express affection to his son. 'I should like him to be good at games,' Carnarvon commented. Perhaps it was the wish of the frustrated sportsman in a failing body.

He was also concerned that Almina was bored and had been suffering some health problems. She was somewhat nervy, but he commented to Winifred that Luxor seemed to agree with her. 'I am glad to say Almina is looking better . . . the air on the hills is so pure and champagne-like. I am afraid she will have to have a small operation on our return, scraping the womb. I consider it comes chiefly from nerves but I am not a very nervous person, so perhaps am not a good judge.'

That first dig must have been extremely trying for any casual observer. After six weeks of hard labour and dashed hopes, Carnarvon brought operations to a close. The sum total of artefacts recovered was a single case for a mummified cat, which Lord Carnarvon gave to Cairo Museum. He was not discouraged. As he assured Winifred, 'this utter failure, instead of disheartening me had the effect of making me keener.'

In 1907, the Carnarvons were back, and this time the Earl was well aware that he had previously been palmed off with a site that the authorities knew was a dud. With the help of Gaston Maspero, Carnarvon chose a site near a mosque en route to the temples at Deir el-Bahri. He had gathered in the local coffee shops that there were rumours of a tomb, and after two weeks of hard digging, his team found it. It proved to be an important Eighteenth Dynasty tomb, that of a King's son: Teta-Ky. There was a principal decorated chapel more or less intact, niches in the courtyard contained *shabti* figures (small servant figurines) and eight more painted *shabtis* lined the corridors to the subterranean vaults. Carnarvon was incredibly excited – and hooked. He spent days taking photographs as a record of everything he found. He also donated a limestone offering table to the British Museum. Carnarvon knew that if he carried on in Egypt he would need professional help and interpretation. Gifts of antiquities were an excellent way of gaining attention. In the end Dr Wallis Budge of the British Museum became a close friend and frequent guest of the Carnarvons in London and at Highclere.

Gaston Maspero was still receiving disparaging letters from his inspector, Arthur Weigall in Luxor, concerning Lord Carnarvon's excavations. To be diplomatic and to improve Carnarvon's chance of success, Maspero suggested that he hire Howard Carter to supervise and advise on the excavations. In terms of subsequent events, the most significant event of this season was therefore the planting of a seed that led to a friendship between Howard Carter and Lord Carnarvon. It was to be another two years before they embarked upon a collaboration that lasted fourteen years and eventually, with the discovery of the tomb of Tutankhamun, ensured that their names are still remembered by anyone with more than a passing interest in Ancient Egypt.

Howard Carter was born in London in 1874, the son of an artist who specialised in animal paintings. He had been in Egypt almost constantly since 1891, when he arrived as a precociously talented seventeen-year-old draughtsman. He rose to become one of the most eminent experts in the field, but in 1905 he had fallen on hard times. He had resigned earlier that year from the post he had held since 1899 as inspector of Lower Egypt for the Antiquities Service. There had been a fracas between French tourists and Egyptian site guards in which he supported the Egyptians, and his position became untenable.

In 1909 Lord Carnarvon engaged Carter to be his man in Luxor and was paying him a salary; the following year he built him a house that became known as Castle Carter. His concern was that Carter should be sufficiently well provided for to be able to get on with the job in hand. Carnarvon installed a dark room, which helped enormously with his photographic work. Castle Carter would also come in handy as a lunchtime rest point. Carter was delighted to have secured a financially generous, committed and serious-minded colleague. Despite the differences in the two men's social background, they were a formidable alliance and became great friends.

This change in fortunes was exhilarating; Carnarvon was ecstatic. He adored the exquisite objects that he was discovering and before long established a reputation for his collector's eye. 'My chief aim . . . is not merely to buy because a thing is rare, but rather to consider the beauty of an object than its pure historic value.' He was not merely an aesthete, though. The book he wrote with Howard Carter about their five years' digging at Thebes was a serious work, published by the Oxford University Press and illustrated with his own photos. Although he was regarded by many as a maverick, he was well liked by the locals, who referred to him as 'Lordy'. Carnarvon was unfailingly courteous, one of the very last of the gentleman excavators.

Almina shared her husband's appreciation of the highly aesthetic and was thrilled that now they were seeing concrete results, an abundance of gorgeous things. But Almina wouldn't have been Almina if she hadn't also looked for an outlet for all her restless energy. Before long, she found a way to stamp her genius for party organising on the local social scene.

One evening she organised an unforgettable dinner party in Karnak Temple. She appropriated all the staff from the Winter Palace Hotel and dressed them in costumes inspired by the *One Thousand and One Nights*. The Carnarvons received their guests in the temple of Rameses. Long tables set with crisp white linen, glass and silverware stretched the length of the chamber. The food and wine were, naturally, of the very best quality. Maspero sat at the head of one table of Egyptologists, the Carnarvons at another. The whole scene was flooded with moonlight as well as candles and lamps that Almina had arranged to throw into relief the columns of the Hippostyle Hall. When the meal finished, everyone wandered down to the Sacred Lake and contemplated in silence the breathtaking view before making their way back to the Winter Palace. Then the staff glided in and removed every trace of the event. It was as if the party had been a vision conjured up by one of the genies in Scheherazade's *Arabian Nights*.

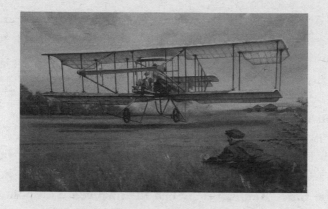

8

The Passing of the Golden Age

The Edwardian era came to a close with the death of Edward VII on 6 May 1910. He had been king for just nine years but had restored the sparkle to the monarchy and embodied the values and vices of the upper classes in spectacular form. Alfred de Rothschild, his longstanding supporter and friend, was terribly grieved. It was the beginning of a long slide into disappointment for Alfred, who was shortly to suffer the pain of having family and friends in both Britain and Germany, as the two countries lurched towards war.

The new king was in precisely the same boat. George V was related to virtually every crowned head in Europe. One of his first cousins was the Tsar of Russia; another was, of course, the Kaiser. Victoria had made little secret of preferring Wilhelm II to George V, but the new King had identified Germany as a serious threat as early as 1904. He was right; there was disaster bubbling under, mud and horror and death on a scale that no one could imagine in an era when mechanised mass warfare was still inconceivable.

But Britain had a last few precious years of peace to relish before the carnage. Not that it was uneventful: 1910 was a year of political turmoil and, in a sign of the pressure of the times, Almina briefly became involved with political activism. But at Highclere, for now, all was calm. Or rather, all was the usual mad swirl of fun and adventure. Throughout 1910, Almina put on parties and balls, accompanied her husband on trips to Scotland for shooting, made the annual trek to Egypt. When they were in town, she and Lord Carnarvon – along with her mother Marie – were often at Alfred de Rothschild's box at Covent Garden.

The Earl, meanwhile, was facilitating a piece of aviation history. He remained fascinated by motor cars and technology of all kinds. As early as 1908 he had begun to invite pioneers of aviation such as John Moore-Brabazon and Monsieur Gabriel Voisin to stay at Highclere. In 1909, when the brilliant young engineer Geoffrey de Havilland was casting around for somewhere to store and test his experimental aircraft, Moore-Brabazon suggested he use his sheds on the edge of Highclere estate and approach Lord Carnarvon for permission to carry out a test flight off the lower slopes of Beacon Hills. In November of 1909, de Havilland and his assistant loaded the biplane that was the prototype for the famous Gipsy Moth into a lorry and took it to Highclere. When Lord Carnarvon and Mr Moore-Brabazon visited the men, who were staying at the local pub, they were hugely impressed. Carnarvon said de Havilland could use the fields, and promised to keep the grass mown.

Over the next ten months, de Havilland made numerous test flights. The first were tiny hops but gradually, as he tweaked the design, the flights grew longer. He was lucky to escape several crashes, but by the end of autumn 1910 he had kept the aircraft airborne for more than 50 feet, banking to the left over the road into Highclere, turning a full circle and then landing. Lord Carnarvon, who witnessed this flight, was 'elated at the success which attended the efforts of the flying men.'

That autumn there was a family celebration. Lord Carnarvon's half-brother Aubrey was getting married, and no one, least of all the groom, could quite believe his luck in acquiring such a lovely wife.

Aubrey was careless with money and physically frail, just like his older brother. He had terribly poor eyesight and unconventional taste in clothes, but his gestures were expressive and warm and, like Lord Carnarvon, he was wholly unpretentious. Mary, his intended, was the daughter of Anglo-Irish nobility: the 4th Viscount de Vesci, and was tall, elegant and very well educated; she also moved in the most fashionable circles. Aubrey met her through his friend Raymond Asquith, the Prime Minister Herbert Asquith's son, who was a great friend of his from Oxford, and whose sister Violet was one of Mary's confidantes. Opinion on Aubrey's spectacular luck divided the Asquith siblings, with Raymond happy to acknowledge that Aubrey would be a very fortunate man on his wedding day and Violet sniffily retorting that he was quite undeserishedly blessed.

Mary seems to have thought that he would brush up well enough to be taken to Gosford Castle in Ulster to meet her grandfather the Earl of Wemyss. She was more worried about curtailing the overflowing parties of drunken diplomats at Pixton, the house in Somerset he had been gifted by Elsie, his mother.

Aubrey might have been a scruff and a dilettante, but he was also an acknowledged regional expert on the Middle East. He had been in Egypt in 1904 and then gone to Constantinople on a two-year diplomatic posting. He was reasonably fluent in Turkish, Greek, Albanian and Arabic as well as French and German, and well liked across the region. (So well liked that, just before the outbreak of the Great War, he would be approached by the government of Albania and asked whether he would like to become king. He cabled home. *Have been offered throne of Albania stop may I accept love Aubrey.* The Earl's reply was terse and to the point. *No. Carnarvon.*)

Aubrey and Mary were married on 20 October 1910 at St James's, Piccadilly. It was a quintessential Society wedding, and Almina was insistent that the couple should begin their honeymoon at Highclere. The children, Porchy and Eve, were particularly delighted with that suggestion, since they adored their bumbling, exuberant uncle.

It wasn't long before Aubrey's dress returned to its naturally chaotic state, and the house parties at Pixton were made only marginally more dignified by the introduction of Mary's elegant friends.

Aubrey and Mary were given her mother's magnificent house at 28 Bruton Street as a wedding gift. They were living just a few doors down from Almina's mother Marie, and round the corner from Carnarvon HQ in Berkeley Square. The family network was extremely handy when Lord and Lady Carnarvon were abroad, as they very frequently were. Porchy remembered lots of stays with his grandmother, who was only too pleased to look after the children and spoke nothing but French with them.

Almina was by this time thirty-six years old. She had been married for seventeen years, had metamorphosed from a slightly suspect young unknown to the public face of the Carnarvon partnership. As her husband's health got worse, she took on more and more of the hosting duties, more of the networking that sustained their lives. These days, Carnarvon preferred to ask connections from Egypt to stay at Highclere. He was beginning to acquire a notable collection of small exquisite works of Egyptian art. Carnarvon appropriated the breakfast room for his 'Antiques Room' and – through the British Museum – organised proper display cupboards to be made. Almina had to ensure that the staff completely cleared the Dining Room at the end of an evening because the family would have to breakfast in there from now on.

Small details like this were not enough to keep Almina occupied. Her vast energy lacked outlets and she was patently looking around for something other than the social whirl and household management to occupy her.

For a while she seems to have thought her passion might be politics. The year 1910 was a big one in British politics. In 1909 the Chancellor of the Exchequer in the Liberal government, David Lloyd George, had proposed the 'People's Budget', which included radical reform of the tax system, explicitly designed to redistribute money from the wealthy to the poor via an increase in social welfare. More controversially, it also included a land tax. The budget was rejected by the House of Lords, causing a furore and triggering a general election in January 1910 that produced a coalition government led by the Liberals in alliance with the Irish Parliamentary Party. The Liberals won just two more seats than the Conservatives and promptly began to try to limit the power of the House of Lords to veto legislation. By the middle of the year, everyone was waiting for another general election to be called since the government was virtually deadlocked, particularly over the budget and the issue of Home Rule for Ireland.

There was a huge feeling of outrage from Conservative voters about the possible break-up of the Union, the Liberals' attempts to reform the House of Lords, immigration and the inadequacies of the National Insurance Bill. Almina felt it was her duty to get involved to champion the Tory Party cause. In anticipation of her increasing workload, she hired a secretary, Miss Mary Weekes.

Mary had previously worked for Alfred de Rothschild and was supremely efficient, used to dealing with the slightly capricious style that characterised both Almina and her father. She was very much the equivalent of the modern PA, booking in Her Ladyship's social engagements in London, organising her at Highclere, travelling with her at all times. She was tall and slim and completely devoted to Almina. She was also a sign of the changing times, a woman in the Countess's employ who was not strictly speaking a servant, certainly not a lady's maid.

Mary helped Almina to push the bounds of her role far out beyond the confines of the Castle. There is a red cuttings-book at Highclere in which are pasted the transcripts of Almina's speaking engagements in the years 1910 and 1911. They must have been typed by Mary, and they range from the straightforward speeches delivered at village fetes: 'I am delighted to declare this bazaar open!' to addresses to the ladies of the South Berkshire Unionist [Conservative] Association.

Almina's tone when she spoke at political meetings was highly charged, her language designed to touch the hearts of her listeners as well as to stir their campaigning zeal. In a speech opposing the Liberal government's attempts to reform the House of Lords, she pointed to the Lords' defence of every parent's right to determine what religious education their child should receive as evidence that the Upper Chamber didn't need reforming. Almina's rhetoric is perfectly judged for her audience, her tone supremely confident. 'We maintain that the poor man has as good a right as the rich to choose in what religion his child should be brought up . . . [Here we see] the importance of a strong Upper House to every mother in the land.' You can almost hear the enthusiastic applause of the mothers in the audience.

Almina goes on to urge her listeners to campaign for their values, which were seen to be under attack by the Liberals, whom she insists on calling the Radicals. Her speeches are eminently readable; she seems to be relishing this chance to get out into the world and talk about something of national importance, rather than being merely the public face of Highclere. There is an exuberance in her words that suggests she was probably a very good public speaker. 'The Constitution under which we have flourished and found the highest civilisation and the most perfect freedom is in peril. Remember, we were caught napping in 1906 [when the Conservatives lost their seat in Newbury in a landslide victory for the Liberal Party] and that the slightest weakening in our work may jeopardise Mr Mount's seat . . .' Almina comes across like a seasoned pro of political speeches, building up to a stirring finish and a direct call to action. 'Don't forget Reading. Urge your friends not to rest content until the flag of national unity, trade reform and social progress waves triumphantly in that important centre of industry.'

In the January 1910 general election, the Conservatives regained Newbury from the Liberals. You can't help wondering what part was played by the army of South Berkshire women Almina sent out to campaign.

Almina might have been a skilled orator and energetic defender of Conservative politics, but she was also a woman at a time when women did not have the right to vote, let alone to stand for election. Any ambition to be involved in politics would have to be channelled into behind-the-scenes campaigning work. It seems that Almina, despite her modest assertions that she was unaccustomed to public speaking, very much enjoyed it, and when Aubrey decided to stand as the Conservative candidate for Somerset South in a 1911 by-election, she relished helping him to write electioneering speeches and campaigning on his behalf. Aubrey won. They must have been a dream team, both of them big personalities overflowing with self-assurance.

Almina's values and politics were very much those you would expect of a woman of her social class at the time and it would, of course, be overstating the case to say that she was a champion of women's rights. She never voiced any support for women's suffrage. Even so, some of her speeches give a very strong sense of her forceful personality, her wit and her faith in women's power to influence public life. She tells the Newbury Unionist Women's Association in January 1911: 'In the dark ages, which are not very far behind us, we used to be called the weaker sex. We never were, and we never shall be weaker in our patriotism. In this as in all similar matters we are neither inferior nor superior, but only very different and I am convinced that we shall do most good to our country and her cause if instead of imitating men we endeavour to widen and perhaps enrich the spirit of public life by being simply ourselves.'

After her successes campaigning in the 1910 general elections and Aubrey's by-election, Almina seems to have cast around for the next challenge and realised that there wasn't one that really suited her. She was too theatrical and too restless to be content with delivering rousing speeches to local political societies, and although now you can imagine her as a fiery, eccentric MP, then she had no such outlet. Her instinct to be useful was clearly very strong because she kept up her public speaking and appearances at various charitable occasions including the East Ham Chrysanthemum Show and the Tunbridge Wells fundraiser for Dr Barnardo's children's homes. But she would have to wait another three years for her big chance to do some good in the world.

And in the meantime there was always something to distract her from any lingering sense of purposelessness. Racing was perfect for that, and on 15 May 1911 Lord and Lady Carnarvon were at Ascot with the new King. There is a striking picture of them in the Royal Enclosure. The

Earl is in top hat and tails, using a silver-topped cane to support his bad leg. He looks like a man who is confident that he is about to have fun in the company of friends. Almina is wearing an ankle-length dress in black-and-white striped satin, a dark fur and a spectacular wide-brimmed, ostrich-feather-trimmed hat. She is leaning away from her husband, seemingly laughing as she extends her hand to someone by her side. She looks as if she is graciously receiving the tributes due to her. It is utterly unlike the sweet and purposeful demeanour in the photo of her in nurse's uniform that was taken barely more than three years later.

Glitz, public life, the dignity of the Carnarvons – these were still very important to her in 1911, and they all combined on 22 June 1911, the day of the coronation of King George V and Queen Mary. The whole household had gone up to town to prepare. Fearnside, Roberts and Jessie Money, Almina's new lady's maid, had been in charge of bringing everything that would be required to the house in Berkeley Square. Meticulously, Fearnside brushed down the Earl's ermine robes. They had last been used eight years previously, at the coronation of Edward VII, and had been carefully kept in camphor and checked twice a year for moths. Roberts and Money laid out Almina's ornate dress, tiara and jewels. Lord and Lady Carnarvon each had a bedroom and dressing room on the second floor of the house and, by the time they arrived to get ready, the running along corridors and frantic unpacking of boxes was all finished and everything was ready for them. The Earl and Countess set off for Westminster Abbey to join the throng of peers and nobles of the realm.

The procession to the abbey was splendid. The King and Queen travelled in the gold State Coach, drawn by eight heavily caparisoned carriage horses with four postillions riding and several footmen accompanying. Lord Kitchener rode in a place of honour to the right of the State Coach. He had been made Field Marshal, the highest rank in the Army, by Edward VII as he lay on his deathbed, in recognition of his service in Sudan, South Africa and India.

As they waited for the ceremony to begin, there was plenty of time to observe the splendours of the abbey, familiar to them of course from all the State occasions they had attended there, and the dress of the other members of the congregation. The church was full of the Carnarvons' friends and all the crowned heads of Europe, but Almina must have been irritated to have to shake hands with Herbert Asquith, the Liberal Prime Minister, leader of the dreadful 'Radicals'.

The Carnarvons watched anxiously for the arrival of the procession and strained to catch their first glimpse of their son, who had been chosen to be one of the Pages of Honour. He had been granted leave from his prep school, Ludgrove, to attend the endless rehearsals for the coronation, all masterminded by the Duke of Norfolk. The Duke was apparently meticulous in his supervision of the pages and required complete attention to detail, but Porchy remembered that, if a rehearsal had gone well, he dished out delicious chocolates to everyone afterwards.

On this occasion, doubtless to Almina's relief, her son acquitted himself perfectly and the whole ceremony was magnificent, with the guns' salute thundering across Hyde Park and the bells of the abbey pealing out over the newly crowned King and Queen as they left the church. It was probably the last great gathering of the old order. Europe's political scene was tense and getting worse; there were just over three years to go before war was declared. Of the eight Pages of Honour on that occasion, only two would survive the coming carnage. Lord Porchester would be one of them.

On New Year's Eve 1911, Almina gave her annual children's party at Highclere, with hundreds of guests, and entertainers brought down from London. Twelve days later she threw a ball for 500 local people. Almina had to greet her guests without the Earl, whose migraine was so bad that he could not attend for more than a few minutes before retiring to his rooms. That wasn't unusual; Almina was increasingly the power that was keeping everything going. She addressed the throng of people at midnight, from the balcony that overlooks the beautiful vaulted Saloon at the heart of the Castle, apologising on Lord Carnarvon's behalf. She was flanked by her mother Marie, her husband's sisters, and by Aubrey and his wife Mary. Prince Victor Duleep Singh stayed to lend his support to Almina as she spoke and then loyally retired to the Earl's sitting room to keep his old friend company. Aubrey welcomed everyone again at supper and then the Mayor of Newbury thanked the Carnarvons and family on behalf of the guests. The dancing began after supper with music supplied by Merier's Viennese orchestra and twenty different dances on the programme. Almina had placed lanterns all along the carriage driveways to light her guests home in the early hours and the party didn't finish until 6.00 a.m.

It had been fun, it had been a success; but by now Almina could manage these occasions in her sleep. It was not the challenge she needed. The Earl's health continued to be poor and she was busy overseeing all his treatments. She loved to take care of him and, gradually, nursing became a preoccupation, not just at home but in general. She attended operations performed by Berkeley Moynihan, the eminent surgeon at Leeds General Infirmary who made occasional trips to London to carry out his duties as a consultant at University Hospital. A plan was forming in the back of her mind, and she wanted to be prepared if the moment for action presented itself.

Almina continued to accompany Carnarvon on his trips to Egypt, where he and Carter were struggling to get access to the sites they were determined to excavate. They had their eye on a spot in the Valley of the Kings, rather than the Valley of the Queens or Nobles, where they had always been based, but at that time the concession was still held by an American, Theodore Davis. Alternatives were proposed and rejected. Private excavations were no longer favoured and Maspero insisted that the pyramid site Carnarvon had been considering must be reserved for official exploration.

Ever resourceful, Carnarvon contacted Lord Kitchener, who was a personal friend, and asked if he could lean on Maspero. After his nine years as Commander in Chief of India, Kitchener had been sent to Egypt in 1909, where he was Consul General and de facto Viceroy. It was inevitable that Kitchener and Carnarvon would meet and socialise out there, since they moved in precisely the same circles. Despite this high-level connection, though, Carnarvon had no success.

Unsure where to concentrate next, he was persuaded by Percy Newberry, a noted English Egyptologist, to apply for some delta sites at Sakha and Tell el-Balamun. Working in the delta of the River Nile put them out of range of civilised amenities: it was going to entail camping. The fact that a man of Carnarvon's fragile health should even consider such a thing is proof of his obsessive love for his work. The fact that Almina went along too is surely proof of her love for him.

Carnarvon asked Percy Newberry to organise tents and provisions for him, Almina, his valet Fearnside, Her Ladyship's maid Edith Wiggal, Howard Carter, Dr Johnnie and himself. Provisions such as tins of soup were shipped from Fortnum & Mason's in London. The expedition duly set off. It was an adventure by anyone's standards, and one imagines Jessie and Almina rolling their eyes together at the privations they were both expected to bear. Jessie was a regular traveller since she accompanied Almina wherever she went, but it was the first time the two women had roughed it and it proved too much.

The delta was muddy and full of cobras but the group stuck it out until the Earl fell ill with bronchitis, at which point they repaired to Luxor and the Winter Palace Hotel. With his weak lungs, he was quite seriously sick, and Almina had to nurse her husband, who was not an easy patient, back to what constituted more or less full health over a number of weeks. Carnarvon wrote at one point to Budge saying he could not put any weight on. He weighed less than nine stone and was five feet ten inches tall.

By Easter, Lord and Lady Carnarvon were back at Highclere and digging was over for another year. The Earl used the summer months to entertain his Egyptian contacts, since without a supportive group of friends in high places, it was likely to prove harder and harder to work out there.

This routine of winter in Egypt and spring and summer at Highclere was disrupted in 1913 when Almina's mother grew very ill. Marie had been a key presence throughout Almina's married life, coming to Highclere for weekend parties and for Christmas with Porchy and Eve, looking after the children in London when Lord and Lady Carnarvon were away. Almina adored her all her life and the bond they had formed when times were much harder was sustained when Almina's circumstances changed. It was a terrible blow when Marie's health began to fail in spring 1913. Almina's instinct was to bring her to Highclere and care for her there, with the aid of Dr Johnnie, but Marie was adamant that she wanted to visit her native France one last time.

Marie Wombwell's death was announced in the *Daily Mail* on 1 October 1913. She had passed away the previous week at her house in Bruton Street. Marie had got her wish and travelled to France, taking the waters in Vernet-les-Bains with her daughter by her side, but Almina had been concerned that the medical care there was not as good as that in London and the women returned to Mayfair. For six weeks Almina put into practice everything she had learned nursing her husband over the years to make her mother's last days as comfortable as possible. She owed her an enormous amount, from her French charm to her determination and self-belief, and when Marie was gone, Almina was lost without her. Alfred was terribly saddened. He and Marie had been companions for almost forty years.

A few days later, Almina's uncle, Sir George Wombwell, also died. He had stood by her all those years when rumours about her paternity circulated and had stepped up to give her away on her wedding day. Sir George and Lady Julia had often been at the Castle when Marie had been visiting and now, with his loss, it must have felt as if one more link to her past and to her mother had been broken.

She went home to Highclere and resolved to resume all her duties, but never had the everyday tasks of hosting her husband's friends and business contacts seemed such a struggle. Earlier in the year, Almina had been delighted to write to Rutherford from Egypt to accept a request to become the Patroness of Cold Ash Hospital, which lay five miles north of Highclere. She had always said she would do anything to help them, and now, more determined than ever that nursing was her vocation, she applied herself to finding out how she could be most useful at the hospital.

The guests at the Highclere house parties had always been eclectic, and now they were becoming more than a little odd. The Earl had been interested in the Occult for years, an interest that deepened the more time he spent in Egypt. By 1912 he occasionally employed a palmist to read his palm and quite frequently engaged a clairvoyant to hold séances at Highclere. There was nothing unusual in that. Spiritualism, which had begun as an import from the United States in the 1850s, rapidly became a craze. The first national Spiritualist meeting in the UK was held in 1890, by which time it was a genuine mass movement. All over the country, people were sitting in circles, hands joined, hoping to make contact with the spirit world and receive messages from the dead. There were celebrity fans such as Sir Arthur Conan Doyle, the author of the Sherlock Holmes books, who wrote extensively on the phenomenon.

Sometimes the séances were private affairs, but sometimes they were offered as entertainment at a house party. Porchy remembered observing several, sometimes with his sister, Eve. They were held in one of the upstairs guest bedrooms, with the shutters closed against any glimmer of light, and could be very tense occasions. Once, Porchy and Eve witnessed a bowl of flowers levitating off the table. Eve got so nervous she reportedly had to go into a nursing home for a fortnight's rest. At one, Howard Carter and a female guest were present, and the lady was placed in a trance in order to channel a spirit message. She began to speak in a strange voice and a language that at first no one could identify. Carter proclaimed, in a tone of amazement, 'It's Coptic!'

Out in the real world, there were things far more frightening than inexplicably floating flowers or even the reappearance of long-dead languages. You didn't need to be psychic to sense that something nasty was coming for the people of Highclere.

9

The Summer of 1914

The summer of 1914 was delightfully warm. Almina arrived back from Egypt in late April and was only at Highclere for a few weeks before she made a week-long trip to Paris. On 11 June, the Earl and Countess were entertaining a large house party for the Newbury Races; amongst their guests were Mr and Mrs James Rothschild. If you were a casual observer, you might say it was business as usual, but a glance at the newspapers, or at Alfred de Rothschild's distraught face as he sat puffing cigars nervously in the Smoking Room, would have told you otherwise.

Europe was on the brink of war, despite the best efforts of numerous people, including Alfred, to avert it. Alfred had placed his considerable powers of influence, his network of contacts and his money at the disposal of the British government, acting as an unofficial intermediary between the unravelling Austro-Hungarian Empire and Germany. Half of Alfred's family and friends were based in Europe and it was agony to him that hostilities were about to open up between countries that had until relatively recently been bound together so closely. The growing certainty that conflict was inevitable left him worried sick about loved ones on both sides and suffering from a sense of helplessness.

The challenge of holding back war was too big for any single individual, family or politician, despite all the desperate, behind-the-scenes negotiations. For months the newspapers had carried stories of Germany, Russia and Austria all conscripting men into their armies and hurriedly constructing more railways to transport them. Germany, although virtually landlocked, had been building up a Navy big enough to rival Britain's.

Almina sensed what was coming and made a decision. She had, after all, been thinking about it for at least two years. She consulted Lord Carnarvon, who was lukewarm, but when pressed, agreed that it might be a possibility. Lady Almina wanted to convert Highclere into a hospital for injured officers, to bring in the most expert medical staff and provide the best of everything a soldier could possibly need to recover, from state-of-the-art equipment and pioneering operations to abundant fresh food and soft clean sheets. Almina's instinct was to create a hospital that soothed and cheered the senses of men who had been half destroyed by horror.

With her husband's assent secured, Almina's next step was to speak to the military authorities. She would need their assistance at least on the administrative side, if not the financing. Almina already had a third conversation planned that would resolve the problem of who was going to pay for everything: the money question could wait. It was entirely typical of Almina's life that when she decided to establish a military hospital, the person she elected to call to discuss her plans should be the highest-ranking official in the Army. Straight to the top – that might as well have been Almina's motto.

Field Marshal Earl Kitchener, Sirdar of Egypt, accepted her invitation to lunch in late June and arrived dressed in an immaculate tweed suit, accompanied by his military secretary Colonel Evelyn Fitzgerald. The famous hero was now sixty-four years old but he was an upright, imposing man, with the piercing eyes and perfectly groomed moustache that would shortly be put to such iconic use in the famous recruiting poster 'Your Country Needs You'.

He was also a longstanding friend of the Carnarvons and Alfred de Rothschild. Almina had prepared a delicious summer lunch and showed Lord Kitchener around, explaining what she wished to do. He was impressed by her enthusiasm and sincerity. She needed his approval and blessing, and a promise that he would encourage the Services, particularly Southern Command, to take her up on her offer. She got it.

Porchy had been allowed to join them for lunch. He was an overexcited Eton schoolboy in awe of meeting one of his heroes, and years later he still vividly recalled the moment his father turned to K, as he called the great man, and said, 'In future, dear K, our telegraphic address will have to be Carnarvon, Amputate, Highclere.'

Almina was euphoric. She had never doubted for a moment that she would bring the necessary people round to her way of thinking. She immediately set about laying plans. The first step, naturally, was to secure the finances. And equally naturally, that was as easy as getting on the train to London and making her way to the Rothschild offices in New Court, St Swithin's Lane, to speak to Alfred.

Alfred had never ceased to be astoundingly generous with his time, money and affection over the years. It was hardly unprecedented for Almina to apply to him for support – the electric lights in Highclere were testament to that. Porchy remembered being taken up to visit his relatives from time to time and relishing the fact that he was likely to find all three Rothschild brothers at work, all of them only too willing to press as much as ten gold sovereigns into his hand. Alfred occasionally used to remonstrate gently with Almina, saying, 'Oh, puss-cat, I gave you ten thousand pounds only last week. Whatever have you done with it, my darling child?' But he never refused her; he simply took out his chequebook and unscrewed the lid of his pen.

Even so, this request was for a lot of money. Almina asked Alfred to give her £25,000 for the set-up costs. He agreed unhesitatingly. Alfred was delighted to help. He had been actively trying to avert conflict, but now that it was coming, he switched his attention to supporting the British war effort. He lent Halton House, his beloved country pleasure ground, to the armed forces for the duration of the hostilities. (It would be used as a training centre, complete with dug-out trenches, for some of Kitchener's 'first hundred thousand volunteers' later in the year.) He also supported other grand ladies in their relief work. (Almina was by no means the only Society hostess engaged in war work – Lady Sutherland was to set up a field hospital in France, and the indomitable Dowager Countess of Carnarvon, Elsie, would play a crucial part in alleviating the suffering of soldiers caught up in the savage fighting in Gallipoli.)

The Rothschilds had always had a strong commitment to philanthropic work and were particularly interested in supporting hospitals. The family interest might have been one of the spurs for Almina's own fascination with nursing, and probably fuelled her belief that it was a perfectly reasonable thing to aspire to do. After all, the Evelina Children's Hospital that was eventually merged with Guy's and St Thomas's had begun as a Rothschild-financed memorial hospital for Lady Evelina de Rothschild, who had died in childbirth in 1866.

Almina left New Court with a sense of purpose and an iron determination. She was going to make things happen.

The eighteenth of July was the start of the last big house party at Highclere for years. There were twenty-six guests, plus all their servants. Among the visitors were General Sir John Cowans, General Sir John Maxwell, Aubrey Herbert and Howard Carter. Lord Carnarvon was very much alive to the threatening state of affairs, and advised Sir John to recall his wife and daughter from Aix-en-Provence in France and Homburg in Germany, immediately.

The Earl, like the rest of the country, was worried that the Germans had been building up their Navy in order to blockade Britain. If that did happen, food shortages were likely. The farm at Highclere would be a crucial resource in the war effort and, in fact, Carnarvon had already received a large offer for his grain stock. Considering that he was morally responsible for the welfare of the entire household, as well as the tenants, he refused the offer and set about adding to his flocks and herds. He also bought one and a half tons of cheese and an immense amount of tea.

Having sorted out the provisions, Carnarvon went to the Bank of England and asked to withdraw £3,000 in gold. The clerk suggested that perhaps His Lordship might consider upping that amount to £5,000, which he duly did. Once he had deposited the gold in his bank in Newbury, he was in a position to provide 243 men, women and children with all essentials for at least three months.

The clerk's tip proved to be very well judged when from 31 July there was a run on the banks as the nation realised with horror that war was now imminent.

Meanwhile, the rest of the family was also caught up in preparations. Aubrey and Porchy were both desperate to fight, despite being either too blind or too young. Carnarvon knew he would never see active service, given his health problems, but he volunteered to advise on aerial photography, should the need arise, which in due course it did.

Lord Carnarvon's sister Winifred and her husband Herbert, Lord Burghclere, had been in Europe since June, but so tense was the atmosphere that they turned around and made their way back from the Vichy spa at which they'd been intending to stay some weeks. They arrived back in London on 25 July, with a copy of the newspaper announcing news of the Austrian ultimatum to Serbia following the assassination of the Archduke. Winifred wrote to Lord Carnarvon that it was 'the last Sunday morning of the old world'. Arriving unexpectedly at her London house on Charles Street, she added that she had just enough servants to contrive 'a picnic existence'.

After all the build-up, the excuse to take the final dramatic step towards war had been the assassination of the Austrian Archduke Franz Ferdinand on 28 June 1914 by a Serb nationalist. Once the ultimatum came and went, Austria declared war on 28 July. That triggered a domino effect as various treaties were invoked and all the great powers waded in. Russia mobilised on 31 July and Germany could therefore claim that it was acting in its own defence when it declared war against Russia on 1 August and against France on 3 August. Britain had signed the Entente Cordiale with France in 1904 and the Anglo-Russian Entente in 1907, both of which dictated that it should fight against Germany, but its hand was in any case forced by Germany's invasion of neutral Belgium. Great Britain declared war on Germany on 4 August 1914.

The Highclere guestbook has 'August 1–4 WAR!' written in a shaky hand across the top of the page that records the names of a few guests who stayed on at the house that weekend. Leonard Woolley was staying as was Lady Maxwell and Dr Johnnie. The scale of the imminent carnage was literally unimaginable to those men and women carefully studying the newspapers and sipping on a brandy to steady the nerves, or downstairs in the kitchens, discussing the latest news as they scrubbed potatoes or washed dishes.

Already it was obvious that recruits would be needed. Porchy, sixteen years old, declared he would join the cavalry. Kitchen maids joshed footmen about whether they were planning to sign up. Teenagers with nothing but bravado to sustain them boasted of their bravery. Everyone thought the war would be over by Christmas.

There was nervousness, of course, but also confidence and a sincere passion to serve King, Country and Empire.

Upstairs and downstairs, the people of Highclere were staring life-changing tragedy in the face. They just didn't know it yet.

IO

Call to Arms

After the tense summer of waiting for something definite to happen, once war was declared there was an explosion of activity.

Almina immediately pressed her sister-in-law, Winifred, for an introduction to a woman called Agnes Keyser, the founder of the Edward VII Hospital. Agnes had been a very rich, very pretty young socialite of the 1870s and 1880s. Somewhat inevitably she came to the attention of the Prince of Wales. They became friends and, later, lovers. Agnes allowed him to use her house in Belgravia for entertaining his various other friends, including Mrs Alice Keppel. The two formed a strong bond and their relationship, which was accepted within court circles and even by Queen Alexandra, lasted until the King's death.

The Prince of Wales's extravagant generosity meant that when he came to visit Agnes in Wilton Place he brought presents for everyone in the household, from the house-keeper to the newest scullery maid. But when the Boer War broke out and Agnes discovered a vocation for nursing, his assistance became more consequential.

Agnes was horrified by the plight of officers returning from the Boer war, whom she discovered were mostly highly self-sacrificing, unable to pay for surgeons' fees and conse-quently medically neglected. She used her own money to finance a hospital but relied on her connection to the King to secure the co-operation of the most distinguished doctors and surgeons. She had a genius for organisation and by 1914 was a very well-respected humanitarian.

Here was the perfect role model for Almina. She was absolutely determined to meet Agnes and ask her advice. But Sister Agnes, as she liked to be known, was already extremely busy with her own hospital. As soon as war was declared, she was offered five private houses to expand the work she was already doing, and had just taken on an extra surgeon and another house doctor when Almina sent a note requesting a meeting.

Almina, very practised in getting her own way, was insistent, and eventually Agnes granted her half an hour, although she stayed standing throughout, saying she was too busy to sit. Almina took her cue from her more experienced colleague and refused a seat. She put her case simply and clearly, and Agnes was so won over by the woman standing in front of her that she embraced her warmly as the two parted. Almina left Sister Agnes's hospital armed with practical advice from a rigorously organised and experienced nurse, and full of inspiration.

Across the country, dozens of well-off women in similar circumstances to Almina were also rushing to establish nursing homes and hospitals. The need was desperate. Queen Alexandra's Imperial Military Nursing Service had just 463 trained nurses when war was declared, although it was rapidly being augmented by Territorial Nursing Services and other voluntary organisations.

Meanwhile, the British Expeditionary Force (BEF) was preparing its departure for France, commanded by Sir John French and under the direction of Lord Kitchener. The latter had previously been planning to return to Egypt to resume his duties, and was in fact waiting at Dover to board a steamer bound for France when he received a telephone call from the Prime Minister requesting his immediate return to London. On 5 August, Lord Kitchener, now the Secretary of State for War, confirmed to the government's Council of War that the Army's forces would cross the channel immediately. Fourteen thousand extra horses had been secured for the purpose by General Sir John Cowans, the General Quartermaster (and Highclere house guest back in July, in what was rapidly feeling like a vanished age).

Kitchener was doubtful about the French capacity to defend against the Germans, but in truth, the British were scarcely better placed. The entire Army's strength was 250,000 men, of whom nearly half were stationed overseas. There was of course the Territorial Army, founded in 1908 and made up of a further 250,000 volunteers, some of whom

had even attended short training camps. The German professional Army, by contrast, was 700,000 strong, and by 10
August a further three million men had been called up.

Still, the nation was buoyed by the fact that its great
military hero was leading the charge and the British
Expeditionary Force began to deploy just three days after
war was declared. It was led by officers in scarlet or blue
coats, carefully pulling on their white gloves as they returned
the salute of the staff officers who were issuing orders to the
men. The commanding officers rode beautifully groomed
and burnished horses. The whole scene was like a pageant,
unchanged in the last two hundred years.

Aubrey Herbert, with amazing bloody-mindedness, dis-
regarded the fact that he had been rejected from both the
professional Army and the Territorials on the grounds that
he was more than half-blind. It was true he was somewhat
disadvantaged in that area, but he was also highly educated,
with a First in history from Oxford; he was also a seasoned
diplomat, fluent in six languages and passionate about the
national cause, and he was damned if he was going to stay
at home. So he got a uniform made, a complete copy of the
one worn by the Irish Guards, in which regiment his brother-
in-law was a colonel. When the Guards marched out of
Wellington Barracks opposite Buckingham Palace early on
the morning of 12 August 1914, he simply fell into step. His
mother Elsie and wife Mary waved him off at Victoria Station
and Aubrey sat with his friends in a train carriage bound for
Southampton, to board the boat to the Continent. He wasn't
discovered until they all disembarked in France, and by that
time it was too late for the Army to send the stowaway back,
so they took him on as an interpreter.

Aubrey had written to Winifred as he prepared to go off to war. His letter is charming in its expression of love for his sister and poignant in its naïve optimism.

My dear one,
It was so dear of you to have sent me the lovely flask. I was on the point of going out to buy one. I had given up the foolish habit of believing one could do without a drink. I suppose it will be very uncomfortable without a servant etc., but one really has the time of one's life before one goes. This war is a most extraordinary thing. It has made the government popular, the House of Lords popular, the House of Commons popular, the Church popular now that the Bishop of London is going, the King popular, the Army popular etc. Thank you again so much my dear, and all love to all of you.

Aubrey's gallant mission to serve as a frontline soldier didn't last long. The Irish Guards travelled northeast on foot and by train, welcomed everywhere by the French Army and civilians. Finally reaching the Front, Aubrey dismounted from his horse to march with the troops through a village and make some sort of reply to the German guns they could hear. He noted that he went into the first fight prepared only for peace as he had left his revolver and sword on his horse tethered in the woods behind. Scarcely had they reached the battle lines at Mons before they came under fire, and less than a day later were swept up in the retreat.

The British force's role was to protect the Fifth French Army's flank and prevent the Germans from executing their long-planned pincer movement to cut off the Allies. The BEF was outnumbered three to one but initially held the enemy with such good marksmanship that German soldiers later reported they thought they were being fired at with machine guns rather than rifles. But once the French Army took the unexpected decision to retreat, there was nothing for it but to fall back, fighting rearguard actions and blowing up bridges all the way to the outskirts of Paris.

Aubrey found a role as a galloper, passing messages between commanders, riding a fast if troublesome horse called Moonshine. He out-galloped several bullets before, on 1 September, one found him, punching a hole in his side and passing clean through. A Royal Army medic dressed it and left him on a stretcher heavily dosed with morphine, slipping in and out of consciousness. Hours passed and suddenly Aubrey found he was being jabbed with the butt of a rifle. It was a German soldier doing the jabbing. The man must have got the shock of his life when the heavily wounded British soldier suddenly started mumbling in groggy but fluent German.

It was probably the fact that he was an object of interest that saved Aubrey's life. That and the heavy dose of morphine that had kept him sedated and immobile. He was taken to a German-run field hospital and eventually moved on to the town of Viviers and deposited with other wounded officers in a makeshift triage station. Stories and information about friends were swapped and Aubrey's spirits recovered, but conditions were tough. The only food was unleavened biscuits, the bandages had run out and the morphine was reserved for Germans. There was no way to get a message to anyone on the British side.

Back at Highclere, reports were filtering through of the Irish Guards' involvement in the battle and the retreat. Everyone was terrified for Aubrey, who cut an unlikely

Lady Almina, the 5th Countess of Carnarvon, 1899.

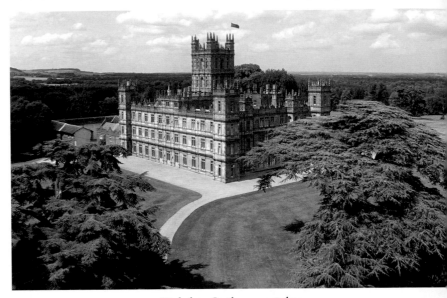
Highclere Castle, present day.

The State Drawing Room of the Castle c. 1895.

The 4th Earl of Carnarvon, 1883.

A drawing of Elsie Carnarvon, the 4th Countess.

Alfred de Rothschild, in the late 1800s.

An early portrait of the
5th Earl of Carnarvon.

Almina just before her
wedding in 1895.

A portrait by Paul César
Helleu on the occasion of
Almina's wedding, with
her married signature.

Almina, the 5th Countess of Carnarvon, in full regalia.

The staff of Highclere Castle in Almina's day.

The bellboard in the lower ground corridor of the Castle, photographed today but exactly as it was 100 years ago.

A group shot, taken by the 5th Earl of Carnavon in December 1895, of Albert, HRH The Prince of Wales, on his visit to Highclere Castle. Albert, later King Edward VII, is in the middle, standing behind Almina, seated with fur stole, on whose left (right in the picture) is Lady Winifred Herbert, the 5th Earl's sister.

COUNTRY LIFE

VOL. XII.—No. 305. [Registered at the] G.P.O. as a Newspaper] SATURDAY, NOVEMBER 8th, 1902. [Price Sixpence. at 1907. $\mathcal{8}$d.]

LAFAYETTE   184 New Bond Street. W.

THE COUNTESS OF CARNARVON.

Almina as front cover star of *Country Life* magazine in November 1902.

Almina & Porchester
Jan. 1899

Almina pictured with her newborn son, later the 6th Earl of Carnarvon, in January 1899. He was always referred to as 'Porchy', never Henry, his real name.

figure as a frontline soldier; after some days of anxious waiting, the Earl decided to take matters into his own hands. He set off in his largest motor car to go to rescue Aubrey from France. This was of course hugely dangerous, but at that point it was still just about possible. Carnarvon was on the brink of boarding a boat from Southampton when he heard the news that the French had retaken Viviers from the Germans. The seriously wounded had been left behind in the temporary hospital to wonder what was going on and listen in frustration to the machine-gun fire rattling around outside. Amongst them was his brother. Lord Carnarvon wired back to his sister, 'Aubrey wounded in the stomach; left behind when Army retired; will wire.'

Winifred then received a rather more detailed account from Almina. It transpired that the information about Aubrey's whereabouts had been given to her by Sir Mark Sykes, a great friend of Aubrey's who shared his passion for the Middle East and was working in the War Office with Lord Kitchener. The moment Sir Mark received news, he called on Almina in London, who cabled Winifred with an update:

Aubrey last seen in vicinity of Compiègne lying wounded in abdomen. English surgeons advised leaving him to care of Germans as to move under existing circumstances too risky. Two things in Aubrey's favour were having had no food for considerable time and assurance that when wounded are tended by Germans they are well looked after. That is all I know of Aubrey so far. I have personally requested American Ambassador, French Councillor and Swiss Minister to make every possible enquiry. Am in London for two or three days, wire if you want me to do anything. Elsie and Mary lunching. Am doing all I can. Almina.

Almina's telegrams caused some acerbic amusement amongst her Carnarvon relatives as they were never conspicuous for their brevity. She retorted that parsimony in communicating important information was a false economy, and she was right in this instance. Due to all the pressure in the form of telegrams flying around, Sir John French allowed Aubrey to be transported to Le Havre by road under the care of a nurse rather than in the somewhat rough troop hospital trains. Almina wasn't going to let a little thing like a war get in the way of her policy of asking for what she wanted and, as usual, she was vindicated.

Winifred had just finished her breakfast when another telegram arrived, this one only as long as it needed to be to convey the good news. 'Aubrey found; disembarks at Southampton today.'

He was met by Elsie, Mary, Lord Carnarvon and Dr Johnnie. Carnarvon wanted to take him straight to Highclere but Aubrey's wife and mother preferred to have him in town, close to them, at a small nursing home run by Almina's sister-in-law, Vera. The family set off slowly in convoy for London. Aubrey was incredibly lucky to have survived his injuries, and what was most extraordinary was that when he recovered, he went back to the front line. His war was far from over.

Fired up by her conversation with Agnes Keyser, and fuelled by nervous energy from fretting about Aubrey, Almina had set about the process of converting Highclere into a hospital. The first step was to find the people to staff it. She had appointed Dr Marcus Johnson, the family's much-loved personal physician, as medical director. Dr Johnnie was a GP. He knew the Carnarvons well, had travelled with them for years and was more like a member of the family than an employee. He had long ago grown used to being teased by the Earl who, indulging his love of practical jokes, once planted a piece of Gorgonzola cheese in one of poor Dr Johnnie's travelling trunks and teased him relentlessly about the smell wafting from his cabin. Dr Johnson moved in to the Castle on 12 August 1914 and proved himself to be a capable administrator and the perfect right-hand man for Almina, whom he adored.

They placed adverts and called on all the nursing agencies in London and, between them, Almina and Dr Johnnie recruited thirty nurses. There must have been quite a run on nursing staff, what with all the grand ladies rushing to perform their patriotic duty by opening hospitals, but Almina had plenty of money to pay for the best people. She had a decided preference for Irish nursing staff and the Highclere nurses also tended to be good-looking; Almina seems to have decided that pretty nurses would be good for morale. As it turned out, she wasn't wrong about that.

Since she was also somewhat prone to self-importance, Almina had a vision of herself in the role of all-powerful matron. She certainly relished using the same organisational and leadership skills she had been honing for years in the running of Highclere and in her political work. For the first time since her campaigning days, she felt herself flexing some mental muscle. She was in her element.

It is deliciously typical of Almina that the thing she did next was commission a high-fashion uniform for her nurses. Their dresses were made of fine wool in a cheerful crushed-strawberry-pink, with starched white aprons and caps. This detail set the tone: Highclere would be a cutting-edge hospital, but also a sensual retreat from the horror of combat. Almina proved herself to be an instinctive master of what we might call, nowadays, holistic medicine. She understood that to treat the injured soldiers as individuals in need of space, time and comfort, as well as medical attention, was the key to success.

Once the staff were engaged it was time to tackle the equipping of Highclere. Almina relied heavily upon Mary Weekes to help her. Mary had already proved herself as a very useful secretary, but now she took on the role of deputy hospital administrator and found herself liaising with visiting doctors, Army Medical Boards and patients' relatives.

The first task was to organise for blinds to be constructed for all the Castle's south-facing windows. Arundel, a bedroom on the first floor in the northwest corner of the house was to be used as an operating theatre. It was right opposite the back stairs, so hot water and other supplies could be rushed up and down as required. There was no question of installing hospital beds in any of the larger rooms to make communal wards. The patients, up to twenty at a time, were to have individual rooms or, at times of great pressure, to share with one other person. All the guest bedrooms on the first floor were readied for use, as well as some of those on the floor above. The men would be made to feel as if they were house guests, sleeping in comfortable beds with soft down pillows and beautiful linen and cotton sheets.

The Castle had its own laundry on the northern edge of the estate. When a new laundress was required in 1915, a servants' employment agency was engaged to find a suitable candidate to ensure an efficient supply of clean linen to the hospital; Harriett Russell was recruited with her husband Harry, and the estate paid for their removal expenses from Folkestone.

Highclere was of course well used to receiving guests, but still, the maids had to double up in their bedrooms, since they were to make way for all the arriving nurses; and everyone, from the kitchen staff to the housemaids and the footmen to the gardeners, had to brace themselves for an enormous increase in their workload. Almina's vision of her refuge for the men stipulated that the patients would be served their meals either in their rooms, if they were not well enough to leave them, or at a large table at the end of the North Library, behind the gilded columns. In either case, they would be waited on by footmen. In effect it was like moving a house party of fifty people into the Castle, on a permanent basis.

Streatfield and Mrs Macnair, who had replaced Mrs Bridgland as housekeeper by 1911 were instrumental in making it all happen. Mrs Macnair received her orders from Lady Carnarvon in the sitting room as usual, but now they concerned the nurses' accommodation and the best foods to give men recovering from fractures or dysentery. Almina had adopted the nurse's uniform she wore throughout the war when working, but her new occupation in no way countenanced any change in the interactions between her and the staff. Almina might have had a job to do, but she was still Her Ladyship.

Almina reported an upbeat spirit of willingness in her household staff as they helped her to make Highclere ready for its first new guests. They must have been run off their feet, but of course they were also involved in an important element of the nation's war work. For everybody, keeping busy was a welcome distraction from wondering when the call-up might come, for themselves or their husband or son. And then again there were some members of the household who considered that, given the usual strict regime of Mr Streatfield, it was a pleasure to have some new blood around the place, a different set of tasks and plenty of new faces.

So it was all change at Highclere. Almina decided that the Library would be used as the men's day room. None of the furniture was moved out but additional chairs were added, so that there was ample space for the men to sit and play cards or to read the books. The room runs the width of the house and is elegant but supremely comfortable. The leather-bound books and veneered wooden shelves, the oriental rugs and the lamps on low tables next to overstuffed sofas make it feel like a place to sit by the fire and be soothed. The French windows open straight out on to the sweep of the drive and look out over the gardens, so on a sunny day the room is flooded with light, and within moments you can crunch over the gravel and feel springy lawn beneath your feet.

Everything had been designed to make Highclere's luxurious country-house lifestyle available to the injured soldiers; Almina had re-imagined the Castle as a therapeutic space, one where the atmosphere in the Library or the excellent cooking from the Castle's kitchen was as important as the services of the radiologist she planned to bring down from London. The first patients arrived in mid-September, members of the Seaforth Highlanders and the Royal Artillery, who had fractures, gunshot wounds and no doubt a large dose of what would soon be called shell shock, and what we now describe as post-traumatic stress disorder. No wonder they reported that when they first laid eyes on Highclere, it felt as if they had arrived in Paradise.

I I

Paradise Lost

As soon as the call for men went out, Highclere answered. Most of the male staff worked on the estate, as gardeners and foresters, gamekeepers and grooms. Naturally they had to ask permission from their employer to go. Lord Carnarvon let it be known that any man who wished to volunteer would be guaranteed his job when he returned. Lord Carnarvon also offered to pay the men's wives half their wages to ensure the families had some income. Arthur Hayter, who had started as a groom and risen to be the head man in the stables, volunteered and was told he was too old, but six other men had gone by the beginning of September.

History chronicles the bravery of the men joining up

– as it should, given that by December 1914 over one million men had enlisted in Kitchener's New Army, and recruitment was maintained at 100,000 a month until August 1915. But the flip side of the coin is the movement in the other direction: 24,000 men a week coming back wounded.

The clearing hospitals in France and Belgium were extremely rudimentary and barely able to cope with the huge numbers of casualties. They were desperately short-staffed. The Royal Army Medical Corps had 1,509 officers and 16,331 other ranks in 1914, and all its procedures were based on experience gained in the Boer War. Conditions in France and Belgium were very different. Bacteria lurked in the soil that was being dug out for trenches; it caused gangrene, which was the biggest killer of soldiers who made it back to a clearing hospital, and tetanus. Typhoid was rife throughout the Western Front and isolation units were often not a top priority, so more men died from infection. Doctors resented the fact that they were expected to turn their hand to anything rather than being encouraged to specialise.

Once the wounded had been evacuated from the field and transported from their unit base, via a dressing station, to the clearing hospital, triage could be carried out. But it was haphazard at best. Surgeons would walk the rows of stretchers lined up under a makeshift cover and have to assess who to give basic treatment to there in the field, who to send home for operations that could only be performed in a fully equipped hospital, and who to allow to die. The lucky few whose injuries merited an attempt to treat them but were too serious to be seen by a doctor in France, got put on an ambulance that bumped its way to the nearest working train station for return to England by boat. The journey from battlefield to a hospital at home could take up to three weeks. Plenty of men died en route.

Southampton was one of the principal points of return for the injured soldiers, and from there they were dispatched all over the country. Some of them came to Highclere. Later on, when the hospital's fame had spread, strings had to be pulled to gain admission, but at the start of the war, you simply had to be in the right place at the right time. This was an era before public healthcare, when all hospitals were funded by wealthy individuals or charitable organisations. Women like Almina and the other Society ladies who stepped in to help with the huge numbers of war wounded were not just on some vainglorious mission; they were fulfilling a need that wouldn't have been met without their actions.

In September 1914 there were just a dozen patients at Highclere. Lady Carnarvon greeted everyone at the front door. She showed the men to their room and, having seen that they were settling in, her next course of action was to send a telegram to their families to let them know that their son or husband was safe. Almina loved these moments of being able to give people the news they were desperately waiting for. Given the length of the telegram she sent Winifred about Aubrey's whereabouts, you imagine that she didn't skimp on her words, wanting to tell the family every possible detail that might reassure them.

The patients knew they had arrived somewhere special from the moment they opened their eyes to realise they were no longer in a dugout in Belgium, but surveying an English park. They spent their first few days at Highclere in their rooms with books, home-brewed beer from the

Castle's brewery and exquisite meals. One patient, Basil Jones, wrote later to Almina, 'You get on as well as they do in fairy tales, however grievous your hurt may be.' He was the first of many soldiers to comment appreciatively on the charming nurses, singling out one Sister Bowdler, whom he thought 'just wonderful'. The patients couldn't thank Almina enough for giving them her home and, as one man, John Pollen, put it, 'personally attending to the many things that make a house a real home.'

Lady Carnarvon assigned a nurse to each patient to bathe their feet, dress their wounds and offer comfort. She wanted to be very much a hands-on nurse herself, though, and enjoyed her rounds enormously, making sure she knew exactly what was going on with every man in her care. She also brought the Earl round to see her charges. Patients whose 'nerves . . . were utterly wrong', even this early in the war, wrote to her later of their enjoyment of the Earl's calls. Almina always encouraged their own families to come to see them. Saturday was visiting day. It was all part and parcel of the deliberate attempt to resist the anonymity of big hospitals and to look after the men in every way possible.

Almina's approach might have been exemplary, but it was also expensive; in fact it was turning out to be a constant drain on the Rothschild coffers. Not that Alfred really minded. Quite apart from the family commitment to philanthropy, not to mention Alfred's keen patriotism, he was also a hospital administrator, being Treasurer of Queen Charlotte's Hospital for 31 years by the time he died. When, after a few weeks of Highclere being up and running, Almina took a day off work to travel again to New Court to ask her father for more money, Alfred's protests were nothing but routine. 'Darling, it was only last month I gave you £25,000, what on earth have you done with it? I know it's all in a good cause, but please do be careful.' Almina reassured Alfred, pocketed another £10,000 and returned to the Castle to put her plans into action. Given the way the war was going, she needed everything she could get.

On 22 October Lord and Lady Carnarvon lent their support at a stirring mass meeting in Newbury to encourage men to join the Army. There was a 'mood of gravity' in the country and, although the pace of recruitment was brisk, more and more troops were needed. The Carnarvons were joined on the platform by Lord Charles Beresford, Admiral and MP, who was a great naval hero and never appeared in public without his bulldog. Lord Carnarvon, as High Steward of Newbury, opened the meeting and expressed the belief that, although the war had been forced upon Great Britain, it would all be over soon, provided the nation stood firm. Then Lord Beresford exhorted the crowd to do their bit, and echoed the sentiment that any boys joining up now could do their duty and be home in time for Christmas. Beresford stayed at Highclere that night; as yet, not quite all the beds were occupied by patients.

By this point the British Expeditionary Force was taking part in the first battle of Ypres. The pressure on the Western Front had increased since the Russians suffered a heavy defeat on the Eastern Front. The Allies were holding the line, but it was already abundantly clear that with more than a million men on both sides dug in across Belgium and northern France, this war was definitely not going to be over by Christmas.

The Carnarvons heard that Winifred's nephew, Bar

Maitland, had been killed by a shell. His brother Dick, a delicate boy who had pneumonia most winters and was an artist, volunteered to take his brother's place and obtained a commission in the Scots Guards. Then came the news from even closer to home. Two of the young lads who had volunteered from the estate, Harry Garrett and Harry Illot, had died while serving in India and France respectively. They had both been gardeners under Augustus Blake who had succeeded Pope in about 1908, and Harry Illot's family had been working at Highclere for the past twenty years.

The casualties were high, much higher than the men in charge of strategy had ever allowed for. As Almina could have testified, the wounded and the dead were frequently experienced soldiers. The cream of the Allied professional fighting forces was being shipped home in bits.

Almina seems to have responded to the horror in a very characteristic way: by using her money and determination and contacts to keep up the pressure to get more done. She decided that they needed more expertise at Highclere and so, by mid-October, Robert Jones was operating in the Arundel room on a succession of men with broken bones.

Jones, who was later knighted in recognition of his work, was already an experienced orthopaedic surgeon who had learned how to treat fractures from years working as the surgeon-superintendent on the construction of the Manchester Shipping Canal. He devised the first comprehensive accident response service in the world, and implemented it along the length of the canal, so he was accustomed to treating lots of people in stressful conditions. By contrast with the on-site service he provided for the canal labourers, the damask curtains and carpets of the

Arundel bedroom must have made a surreal backdrop. Jones was fifty-seven years old and felt a huge duty to do his bit on the home front, given that so many of his younger colleagues were in the field hospitals, battling with conditions that made the ship canal look like a Sunday stroll around Highclere's gardens.

Two-thirds of all casualties during the First World War (those who survived long enough to reach a hospital) had injuries to bones from shrapnel and gunshot wounds. There was a lot of work for orthopaedic surgeons. (Abdominal wounds, by contrast, were considered too complex to treat and these men, like Aubrey Herbert, were simply dosed on morphine; and, unlike him, most died.) Jones was adamant that by using a particular technique called the Thomas splint, which had been developed by his uncle Hugh Thomas, in the treatment of compound fractures, the mortality rate could be brought down from 80 per cent to 20 per cent. It seems odd to us now to imagine that a broken leg could kill you, but on the battlefields of the Great War, it frequently did. The femur is the longest bone in the body and the muscles surrounding it are correspondingly strong. When the femur breaks, the muscles contract, pulling the bone ends past each other, causing additional injury, dangerous loss of blood, nerve damage and a lot of pain. Jones's idea was to use traction to ensure that the two broken pieces of bone were held end to end so healing could take place. It was a brilliantly successful treatment and saved countless lives at Highclere and throughout the war. The patients who benefited were so grateful and so conscious of others' needs that they frequently returned their splints to Almina's hospital once they were done with them.

Almina and her team got to December before having to deal with someone dying in their care, which suggests that someone at Southampton docks was making the right decisions about whom to prioritise for their attention. Robert Jones left Highclere, having instructed Lady Carnarvon and Dr Johnnie, who assisted at numerous operations, how to carry out the more straightforward procedures themselves. The next eminent medical man to come down to the hospital was Hector Mackenzie. He was a renowned specialist in chest surgery but, despite all his best efforts, one of the patients he operated on, a man called Thompson, died. When it became clear that her patient was not going to recover, Almina sent a wire to his daughter and invited her to come to stay at Highclere. Agnes Thompson wrote to Almina later. 'I will never forget my few days' visit to Highclere and that I saw the death of Daddy and the very kind treatment that he received from your hands. I do hope you are feeling better . . . you looked very ill.'

The family spent Christmas 1914 at Highclere. Almina did her best to decorate the house and create a special Christmas for everyone. There was the usual enormous Christmas tree in the Saloon, beautiful winter flowers scattered on the tables and garlands of greenery. The visitor book records that the house was full to bursting with wounded soldiers as well as a few close friends. Those who could leave the house attended services at the village church, along with the entire household, from the nurses, who would not be taking any holiday, to the maids and estate staff. The kitchen staff had been preparing for a celebratory dinner for days. Lord Carnarvon's worries about securing enough food for the hospital were getting more acute, but this was not the day for stinting, and Streatfield and his team of footmen served the patients soups, then roast goose followed by a plum pudding, in the north Library. Lord and Lady Carnarvon joined them in the Library afterwards and they shared a brandy in front of the fire.

Out on the Western Front, there was a strange meeting taking place, an event that has assumed an almost mythic status. It began when German and British soldiers called out Happy Christmas to each other across No Man's Land. Tentatively, disbelieving, the soldiers negotiated their own totally unofficial truce for a day. Unarmed soldiers from both sides went over the top to collect their dead and, when they met in the bog of blood and mud that lay between them, they shook hands and agreed to bury their fallen comrades together. Somebody suggested a game of football. Provisions were produced and exchanged: sauerkraut and sausages for chocolate. That night, as the men at Highclere thanked their lucky stars they were tucked up in warm beds, comfortably full of brandy and pudding, the sound of 'Silent Night' being sung in German and English rose from the trenches. For almost twenty-four hours there was peace on the Western Front.

It was the tiniest respite. The first battle of Ypres in October and November had left the British Expeditionary Force scrambling to adapt its tactics in the face of morale-devastating losses. The following year, 1915, was set to deliver loss of life on an even greater scale.

At Highclere, Lord Carnarvon invited a few friends, including the stalwart Victor Duleep Singh to stay on for a week between Christmas and New Year. There is a dejected scrawl in the visitors' book. 'Seeing the New Year in . . . the saddest and most trying owing to the awful war.'

149

In early January the household readied itself for the arrival of more patients. Most of the twenty men who arrived for treatment were from the 9th Bhopal Infantry and the 8th Gurkha Rifles, but not all of them. In a letter to Winifred, Lord Carnarvon related the story of one patient, a sailor, who had arrived in the first week of January. The man was called S. W. Saxton, and he had had an extraordinary escape. He had been serving on HMS *Formidable*, which was out on exercises on New Year's Day when it was torpedoed by a German U-boat. As the ship went down, Saxton clung to the propeller, despite his injuries and the immense waves, strong winds and hail that threatened to wash him away. When he lost his grip on the blades of the propeller, his instinct to swim pushed him to head for a distant trawler boat, but when he eventually made it, he found he was totally incapable of hauling himself up the side of the boat. He was about to give up and let himself drown when a huge wave caught him up and swept him on deck. Saxton arrived at Almina's hospital with broken bones, shock and hypothermia – but he was one of the lucky ones. The *Formidable* was the first dreadnought sunk in the war, and only 199 men of the 750 on board were saved.

Saxton responded brilliantly to the regime at Highclere and was soon well enough to be sent out to one of the convalescent homes that were used as staging posts before the men were returned to their duties. Many of these homes were run by acquaintances of Almina's, and she would arrange transport and ensure that the men were transferred with all their records of treatment. Trotman, the Earl's chauffeur, would drive them to the station to catch their train, all wrapped up in rugs for the journey and with a store of provisions. Sometimes Trotman drove them all the way to their destination. On several occasions, Almina accompanied him, and would later receive a letter from a grateful parent who had not realised that the lady who had escorted their boy back home was the Countess whose hospital had restored his health.

By the end of January 1915, the British High Command had decided that any recovered British Expeditionary Force officers should not be returned to the front line to face almost certain death, but retained in Britain to train the men of Kitchener's New Army, hundreds of thousands of whom were needed. Vast numbers of those men would of course be heading for their own deaths in due course. The year saw the war expand to Italy, the Balkans and the Middle East, and conflict deepen everywhere.

In the meantime, although Almina felt she had found her vocation in life, exhaustion was setting in at Highclere. No one had had any time off since the hospital opened. The nurses were shattered; the staff were at breaking point. The scale of what they were dealing with was now becoming horrifyingly apparent. Almina had been working constantly since her decision to open the hospital back in July 1914 and was exhausted, physically and emotionally. She decided that they all needed a break. The Castle was closed for six weeks so that it could be readied for more patients in March, and Almina and Carnarvon headed for Egypt and a rest.

12

War Heroes

After six months of listening to horror stories from the Western Front and tending desperate patients, the familiarity of the winter trip to Egypt must have felt like a return to a rapidly vanishing world. Travel to North Africa was still possible, though difficult.

They were following in Aubrey, Mary and Elsie's footsteps, all of whom had separately made the journey just before Christmas. Aubrey had recovered from his injuries and been passed for active service. In four months he had gone from being an object of mild fun, stowing away because the Army didn't think him fit enough to serve, to desperately needed and rubber-stamped for duty. Attitudes had changed since the war had shown itself to be a bloody nightmare. Now, virtually everyone was welcome in His Majesty's service.

Aubrey headed for Egypt on the strength of his expertise in Middle Eastern affairs and knowledge of several local languages. He set off with nothing but a few random clothes and his typewriter, and arrived to find that General Sir John Maxwell, commander of the Army in Egypt, was still feeling confident that the Turks would be unable to pose much of a threat. Life was carrying on much as it ever did in Cairo, with the usual entertainments still in place for the winter tourists and the same cast of oddballs and adventurers flitting around. Aubrey met T. E. Lawrence, who went on to become a close friend but whose initial impression of Aubrey was the entirely typical one of amusement. 'Then there is Aubrey Herbert, who is a joke but a very nice one: he is too short-sighted to read or recognise anyone but speaks Turkish well, Albanian, French, Italian, Arabic, German.' Aubrey described the man who would be Lawrence of Arabia as 'an odd gnome, half cad – with a touch of genius.'

Aubrey's mother, Elsie the Dowager Countess of Carnarvon, sailed across the Mediterranean to Alexandria to be with him, but arrived in Cairo just a few hours before he was sent to the Dardanelles. She found her daughter-in-law Mary already there and, having decided she could be useful, began the task of organising the logistics for the hospital ships: once the campaign got under way, they would be coming and going out of Alexandria's port. Within four months there were dozens a day, ferrying the survivors from the slaughter at Gallipoli back to Britain.

Almina and Carnarvon stayed at Shepheard's Hotel, as

they had been doing for more than ten years, and Almina focused on recuperating enough to be strong for her return to work. The problem was that Egypt was turning from an upmarket tourist destination to the next theatre of war. The aim of the campaign was to use combined naval and military power to capture the Turkish capital Constantinople, thereby securing the sea route to Russia via the Black Sea. That way the Russians fighting on the Eastern Front could be properly supplied and some pressure would be taken off the Western Front, which was in a state of hopeless stalemate. A young Winston Churchill, then the First Lord of the Admiralty, was one of the chief architects of the plan.

Cairo was filling up with volunteer troops from New Zealand and Australia in their thousands. These were the men who formed the ANZAC force that went on to suffer staggering losses in the Dardanelles over the next year. Almina wandered the streets; they were thronged with young men still full of the optimism and determination that she had seen in Aubrey and his friends before they set off for northern France. She knew what those boys looked like when they returned, with legs in need of amputation and nerves shot to pieces. It was heartbreaking to see the same thing happening all over again, and it made Almina desperate to get back to Highclere and do everything in her power to help.

By early March, Highclere had regrouped. In Almina's absence only the very sickest men who were too ill to be moved had stayed, with a couple of nurses in attendance. Once they had been seen off to convalescent homes, the entire staff had a rest. The pause didn't last long. By April the Allies were suffering huge losses in France and in the Mediterranean and the hospital was busier than ever.

On the Western Front the second Battle of Ypres was under way. The Germans launched a major attack to try to break through the Allied lines and, on 22 April, introduced a new and particularly horrible weapon. Gas. They followed up the artillery shelling with the release of 168 tonnes of chlorine gas into the Allied positions. It was totally unexpected and terrifying. Five thousand French soldiers died within ten minutes of the gas dropping down into the trenches. A further 10,000 were blinded and maimed as they tried to flee. Everything was chaos as the Germans advanced, fitted with their rudimentary gas masks, picking off the desperate French soldiers as they went. The Allies were completely wrong-footed and, over the next month, the Germans gained three miles. They repeated the gas attack, with the same devastating results, on the British Expeditionary Force. One hundred thousand men died, more than two-thirds of them Allied soldiers, and thousands more were sent back to Britain with a whole new raft of symptoms for the medical staff to treat.

Things were no better in the Mediterranean. Three days after the Germans used gas for the first time, the British, French and ANZAC forces arrived beneath the towering cliffs of Gallipoli and began to disembark onto the beaches. The Turks had had plenty of time to install artillery on the cliff tops and lay out barbed wire on the beaches to protect machine-gun posts. As the first troops waded from their ships on to the beaches, the Turkish Army opened fire. The Allied soldiers died in their hundreds, their blood turning the sea red. Of the first 200 soldiers to disembark, only

21 made it ashore. Those who managed to struggle up the beach met the machine gunners, who were running out of ammunition but not determination. The Ottoman 57th Infantry Division were wiped out; the regiment lost every single man as they fought with nothing but bayonets. Their sacrifice allowed enough time for more troops to arrive and the battle to grind on.

Any Allied survivors were forced to cling to narrow ledges on the cliffs and watch as their comrades died around them; medics picked their way through the chaos with stretchers, hunting for the wounded. By the end of the first few days of landings, it was obvious that the anticipated swift victory was not going to happen. As the campaign continued, it turned into a brutal disaster with enormous numbers of casualties on both sides. The ships that the Allied forces had arrived on were transformed into floating hospitals, and morgues.

Aubrey Herbert was there, forcing his way through the battle, picking his way past the trenches that were full of men trying to stay sane enough to fight, despite the hell that was unfolding around them. Aubrey was trying to reach the Turkish commanding officers to negotiate armistices to bury the dead. One month after he landed at Gallipoli, Aubrey negotiated with Mustafa Kemal, who later found fame as Atatürk, the first President of the Republic of Turkey; Aubrey offered himself as hostage while the Turkish Army collected 3,000 bodies from Kabe Tepe. Aubrey wrote in his letters to Elsie in Alexandria that the thyme-filled gullies in the hills behind the beach stank of nothing but death.

The battle dragged on for months, despite the desperate loss of life and the fact that no headway had been made.

Aubrey survived summer on the cliffs but became very sick in early September. It was hardly surprising: conditions in Gallipoli were notorious. The summer was blistering hot, causing the corpses littering the area to decompose even faster and cause even more disease. The winter was cold, sleety and prone to storms that washed away the shallow graves and sent bloated corpses flooding into trenches.

Aubrey was shipped to Alexandria, where he was received by his mother in her capacity as co-ordinator of hospital ships. Elsie was delighted to see him but, once having established that he was not in any immediate danger, dispatched him to Cairo for a rest and got on with the job. Aubrey spent a few days in Shepheard's Hotel, now almost totally closed up and full of ghosts from happier days. Mary joined him and the couple had a few days' rest. His fever cleared up but he was restless and guilt-ridden at being ensconced in the last shreds of luxury to be had in Egypt. As soon as he was well enough, he returned to Gallipoli, but he fell sick again almost immediately and was shipped out for good in mid-October, worn out and low in spirit. The Dardanelles had nearly destroyed Aubrey's peace of mind.

By then the Allies were having to face the fact that the campaign had failed. There had been calls for evacuation from October onwards, but only after one last, disastrous push. Back in August, the lack of progress had already been beginning to cause political problems for the commanding officers, but there was an insistence that reinforcements should be brought in. One of them was a man called David Campbell, who made his way to the slaughterhouse of Gallipoli from his home in Ireland.

Campbell had volunteered for the 6th Royal Irish Rifles, answering Kitchener's call for men to join up. Following training in Dublin and then at Basingstoke near Highclere, the battalion embarked for Alexandria and the Dardanelles. They had no idea what they were sailing to: press reports in Britain at that point were still dominated by propaganda. The men arrived at Gallipoli on 5 August, in the intense heat of high summer. They could smell the decaying bodies on the beach from half a mile away. Two days later they moved out, rattled by shells landing around them and tense with nerves, up Dead Man's Gully. Occasionally, breaks in the cliffs framed stunning views of the dazzling sea, whilst inland, tongues of fire showed them where the shells were coming from.

During a mission to take a summit at Suvla, Campbell was shot in the calf. As a fellow soldier helped him to dress the wound, the man was shot in the foot. David now helped in turn to dress the man's wound, but gunshot was still raining down all around them, and up ahead they could see a wheat field full of the bodies of dead soldiers. Sure enough, David was hit again, by a bullet that drilled through his foot. Unable to move, losing blood from his two gunshot wounds, David passed out. Coming to, he saw that the man who had helped him was dead.

He decided to try to crawl back the way he had come. He fell in with a stream of other bloodied soldiers, but before long he collapsed, too weak from loss of blood to carry on. Then David felt himself being lifted up and realised that a Gurkha was manhandling him over his shoulder and carrying him, dodging from cover to cover, back towards the first-aid post. It took them two hours to get there, and

David was shot again in the leg, but they made it. The Gurkha deposited him and melted away into the crowd, even as David was thanking him for saving his life.

The orderlies on duty dressed his wounds but there were no stretchers left, so David hopped between two other men until he had no energy left to do anything but crawl. Exhausted from the effort, he and his helpers finally made it to the field ambulance station and David was placed on a stretcher and left overnight to try to get some sleep between the shouts of the other wounded and dying men.

In the morning, stretcher-bearers began to transport those who had survived to the evacuation point. They had to cross the beach to get there, and once again the snipers picked them off, until there were not enough stretcher-bearers left alive to carry the wounded, who could only lie there, helpless, wondering whether each shot would be the final sound they heard. The sun burned down on them and they had no water to drink. David came to the conclusion that the only way he would survive was by dragging himself to the evacuation point. When he finally got there he was treated immediately. There was no pressure on the medical staff because hardly any patients made it to them alive. The hospital ships were full but an officer managed to commandeer a fishing trawler and David was one of the men loaded onto it and, the next day, onto a British Army hospital ship. He was assigned a cabin with three other officers. All three died in the night and were replaced with three more.

David Campbell couldn't have known it, but the harbour master overseeing the arrival of his ship at Alexandria was Elsie Carnarvon. Sir John Maxwell, Commander in Chief of the Mediterranean Expeditionary Force, commented to his staff that she was doing really good work and she was given a motor launch to meet the incoming ships, which made her job easier.

Even by the beginning of May it was obvious to everyone out there that the casualties in the Dardanelles were catastrophic, far exceeding what had been expected. Sir John's confident prediction that the Turks wouldn't be able to do much damage had proved to be laughably ill informed. Once Elsie got a sense of how bad things were, she took matters into her own hands. She contacted Almina and between them the two women arranged for twenty-seven nurses to travel out to Alexandria. The nurses left Tilbury on 15 May 1915 on board the P&O steamer *Mongolia*.

Aubrey's wife Mary helped Elsie to sort things out in Egypt. The bureaucracy proved difficult since the nurses had no permits to work or visas to stay, and the military authorities were initially more concerned with the rule book and the budget than anything else. Mary and Elsie argued that they were prepared to pay the wage bill of £2 2s per week per nurse, which removed one obstacle; they also suggested that, given that the nurses were here now and they were certainly desperately needed, perhaps it was time to change the rules on visas and permits. It was a persuasive argument, and eventually Elsie got her nurses. It probably helped that Sir John Maxwell was a great friend of hers.

Elsie, now in her sixtieth year, was one of those formidable women with an enormous capacity for getting things done. The intense heat never seemed to bother her and she never ever complained. When there was a shortage of stretchers she went out and scoured the city for sewing machine and fabrics, organising work teams to make up the equipment that was so desperately needed. She started a canteen for the ANZAC forces and provided all the cutlery and crockery. One day the men got so rowdy that plates and cups were smashed, and Elsie took it upon herself to march in there and demand what they thought they were doing. What would their mothers say? Something in her manner brought the fracas to a halt, and when the men realised who she was and what she had done for them, they lined up to apologise to her.

Meanwhile, David Campbell had struck lucky. He was assessed as suitable for return to Britain and, having avoided the Egyptian military hospitals, he sailed out of Alexandria on the *Aquitania*. Conditions aboard could most generously be described as basic. Everyone got dysentery, including David. He had splinters of lead removed from his gunshot wounds without any anaesthetic. Unsurprisingly, his foot became gangrenous, and was marked for amputation, but then the surgeon fell sick and was too ill to carry out the operation, so David arrived back in Britain still in possession of both feet. In Southampton his luck held and he was tagged for Highclere. So, in mid-September, he bumped up from the south coast in an ambulance with three other patients, all of them groaning every time they were jolted over a pothole. The trailer rumbled up to the front of the house and David was helped out and into a wheelchair by a footman, who pushed him carefully across the gravel drive and in through the front door of Highclere.

As always, Almina was there to welcome the new arrivals, accompanied by two nurses. It took two footmen to help David make his way up the ornate carpeted stairs, past the

Italian marble statue of the 4th Earl and his sister Eveline at the bottom landing, up past the seventeenth-century Flemish tapestry and into his bedroom. There the nurses helped him to wash. He was still caked in the filth of the battlefields and all his clothes had to be taken away and burned. Pyjamas and a dressing gown were provided and then, once he was clean and comfortable, Almina and Dr Johnnie visited him to make their assessment.

The foot looked ghastly. It was swollen and dark and almost too painful to touch. But Almina had decided something. She wanted to avoid amputations wherever possible, believing that they were too frequently performed, sometimes for the doctors' convenience rather than the good of the patient. In the field it might be a matter of life or death, but here at Highclere where the risk of infection was so much lower, she took the view that they could be ambitious about reducing the number of amputations.

Almina washed and dressed David's foot every day, and came at mealtimes to check that he had everything he needed. The excellent nursing paid off – after a week he was encouraged to go and sit outside and then he progressed to crutches. Some friends came to visit and hardly recognised him because his frame was so shrunken and his face so hollow from the effects of the dysentery and the mental fatigue. But he was healing in mind as well as body. He wrote to his family, 'there can be no better solace than to wander over the cool green grass and sit under the cedars.'

Actually, David wasn't quite right about that. One lucky patient received even greater solace, in the form of the attentions of Highclere's sweetheart, a particularly pretty auburn-haired nurse. Porchy, by that time a seventeen-year-old schoolboy who had fallen slightly in love with her himself, delighted in recounting the story of how one evening, on her patrols, Almina stumbled across the fortunate Major George Paynter, from the Scots Guards, in the nurse's embrace. Almina tactfully withdrew from the bedroom, but the following morning she called the nurse to see her. Apparently, Almina's championing of holistic care had its limits. 'Look here, my dear, I'm afraid you'll have to go. I cannot have my nurses behaving in this fashion. It must have put a great strain on the patient's heart. He might have died as a result!' The flame-haired beauty left, much to the patients' sorrow.

David was soon considered well enough to be discharged, and was ordered to appear before the Army Medical Board on 4 November. He was loath to leave Highclere, but he had to make way for other patients and report to the authorities. He was given one month's leave before he had to report again, so he set off for Ireland. The journey proved to be too much too soon for his foot and he ended up back in hospital in Dublin. David spent a month there before he was discharged and finally made it home, but it was only two weeks before he received another telegram telling him to attend for assessment by the Medical Board. This time David was passed fit and ordered to report to the Irish Rifles for active duties immediately.

13

Hospital on the Move

Christmas 1915 arrived and Almina had no spare energy to devote to festivities. The hospital was a success: she could see the good it was doing her patients; could read the gratitude in their letters. She was training a select band of nurses, engaging the most eminent doctors of the day to perform pioneering operations that saved countless lives. She had the means to enable her staff to treat all their charges with every possible care and attention. She was gaining the respect of the Southern Command of the military authorities, who came to trust her judgement completely – so that if she said a man was not yet well enough to attend the Medical Board, they believed her. By any account, Almina's hospital at Highclere was thriving; she knew for certain that she had found her life's work. Still, she was exhausted and frustrated that she couldn't do more. And there was nothing but bad news, from all directions.

Reports of another Highclere death had filtered back. George Cox, a groom, had been killed at Ypres back in May but it had taken six months for the authorities to inform his mother. There had been no system in place for registering casualties when the war started, and the scale of the losses meant that it wasn't until the end of 1915 that what became, two years later, the Imperial War Graves Commission managed to establish a workable system. Following the French government's gift of land for war cemeteries for Allied soldiers on the Western Front, the task of logging graves began. Army chaplains had used bottles containing slips of paper with the soldier's name scrawled on it to mark graves, and these could now be replaced by wooden crosses. George Cox's body had lain in the fields of France for six months while his mother waited with dwindling hope for news, but none of that deterred two more Highclere men from joining up.

Maber and Absalon were both gamekeepers who elected to join the newly centralised Machine Gun Corps. They handled guns every day of their working lives, so were presumably regarded as an asset. Despite the strategic failures, the lack of progress and the morale-sapping casualty rate, the public mood at the end of 1915 was still determined. There was, as yet, no shortage of recruits.

But the last few months had been depressing for even the most vehement and positive patriot. On the Western Front the Allies had lost nearly 90,000 men compared to the Germans' 25,000, and Sir John French, the commander

Lady Almina in uniform at the Castle. Her nurses were always exceptionally well turned out and Lady Carnarvon paid for all their uniforms personally.

One of many pictures from the Castle Archives of Great War soldiers recuperating at the Castle.

The south elevation of Highclere Castle during the Great War, complete with sunblinds, since removed.

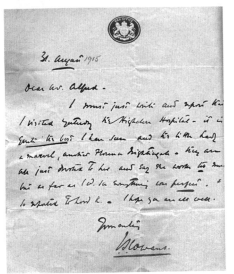

A hand-written letter from General Sir John Cowans, QuarterMaster-General of the British Army during the Great War, to Alfred de Rothschild, after a visit he made to 'Highclere Hospital'. '... It is simply the best... and its little Lady is a marvel, another Florence Nightingale...'.

Major J A Rutherford with his five sons, all of whom served in the Great War. Major Rutherford was the Estate Manager to the 5th Earl of Carnarvon. Three of his sons were invalided from the Army with war wounds. There are 75 names on the Highclere Estate Roll of Honour for those who went to fight during the Great War. 13 are listed as 'Killed'. Major Rutherford is 'Mentioned for Valuable Services'.

A wounded soldie
on the South Lawn
of the Castle near th
south east corne

Mary Weekes, Almina's loyal secretary, and her husband, Charles Clout.
Charles was sent to Highclere when he was injured in World War One,
and they soon fell in love.

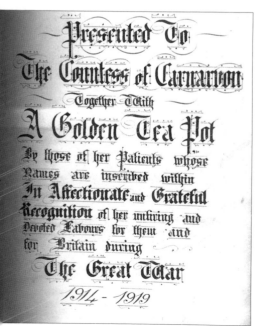

Presented To
The Countess of Carnarvon
Together With
A Golden Tea Pot
By those of her Patients whose
Names are inscribed within
In Affectionate and Grateful
Recognition of her untiring and
Devoted Labours for them and
for Britain during
The Great War
1914 - 1919

A certificate from
the recuperating
soldiers, thanking
the 5th Countess
for her efforts.

A portrait of Lady Evelyn Herbert (1901-1979) during the Great War.

A group photograph at the wedding of the 5th Earl's son, while he was Lord Porchester, to Catherine Wendell in 1922. This was taken four months before the 5th Earl's discovery of the Tomb of Tutankhamun in November of that year.

The Earl of Carnarvon with his daughter Lady Evelyn at Deauville Races, August 7, 1922.

The Earl of Carnarvon with
Lady Almina at Ascot, 1923.

A portrait of the Earl of
Carnarvon, drawn by William
Carter, Howard Carter's brother.

General Edmund
Allenby, High Com-
missioner in Egypt,
with his wife, Lady
Adelaide, and the 5th
Earl of Carnarvon.

Howard Carter and the Earl of Carnarvon at the opening of King Tutankhamun's tomb, 1922.

The Pall Mall Gazette's front page from the 5th April 1923, announcing Lord Carnarvon's death.

The 5th Earl of Carnarvon's faithful dog, Susie. She is famously said to have howled and dropped down dead at 2am on the morning that her master died.

The Christening of Porchy's daughter, at Highclere castle in 1925. Left to right: Sir Brograve Beauchamp, Mr Jac Wendell, the 6th Countess of Carnarvon and baby, the 6th Earl of Carnarvon, Lady Evelyn Beauchamp, Mr and Mrs Portman with little Lord Porchester and Mrs Wendell.

A portrait of Lady Evelyn taken shortly after her father's death in 1923.

Almina's son Porchy, the 6th Earl of Carnarvon, with his wife and daughter, in the 1930s.

AT A MEET OF THE CRAVEN AT HIGHCLERE CASTLE

The Earl and Countess of Carnarvon with their daughter, Lady Penelope Herbert, photographed at a recent meet of the Craven at Lord Carnarvon's Hampshire seat, Highclere Castle.

of the British Expeditionary Force, continued to dither and to fall out with both his own colleagues and the French command. In December he was recalled to Britain and replaced by Sir Douglas Haig.

It was the same story in the Dardanelles. Kitchener finally gave permission to evacuate; ironically, that part of the operation was the only success story, with relatively few casualties. But the ANZAC and the Mediterranean Expeditionary Forces lost nearly 35,000 men between them, up to 70 per cent in some regiments, and total casualties – including the horrific effects of illness – were close to half a million. The whole thing was such a disaster that it triggered the collapse of the Liberal government. Winston Churchill, who had been one of the Gallipoli campaign's principal and earliest cheerleaders, was forced to resign his position at the Admiralty. As Secretary of State for War, Kitchener was hit hard by these two failures and the great hero never recovered his reputation for invincibility. The country was at a desperately low ebb.

One of the few bright spots for Almina was her relationship with her daughter. Almina had been getting a lot of help and support that year from Lady Evelyn. She was fourteen in 1915 and still being educated at home by her governess. She missed Porchy, who was away at Eton, terribly; although unlike her brother, Eve was close to both her parents. She often tried to mediate between her brother and her parents but with only limited success. As Winifred commented in another of her letters to her husband, Lord Burghclere, 'Almina was a genius when organising a hospital, but not so with her first-born.'

But then, Eve presented none of the difficulties that

Porchy did. She was more diffident, so she didn't rub her flamboyant mother up the wrong way. They had a tremendous amount in common since they both enjoyed parties and fashion and possessed a restless energy that meant neither of them could sit still for long. Almina and Porchy, on the other hand, clashed partly because they were such wilful personalities, who both liked to be the centre of attention. Eve was also harder working and more scholarly than her charming but feckless brother, and had a genuine enthusiasm and curiosity about her father's explorations in Egypt that Porchy never shared. Perhaps the weight of expectation on both sides was also a little less, since Eve would not inherit. Whatever it was, she was never short of family affection. Lord Carnarvon doted on her throughout his life, as did Porchy, and she and Almina adored each other. They looked remarkably similar; Eve was tiny, just fractionally more than five foot tall and very slim. She grew up to be a beautiful girl, all rosebud lips, high cheekbones and dark eyes.

When war was declared and her mother decided to make the Castle into a hospital, Eve was plunged into a very different routine from the one she had enjoyed in her girlhood years. Rather than quiet days at lessons and occasional expeditions to town with her mother to see Alfred and visit the Wallace Collection, where her grandfather was a trustee, she found herself living in a house full of grievously injured soldiers. The atmosphere could change from tense to triumphant, depending on how well things were going in the operating theatre or how many names of friends there were on *The Times*'s daily list of casualties. It was a sharp jolt out of a very privileged life and forced Eve to grow up fast. Almina's philosophy of the desirability of public service extended to her daughter's leisure time. Once she'd done her lessons, Eve used to help Almina on her rounds, chatting to the patients and doing basic nursing tasks. This sweet pretty girl was understandably a great favourite of the patients. One of them had smuggled an Alsatian puppy back from France with him, which he gave to Eve. The dog slept in her room on the second floor of the Castle and became absolutely devoted to her. Eve was a good horsewoman and often went out riding in the Park with the head stable man, Arthur Hayter. The puppy always went with her, racing to keep up.

Even Lady Evelyn's assistance couldn't conceal the fact that Highclere was reaching the limits of what it could achieve. The team of Almina, Dr Johnnie and Mary Weekes, backed up by Streatfield and Mrs Macnair, was running at maximum efficiency, but Almina was still tortured by the sense that she needed to do more. By the beginning of December she had decided that they had outgrown Highclere and it was time to move the hospital to London. She could have converted the downstairs rooms into huge wards, of course, and been able to house up to twenty men in each, but she was convinced that a great part of her success hinged on the fact that the nurse-to-patient ratio was high, and the men had the luxury of peace and personal space. The hospital was run as a personal labour of love and she wanted it to stay that way. It would be a wrench: there was something uniquely healing about Highclere. Almina was particularly sorry to lose the wonderful gardens and the abundant supply of fresh fruit and vegetables, so she decided that her new premises would at least have access to a garden, and that she would continue to source food from Highclere and have it sent up to the hospital.

Almina secured the lease on 48 Bryanston Square, a delightful town house in Mayfair overlooking a peaceful garden behind railings. The Cadogan Trustees noted in their minutes that 'they were loath to entertain the application' from Lady Carnarvon but, if they declined it, the War Office might use their powers to commandeer the premises. So they agreed to Almina's request. The house had two distinct advantages over Highclere: specialist doctors were never more than half an hour away, and it could be far better equipped to treat a wider range of injuries than the Castle ever could. Almina installed a lift, a purpose-built operating theatre and an X-ray machine. Then she transferred all her staff from the country up to town and put them under the charge of Sister Macken, the head matron.

The London hospital was not only going to be better, it was also going to be bigger: Almina sacrificed her cherished notion of individual bedrooms in order to double capacity. There were now 40 patients at a time, with some single rooms but, more usually, two to four men to a room, and she gave the mini-wards the same names as the Highclere bedrooms: Stanhope, Sussex, Arundel, and so on. It still felt to the patients like a home away from home, with comfortable beds, the best-quality bed linen and spare pyjamas and clothes until their families could send their own. Almina continued to make liaison with family a priority, sending telegrams and letters with regular updates when patients were themselves unable to do so. True to her vision for the new hospital, the men could spend time in the residents' garden in the square, and they still dined on the vegetables and cheeses sent up every day from Highclere.

The London hospital had barely opened when it was

honoured by visits from two of Almina's earliest supporters. On January 4 Lord Kitchener came to inspect the new premises and pronounced himself very impressed. Two weeks later, Sister Keyser, who had been instrumental in providing inspiration and advice at the start of the war, also came. Almina was almost bursting with pride as she took her guests around the building.

The Castle returned to something approaching normal life, except of course that even if the hospital had gone, the war was still raging. The nurses had transferred to town, as had Mary Weekes, but Dr Johnnie was based between London and Highclere. Almina had engaged the additional services of Dr Sneyd for Bryanston Square. Streatfield, Mrs Macnair and the rest of the staff stayed at Highclere – after the frantic pace of the last sixteen months, they well deserved to take a breather. Lady Evelyn and Lord Carnarvon would continue to live between their house in Berkeley Square and Highclere, and Almina visited for weekends when she could take them. There would be precious little grand entertaining for the foreseeable future, but of course the Carnarvons had no desire to see anybody let go, so the staff simply had fewer jobs to do.

It was a sad crowd of mostly women who kept up appearances at Highclere during 1916. All the talk in the servants' hall was of the war, and of the fortunes of the Highclere men in particular. Florence, one of the housemaids, had left because she had married the gardener Tommy Hill. They had planned to make a different sort of life. Now she was terrified that her Tommy was going to enlist and she didn't think she could stand it if he did. They had been married for less than two years and Florence wanted to start a family.

The only news that filtered back was of those on the casualty list or killed in action. There was always tension between the sincere sense that sacrifice was required from everyone and the entirely natural terror of losing a loved one. The public's stomach for sacrifice varied throughout the war, with a general feeling of revulsion growing over time. Blessedly, Florence couldn't know that Tommy would be caught up in the events of 1916 that tipped the mood of the nation into furious despair.

Another long-running romance between staff members came to a happy end later in the year. Minnie Wills had been working her way up through the kitchen ranks since 1902, when she had started as the most junior maid. By 1916 she was the cook, first at Highclere, and then, when Almina moved the hospital to London, at 48 Bryanston Square. Minnie wore a long white apron over her uniform and a tidy white cap, and swore by the powers of Mrs Beeton's *Book of Household Management: A Guide to Cookery in All Branches*. Having reached the pinnacle of her profession, she decided that now was the moment to accept Arthur Hayter's proposal of marriage. After the wedding they left the Carnarvons' service and bought a pub. The female staff at Highclere were all delighted for her but said it was such a shame that it wasn't a restaurant: they couldn't visit her in a pub as they were very much men-only places.

The urge to join up gripped Porchy just as much as it did Tommy. In early 1916, Porchy was only seventeen, but he was absolutely desperate to leave Eton and enrol at Sandhurst. Both Lord and Lady Carnarvon had grave misgivings on the grounds of his age, but their son was insistent and they also felt it was wrong to try to dissuade him from doing his duty. Porchy went to take the entrance exam and scraped through every subject except maths, which he failed spectacularly. It was mentioned that Lord Kitchener was a close friend of the family and, mysteriously, Porchy's shortcomings seemed to fade from sight. So he went off to Sandhurst and left his sister and parents fretful on his behalf. Porchy was destined to be a cavalry officer, which was fortunate since he had fallen arches and flat feet.

Almina needed the distractions of work more than ever and flung herself into life at Bryanston Square. She had brought much of the hospital equipment from Highclere and spent her own money on topping it up with more beds, linens and crockery. But Alfred was continuing to pay for staff costs, both for the nurses and the household staff. There was a cook, a dozen maids and several footmen. Even more crucially, he supplied more reserves to install the state-of-the-art equipment and essential medical supplies that Almina needed to save more lives.

Alfred was by this time a broken man. He had been something of a hypochondriac all his life but now he was genuinely suffering. He was plagued by the combined effects of years of high living and emotional fatigue. He had been sick at heart ever since the declaration of war, and nothing that had happened since had done anything to relieve his gloom. His closely knit but far-flung extended family had found themselves on opposing sides, just as he feared. There were branches of the Rothschilds in central Europe that were now lost to him, and the world in which he had lived his life – the banks, the family holidays with Continental cousins and the social whirl – had been comprehensively destroyed.

Alfred's only consolation was his support for the Allies' war work. Later in the year, once the bloodbath of the Somme got under way, he offered the glorious beech trees from Halton House to the Timber Control Board, to be used as props in the waterlogged trenches of northern France. For now, he concentrated on maintaining Almina's hospital.

Almina's X-ray machine was her pride and joy. X-rays had been discovered in 1895 and their relevance to military surgeons was immediately obvious: being able to locate a bullet precisely without messy interventions was incalculably useful. Bryanston Square now had the means to carry out cutting-edge procedures on fractures and gunshot wounds. There was no shortage of patients in need.

In February, the Battle of Verdun, which eventually claimed 306,000 lives, got under way, and a man called Bates arrived at Almina's hospital. Harold Bates was a padre, an Army chaplain, a reserved and stoical person who, even forty years later, refused to discuss what he had seen and done in the Great War. He had been on the Western Front since August 1914 when he was sent out with the 6th Division. At some point late in 1915 he was wounded at Ypres, shot in the leg.

There have been Army chaplains for as long as there have been armies, but their role expanded, of necessity, in the Great War. For the first time in history, large numbers of men were living on the battlefield in atrocious conditions, for weeks and months at a time. They were in desperate need of comfort and guidance, and the padres, while being unarmed non-combatants, were often in the thick of the horror. Clearly Mr Bates was close enough to take a hit, and quite a nasty one, since he ended up spending seven months in Almina's care at Bryanston Square. He was a dedicated churchman who went on to serve the Church of England until his death in the 1960s.

At the hospital he carried out his duties with determination and dignity, accompanying Almina on her rounds from the moment he was able to get out of bed and limp. Despite the X-ray machine, the operation and excellent nursing, Bates, who was a tall, broad man, was lame for the rest of his life. He used a stick and always struggled with stairs. When he was finally well enough to leave the hospital, he was discharged from the Army. He was an excellent padre, but his days of wading through mud to comfort injured soldiers were behind him. He had got out just in time.

14

Death in the Trenches

Mr Bates's war was over, but Aubrey Herbert, despite his severe disillusionment in the aftermath of the Gallipoli campaign, was gearing up to return to the Middle East. In March 1916 he was sailing for Mesopotamia in the company of the Commander-in-Chief of Egypt, the Commander-in-Chief of the Mediterranean and the Prince of Wales. It was the first time Aubrey had met the eldest son of George V and Queen Mary, who was briefly Edward VIII before his desire to marry Wallis Simpson sparked the abdication crisis. Aubrey, clearly somewhat underwhelmed, commented that at least 'he was more imaginative than I expected. He said that he hated being at home, it worried him thinking of the others in the trenches.'

British military involvement in Mesopotamia had started

out as an operation to safeguard the oil fields in what is now Iraq; crucial given that the naval campaign in particular was heavily oil-dependent. But it was spiralling into a humiliating disaster, and Aubrey's language skills and local knowledge again made him indispensable.

The 6th Indian division had been dispatched to the region from the Army's bases in Bombay, under the command of General Townshend, but they were woefully poorly supplied in terms of both food and transport. As the military problems escalated, such cost-cutting measures proved catastrophic. Aubrey had a very bad feeling about the whole thing, but was hoping to be proved wrong. When he arrived he wrote back to his great friend Sir Mark Sykes, who was still based at the War Office. 'Well, the position here is absolutely bloody.'

General Townshend had retreated to Kut al-Amara, which he was trying to defend against the vastly superior Turkish forces. Attempts to relieve him and break the siege had failed. His troops were starving; some aerial drops of rations had been made but, even so, by April, the men were down to four ounces of food a day and riddled with disease. There was no choice but to surrender.

Aubrey wrote to Colonel Beach, the head of Military Intelligence in the region, offering to accompany General Townshend to the negotiations – he knew some of the leading Turks very well. While he was waiting for a response, he visited Turkish prisoners of war in the British Army camps and noted that their morale was high. They believed that after Gallipoli, Salonika and now Kut, they were going to win. Aubrey's response was typical of the bullish determination that persisted in the British forces and public, despite the shock of failures. He informed the confident Turks that it was his country's 'national habit to be defeated at the beginning of every war and to win in the end.'

A year to the day after Aubrey's arrival at Gallipoli, he was reunited with his friend T. E. Lawrence, and sent to go and talk terms with the Turkish High Command. The two men's hopes were limited to being able to secure a truce to allow the wounded soldiers to be shipped out, but the British government seemed to have a longer-term goal in mind. The men were authorised to offer £2 million and the promise of not launching further attacks on the Ottoman Empire. This offer was rejected and, although there was a truce to allow for an exchange of prisoners, on 29 April 1916 General Townshend surrendered. Thirteen thousand British and Indian soldiers were taken prisoner.

The whole incident was a tremendous humiliation for the British Army. It must have been hard even for Aubrey to remain positive about the national chances as he surveyed the River Tigris, full of bloated corpses. They washed up on the riverbanks and bumped up against the small boats that plied their way up and down. There had been a cholera outbreak that raged through the already weakened troops. Of the 13,000 prisoners of war, more than half died of starvation or at the hands of their captors.

Aubrey wasn't the only Highclere man out in the region. Major Rutherford, the Earl's agent, had a son serving as a Lieutenant in the 1/4th Hampshire Regiment. He eventually made it back to Almina's hospital and survived the war. Lord Carnarvon wrote to Aubrey asking him to find out what had happened to '[his] boys from the stud farm and the estate.' He 'hoped to send money or some small comforts.' The news trickled back agonisingly slowly. Albert Young, Charlie Adnams and George Digweed had all been gardeners and joined up together, also serving in the 1/4th Hampshire Regiment on the ill-fated attempt to take Baghdad. Perhaps when the flies and the stifling air and the stench of the cholera-infested corpses became too much, they dreamt of the peaceful walled gardens and talked about the Dutch azaleas that would be flowering on the Castle's east lawns. They were all buried in Mesopotamia. Adnams and Digweed were taken prisoner at Kut and died in captivity. Thomas Young was killed in action at the crossing of the Shumran Bend on 21 January 1916 as was Frederick Fifield. His body was never found. His young brother was still at home at Highclere, working in the buildings department. Only Tom Whincup, who worked under his half-brother Charlie Whincup at the stud, and Charles Steer who had also worked there, survived the campaign and were lucky enough to avoid being taken prisoner.

Aubrey made it back to Britain in early July and went to Highclere. He wanted to see his brother. All his life, even after he had established himself as a man to call upon to negotiate for soldiers' lives, Aubrey felt the need to touch base with his brother. Lord Carnarvon was of course delighted that Aubrey was safe and in a position to tell him exactly what had gone on. He was also infinitely frustrated that he could only play a part on the sidelines. Through his friendship with Moore-Brabazon he had become closely involved with the development of cameras and interpretation of aerial photography carried out by the Royal Flying Corps, but he wished ardently that his health permitted him to do more.

It was the second time in a year that Aubrey returned

from the Middle East feeling helpless and despairing. He wanted the comfort of being home.

Just weeks later, seven more men left the Highclere estate. Henry Berry from the saw mill, Charles Brindley, a plumber, Charles Choules, a woodsman, Willie Kewell who worked at the farm, Ernest Barton also a woodsman, Gilbert Attwood and William Bendle, both from the buildings department were all spurred on by the news Aubrey brought of their colleagues' deaths. They headed for France. They were heading for the Somme.

Summer 1916 was dominated by the nation's dismay and grief over the death of Lord Kitchener. K might have lost his aura of the unimpeachable hero, but in death he was restored to mythic status. The naval battle had been escalating brutally as the effects of the British blockade on Germany's trade routes and food supplies began to bite. The war at sea claimed its most high-profile casualty when the HMS *Hampshire* was sunk by a mine on 5 June. Six hundred and forty-three men, including Lord Kitchener, lost their lives.

The Carnarvons were even more devastated than most as he had been a family friend. Porchy, who had two more months to go at Sandhurst, was utterly laid low: K had been his great inspiration for a career in the Army. He was due to go to Ireland for four months' training at the end of the summer, but was mopy and uncharacteristically reflective for weeks. If K's loss was a hammer blow to British morale, already shredded by stalemate and surrender, nobody could have predicted how much worse things were about to get.

The Battle of the Somme was planned by General Haig as a decisive breakthrough in the stalemate in France. Instead it has passed into British and Canadian consciousness as the epitome of catastrophic and futile loss of life. On its opening day, 1 July 1916, the British Army suffered 60,000 casualties – still the highest number ever sustained in a single day of combat. The 1st Newfoundland Regiment was totally anni-hilated as a fighting unit, with 500 of 801 men killed. Over the course of the battle's four and a half months, that story was repeated over and over again. Whole battalions of men, who had joined up together and came from tight-knit communities, were wiped out, creating lost generations back home. Highclere, like thousands of other places all over the Empire, was about to suffer a test of its ability for self-sacrifice the like of which it had never known before.

The impact on every hospital in the country was enormous. Four hundred doctors were killed and injured in July, increasing the pressure on the already horrifically over-stretched medical corps. Patients were sent back to Britain in a barely controlled flood. The Somme was characterised by the use of very heavy artillery. It was also marked the debut of a new weapon – the tank. As well as their physical injuries, the men were suffering from devastating shell shock. The human frame couldn't withstand the impact of this new, fully mechanised slaughter on a grand scale and the number of cases of mental breakdown began to increase exponentially.

Lady Almina had to step up to the task. The staff at Bryanston Square had been working steadily, with the same attention to every little detail as ever. The work was tough, but the routines were in place now and there was a palpable sense that the results were enough to justify all the labour involved. Everyone was tired and demoralised by the war, but at the same time keenly invested in and positive about the hospital. Into this stability crashed the vast numbers of officers arriving with complex injuries and severe trauma from the battlefields of the Somme.

One such man was Charles Clout, twenty-one years old, a Cambridge-educated linguist from a modest middle-class home in south London, who had been recruited by the War Office in August 1914, on the strength of his military cadet training at Cambridge University. Clout joined the Territorial Army and was gazetted to the rank of 2nd Lieutenant in the 20th Battalion the London Regiment. He was a serious-minded man who, even in later life, disapproved of the use of first names except between close friends of the same sex. This seriousness made him an excellent officer, and he took pride in training his men up before they shipped out to France on 9 March 1915. Clout was terribly disappointed when on disembarking he was moved to another battalion that was in need of a good officer to lick it into shape.

By August 1916, Clout had seen almost a year and a half of action on the Western Front. He had been in reserve for the first battle of Neuve Chapelle and fought for months at the Battle of Loos. He had seen a man shot in the head by a German sniper as he ran towards him down a trench. The bomber's brain was 'excised as if on an operating table' and fell in two neat hemispheres on the ground behind him and lay there 'steaming in the sunlight'. When Clout's men refused to touch the man's brains, Clout took a spade and shovelled the remains out of the trench.

In August 1916, after two weeks' leave in which he visited his parents in Blackheath, he found himself back out on the front line at the Battle of the Somme. His first job was to accompany a more inexperienced officer as he ventured out of the trench to collect all the property of the dead men who lay scattered in the mud, so that it could be sent back to England. Clout was sitting reading a map, trying to locate the final resting place of the battalion they had been sent to search for, when a sniper shot him in the face. The bullet entered directly between his eyes, passed through his palate and shattered the right-hand side of his jaw. Part of the bone severed an artery in his throat. Instinctively he clutched his neck and, finding the place where blood was gushing, he tried to stem it as he staggered back in the direction of the headquarters' dugout, shouting at his junior officer to stay low since the sniper was certainly still looking out for them.

He was almost unconscious when they got back and was immediately sent to the base hospital at Le Touquet on the coast. The hospital was funded by the Duchess of West-minster and – in another of the surreal contrasts of the Great War – had been set up in the casino of the elegant holiday resort. Clout had been unlucky to be hit on his first day in the new post (although luck like that was not terribly unusual on the Somme), but he must have been both fortunate and tough to survive his wound even as far as Le Touquet. The science of blood transfusion was in its infancy in 1916, and such procedures were very rarely attempted, so the only hope when treating a patient losing a lot of blood was to keep them immobile and administer drugs like morphine to slow the heart rate.

Clout was operated on to remove part of the bullet lodged in his jaw and, two weeks later, once he was stable, he was transferred to a hospital ship for return to Britain. From Dover he went by train to Victoria Station; there, as he lay on the platform with hundreds of other wounded men, he was labelled for the Countess of Carnarvon's hospital at 48

Bryanston Square. Clout tried to insist that he would rather go to the General Hospital in south London. He must have been thinking of visits from his family, and of getting as close to home as possible. He was dispatched to Bryanston Square in any case, and arrived late at night on 2 October 1916.

Clout always recalled the pleasure of being allowed to sleep late at Almina's hospital. At Le Touquet the matron made her ward rounds at the crack of dawn. In the slightly more tranquil surroundings of Bryanston Square, the men slept until breakfast, and then they saw the medical staff. Clout was there until 13 November and made a reasonable recovery, although he had to return in January for a series of operations to continue removing fragments of bone and shrapnel. He later had reconstructive surgery to enable him to eat solids, but his speech was impaired for years. He took to wearing a bandage on his throat because he was embarrassed by his speech and concerned that people wouldn't appreciate that it was the result of a war wound.

About two weeks after his arrival, when he was able to sit up in bed and the swelling and pain in his face had improved enough for him to take an interest in the world again, Charles noticed that Almina had a very charming assistant who accompanied her on her rounds, taking notes on a clipboard as Almina directed. Mary Weekes, who was rather tall and neatly dressed with a kindly and efficient manner, was by then 26 years old. She had been with Almina first as a secretary then as a hospital administrator for five years, and the two had become completely dependent on each other. Charles wrote in his memoirs that Almina regarded her more as a daughter than an employee, which is certainly borne out by Almina's generosity to her.

Charles caught Mary's eye. There was small talk and she made sure she visited him every day; an attraction formed and within weeks it had progressed to a definite courtship. Charles and Mary frequently went for a turn in the gardens behind the railings of Bryanston Square. Almina thought that going out for a walk or going to the theatre was very therapeutic. Perhaps she had been quietly encouraging Mary. Charles asked Mary to marry him in early 1917.

Despite his insistence on formality, Charles definitely had a roguish streak, and he certainly looked good in a uniform. He recorded in his memoir that when he returned to King's College Cambridge after his Army training to inform the authorities that he was heading to France, he also called on a lady student from Newnham whom he'd met at a university society for reading plays in foreign languages. The Tabard Society was one of the few opportunities the undergraduates had to meet the opposite sex, and although the girls were chaperoned, sparks had clearly flown as the young people recited lines together. As they sat over tea in her rooms, 'her flattering comments on my appearance in uniform put me out of countenance, especially as a number of other girls were summoned to meet me. It seemed I was something of a trophy to be displayed to her friends.'

On another occasion, before Charles was wounded and hospitalised back to London, he found very attractive billets. Since he spoke French, he was often asked to help out when another officer was having problems with his accommodation. Officers were billeted with local people, but it was not obligatory for households of women to take in a guest. A young lady living with her mother had refused to allow a British officer to lodge with them but the communication problems meant there was a lot of misunderstanding. Clout went to investigate with his fellow officer and the matter was resolved and alternative accommodation found. 'I offered to escort the lady back to her home. On the way, with a side-long glance at me, she said, "If it had been you who wanted our room I would not have refused."' Charles was not about to pass up this opportunity. 'As she was a very attractive person, I immediately took up the offer and had my orderly move my kit into her home. My friend would never believe that I had not "pulled a fast one" on him. That night the lady came into my bedroom, and for the rest of the period that we were in action in this section of the line I was always able to visit her during any rest period, which probably helped keep me sane.'

Mary and Charles were married in July 1918, when Charles 'believed that the war might drag on for years yet'. They had decided to wait until his recovery was complete and all the work on his jaw was finished. Lord and Lady Carnarvon were their guests of honour and, in fact, their witnesses. Almina arranged for them to be married at the fashionable church St George's, Hanover Square. She then set them up in a house in Paddington, buying all their furniture. They went on to have three children, and until Mary became briefly ill after the birth of her third child, she continued to work for Almina.

All her life, Almina had wildly cavalier attitudes to money. She could be a bully about it, but she was also generous to a fault, often indiscriminately so. It was a habit that got her into a great deal of trouble in later life, but on this occasion her generosity was born out of sincere affection and in recognition of Mary's years of hard work. She also lent the couple the Lake House on the estate at Highclere for their honeymoon, and, as a souvenir, she gave Mary a specially made fan, painted with a view of the building. It is a beautiful house, an elegant, low villa right on the water's edge, and a peaceful idyll for two people who had been working surrounded by death and destruction for years. Almina, who was good at detail, made sure that food and staff were laid on so that the couple would not have to lift a finger.

Charles wrote a letter to Almina on the evening of his wedding day, just after the couple arrived at the Lake House, thanking her for her gifts to him and for everything she had done for them. 'My dear Fairy Godmother I should like to call you, for that is how I shall always think of you . . . thank you for the links and studs, which are charming, and the gift of plate, which is so fine I think I will never wish to dine away from home . . .' The man who wondered about the propriety of using first names expressed himself fulsomely to Almina, who had nursed him back to health, introduced him to his wife and set him up in life. 'I will try to live up to the trust you have placed in me. With very best wishes and love from, yours sincerely, Charles Clout.'

The following day Mary wrote to her 'Dearest Little Lady' to tell Almina of her perfect happiness at the Lake House and to add her own thanks. 'How can I even try to thank you for all you have done for me. I long to tell you what I feel about your wonderful love and affection but alas no words of mine could adequately express what I really feel . . . I hope I will always be a credit to the kindest lady I know, who has indeed been a mother to me for the last seven years and I know will go on being so . . . With love from us both, yours affectionately, Mary.'

The Shake House
July 2nd

My Dear Lady Carnarvon,

My Dear Fairy Godmother I should like to call you, as it is as such that I shall always think of you. I am trying in this little note to express some of my thanks to you for all you have done, and

Letter from Charles Clout to Lady Almina, 1918.
See p.295 for full transcript of the letter.

189

Letter from Mary Weekes to Lady Almina.
See p.296 for full transcript of the letter.

could not have done more. What a
wonderful memory I have to carry
into the future and if I can only be
half as good and kind as you are
I shall be pleased. I hope I shall
always be a credit to the kindest
little lady I know, who has indeed
been a Mother to me for the last
7 years & I know will go on being
so in the future.

I think Charles wrote you ... want for. The
last evening after tea. I was ... attention on all
rather tired so had a bath
and went & lay down. ... to write to Lord

It is glorious down here and there ... too sweet to me on
... made me long to know
... better. What a wonderful Father
& Mother Eve & Porchy have got and
it made me wonder on Tuesday if
they realized it.

Well, my darling little lady,
a thousand thanks for all you
have and are doing for me.
With love from us both.
Yours affectionately,
Mary (C)

These voices from a supposedly buttoned-down age overflow with sincere emotion. There's no doubt that Almina could be frivolous and domineering, but she also transformed people's lives with her energetic desire to make others happy. For that, many of them loved her back with devotion.

15

The Dark Times

The romance between Charles Clout and Mary Weekes was an untypical bright spot in a gloomy year. Charles was never sent back to the front line – his injury was too severe – and he spent the rest of the war helping to train battalions of new recruits. But the sickening rhythm of injury, recovery and return to the war was repeated over and over again for hundreds of thousands of others. Some men had to find the strength to return two, three, even four times, in the full knowledge that whilst they had been lucky so far, their luck could not hold for ever.

At the same time that Charles Clout was being shipped out of the Somme with a bullet lodged in his shattered jaw, Almina was frantically pulling strings to secure a pass for the father of a young man she had treated back in February, to go over to France. Monty Squire had been at '48', as the Bryanston Square hospital was known, for a month and had made a full recovery as a result of the excellent nursing he had received there. Almina had as usual made it her business to contact and befriend Monty's family, and his parents wrote a grateful letter to her after their son's release. As soon as he was well, he was sent back to France, and to the Battle of the Somme. Some time in August, Mr and Mrs Squire received the news they had been dreading. Monty was hit, he was being held in a base hospital in France and treated there. It was an admission that he was going to die.

They wrote again to Almina, this time begging her to do anything in her power to help them secure permission from the military authorities to travel to be at their child's bedside. Once again, Almina's connections, and her willingness to use them, got results. A pass was secured to speed Mr Squire out to the field hospital where his son lay dying. Monty was unconscious for his last four days, during which time his father sat by his bedside talking and reading to him. Monty's mother Alice wrote to Almina afterwards to say that she had been comforted by the fact that Monty was not alone when he died. 'I have to be strong for my husband, as well as my son,' she wrote.

Winifred Burghclere's nephew Richard Maitland, whose brother had already been killed, was also serving at the Somme. He was badly wounded in the leg and sent back to Southampton and from there to Bryanston Square. He spent five months there and survived the war though, even after his final operation in 1917, he walked with a limp because of a stiff knee.

No family was immune to death, and the Carnarvons, although they were becoming almost numb from the endless loss of friends, were still devastated to hear in November that their cousin, Bron Herbert, was missing in action. Aubrey Herbert was especially close to Bron, who had joined the Royal Flying Corps. He had lost a leg in the Boer War and then followed family tradition by becoming a politician and serving in Asquith's government as Under-Secretary of State for the Colonies, the same post as his uncle, the 4th Earl of Carnarvon, had held. He was confirmed dead in December. Aubrey wrote to his cousin, Bron's sister, 'Oh my dear, I can't write, I am too selfishly sorry. I did love him so.' In his letter to his wife Mary, Aubrey said, 'Bron is more than I can bear, for him this time as well as myself.'

Mary was worried that the news would push Aubrey over the edge and make him do something stupid. His nerves had been frayed by the horrors he had seen in the Gallipoli campaign and the futility he saw everywhere. Aubrey could no longer bear to read *The Times* for news of the death of friends, and began to express the view that the 'military solution' had failed and could not go on. That was not a popular position, in spite of everything, and Aubrey was increasingly seen as a crackpot and a potential danger to himself.

Aubrey was still a serving MP, though, and took the job extremely seriously. He was well placed to substantiate his opinion that the new government was not to be trusted. In December Mr Asquith, who was increasingly blamed for the drift in strategy and the lack of decisive progress, had been ousted. David Lloyd George, who had been made

Secretary of State for War after Lord Kitchener's death, took over as Liberal Prime Minister of the Conservative-dominated coalition government.

It was not a good moment to take on the top job. The public was restive, the generals were patently confused and the war was a disaster. On top of that, the Easter Uprising in Dublin had reawakened the question of Home Rule for Ireland, which had been the recurring nightmare for every British Prime Minister for more than fifty years. Overshadowing everything was an almost unimaginable number. When the Battle of the Somme finally petered out in November 1916, 415,000 soldiers from the British and Dominions Army had been killed or wounded or were missing in action. The total number of casualties across all the nations that participated was 1.5 million. Eventually, of course, Lloyd George would be associated with victory, regarded as one of the greatest politicians of the twentieth century, but for now, he had inherited a very poisoned chalice.

Lord Carnarvon had been ill again in the autumn of 1916 and Almina begged him to come up to London and stay at the house in Berkeley Square so she could keep an eye on him. He was fretful about the new government, particularly their agricultural policies for land requisition, and wrote to Winifred that he was worried about his son, Porchy, who was suddenly looking far too young to be serving in the Army. On Boxing Day 1916, Lord and Lady Carnarvon had to wave Porchy off when he sailed with his regiment, for war. Their big consolation was that he was heading not to France or the Balkans but, for now at least, to the backwaters of India.

Lord Porchester was just eighteen when he landed at Bombay and was a boisterous, self-important teenager who had been enjoying his first love affairs in between training to join the cavalry. Porchy's attitude was the embodiment of the young man's inability to grasp that he may die, that something bad might happen to him. He always recalled the awful sinking sensation of scanning the casualty lists for the names of his schoolfriends, but as a boy he was quite capable of resisting the melancholy and hopelessness that his uncle Aubrey could not.

Nothing Porchy found when he arrived at Gillespie Barracks to join the 7th Hussars disabused him of his good-natured expectation that his life would continue to work out very well indeed. As he wrote in his memoirs, 'the changing pattern of warfare on the Western Front hadn't filtered through to India. The Indian Army still trained and drilled to a pattern that hadn't altered in 200 years: sword-play exercise, mounted combat with lances, revolver practice and polo, to practise horsemanship.'

The niceties were meticulously observed out in Meerut. The Anglo-Indian military's way of life was totally impervious to the austerity that was biting back home. There were four changes of kit a day and dress uniform was worn for dinner, which was always served on the best silver plate by a retinue of staff that put Highclere's to shame.

Porchy enjoyed himself, but he was also frustrated, as was the whole regiment, that despite the awful news from France and the Eastern Front, there was no sign of them being called up and given any work to do.

Porchy would have to endure the luxurious calm until the late autumn, but everywhere else, all was chaos. The naval battle was being stepped up by Germany, since it had been decided that domination of the seas was the way to break the public support for the war in Britain. From February 1917 there was a 'sink on sight' policy and civilian boats were increasingly targeted. US boats were also being sunk in the Atlantic, and Germany was gambling that British morale would collapse before the United States' neutrality was tested too far. German High Command misjudged it and the US declared war on the Central Powers on 6 April 1917. That would eventually prove decisive, but initially the Americans' involvement couldn't alter the fact that Germany was winning the war.

Both the French and the Russian armies were mutinying. The Russians' ability to fight on the Eastern Front, which had been ebbing away since 1915, was on the brink of collapse. In March 1917 the Russian people's loathing of the war and contempt for their government's leadership spilled over into violent demonstrations. The Tsar abdicated; the Russian Army had only one eye on the job of trying to win the war. The provisional government launched a highly unpopular big push against the Central Powers in July and that was enough to prepare the ground for the October Revolution in which Lenin and the Bolsheviks seized power.

At Bryanston Square the hospital was busier than ever. In January and February there were still men staying who had come from the Somme, men who needed too much nursing to be sent out to convalescent homes, some of whom had been there for five months. New patients were arriving from France every day. They begged Almina to be allowed to come back to her hospital the next time they were wounded. No one had any hope that the war would be over soon, and no one wanted to go back to the Front. A condition of stasis gripped people; it began to feel as if war was a permanent state. Almina instructed her nurses to spend as much time as possible sitting with the men, talking, listening and playing cards. She lived by the principle of taking one day at a time and staying busy. There was very little alternative.

In February there was a boost to the spirits of the residents of '48' when King George and Queen Mary paid a visit. Almina had met the royal couple of course, had been to their coronation dressed in her finest silks and jewels. Now she greeted them on the doorstep wearing her nurse's uniform with a large starched cap and floor-length apron. Only her trademark waved hair and enormous smile were the same. She could never resist the opportunity to be charming, and she welcomed her guests effusively. They spoke to every single patient, nurse and doctor, walking from ward to ward and commending the excellent equipment and standard of care. Almina was naturally overjoyed by this recognition and delighted when, following the King's glowing report, she welcomed his uncle, Prince Arthur, Duke of Connaught, the following week.

The King and Queen were accompanied by Admiral Louis Battenberg and Sir Thomas Myles, a high-ranking member of the Royal Army Medical Corps. Admiral Battenberg was a German Prince and a cousin of George V. He had been serving in the Royal Navy for forty years when war broke out, and had been First Sea Lord since 1912. He had begun to draw up the Navy's plans for war, but a huge wave of anti-German feeling had forced his retirement. Just as Alfred de Rothschild's family had found itself on two different sides of the conflict, so the British Royal family had to contend with the perception that some members might have split loyalties. The issue came to a head in the summer of 1917 when anti-German sentiment was so insistent that King George issued a proclamation changing the name of the Royal family from Saxe-Coburg and Gotha to Windsor.

Loyalty was an increasingly vexed issue in 1917. The Military Service Act of January 1916 had introduced conscription for all single men between the ages of nineteen and forty-one. That was adjusted in May to include married men without children. The fact was that by 1917, although the Army managed to reach its target of an additional 800,000 men, the number of fit soldiers able to serve at the front line was falling. Those who were serving were able to take only half the leave they were entitled to. Feelings of resentment towards those who were not perceived to be doing their bit were increasing.

The Western Front continued to stack up with the bodies of young men. In June 1917 the British scored a significant success when they captured the Messines Ridge, near Ypres, using a different tactic: the deployment of mines before the artillery attack. But any forward momentum was lost when there was an eight-week delay before the launch of the next attack. After the strategic success at Messines and the relatively low casualties, expectations were high. Passchendaele crushed them all back into the mud.

The battle opened on 31 July and lasted until early November. It was another exchange of pitiless attrition, with heavy shells pounding into both armies' defences and no-man's-land between them, day and night. The ground, which was boggy even in a dry summer, was destroyed by the explosions, which left behind overlapping craters, huge pockmarks that filled with water, mud and bodies. Then it began to rain. It rained every day apart from three in August. The mud was inescapable. Trenches collapsed, burying men alive; they drowned in mud up and down the lines. There was no relief anywhere, from the noise, the fear, the threat of a gas attack. Depending on the amount of poison released, gas was sometimes merely one more irritant, but other times it was a terrifying choking fog that caused blindness. In very heavy gas attacks, men drowned in it as it dissolved their lungs. There were many ways to die in the Great War.

The little band of Highclere men who had joined up in the summer of 1916, who had trained together and been out in France for six months, dodging bullets, staying lucky, fought at Passchendaele. Stan Herrington survived several months but was killed in September, aged nineteen. In October it was Tommy Hill's turn. His wife, Florence, had borne his absence as best she could, cherishing every letter, refusing to believe that her Tommy wouldn't make it back. His body, like so many others at Passchendaele, was never found.

When she got the telegram to say that he was missing in action, Florence decided to wait for better news. Perhaps she believed he had been taken prisoner. Florence waited and waited until finally, more than two years later, after the Armistice, she had to accept that her husband was dead. She never remarried. When her nephew was born, he was named Tommy, in honour of the uncle he had never known.

Henry Crawley had been fighting in Ypres in 1917 and was wounded and sent to Lady Carnarvon's hospital. He had already fought at Gallipoli and now he had also survived the Somme. His parents lived in Bethnal Green in London so it was easy for them to visit their son. Apprehensive after the stress of the previous three years, they said goodbye as he left again to join his battalion in France. This time the letters stopped, and like so many other parents they could only visit his named grave in the war cemetery in France. He was killed in May 1918.

By contrast, Almina was thrilled when David Campbell turned up on her doorstep at Bryanston Square. She had not heard from him since he left Highclere. 'She gave me a terrific welcome,' he wrote, and then she whirled him upstairs to show him round her wonderful hospital and meet all the patients. She was thrilled that he had been awarded the Military Cross and made him promise to come again the following week so she could spoil him and take him out to lunch.

16

The Promised End

Highclere in 1917 echoed with ghosts. It was virtually shut up; Lady Evelyn was the only member of the family still spending most of her time at the house. Lord Carnarvon was back and forth between London and the Castle, depending on the state of his health and the need to work on estate matters. Almina hated to leave Bryanston Square unattended, but she fretted about her daughter and popped down for the odd weekend to be with her.

Eve missed Porchy and was lonely and unsure of herself; she was sixteen years old with a sense of waiting for her life to start that was exacerbated by the nation's endless suffering. The house felt sad without the bustle of the hospital, which Eve had enjoyed, and although she was

naturally inclined to work hard on her lessons, it was difficult to feel confident about a bright future. The old
path for a girl in her position – the debutante season that
would lead to making a good marriage – was something
of a sideshow compared to the trauma the country was
experiencing. Eve looked forward anxiously to her trips to
town and her parents' visits, and devoured the letters from
her brother that connected her to a bigger world.

When her father was at the Castle they dined together
in the State Dining Room, seated below the Van Dyck
portrait of Charles I on horseback. The wonder of a house
like Highclere is that, although change rages around it, its
physical fabric stays so recognisable. There is a comfort in
the way so many things endure. Eve might have been
lonely sometimes, but she could never feel completely lost
when she was at home in the house she had lived in all
her life, a house that was a monument to her family's
permanence.

Eve and her father had always been devoted to one
another and now their conversations about estate business,
the war and the hospital brought them even closer together.
Lord Carnarvon was desperate to get back to Egypt and
resume his life's work, and Eve, who was as fascinated by
the elegance of Ancient Egyptian art as her father, loved to
listen to his plans for resuming the excavations. There was
sporadic news from Howard Carter, who had reported for
duty in Cairo and been assigned to the Intelligence Department of the War Office. He wrote to tell Lord Carnarvon
that he had been able to undertake some clearing work in
the Valley of the Kings, but there could be no real progress
until the war was won.

One topic that, given his instinctive reticence, Lord Carnarvon probably chose not to discuss with Eve was his concern to avoid giving up any of the land at Highclere to the government. Since 1916 there had been a policy of land requisition, with compensation for owners, so that more food could be produced. But Lord Carnarvon found the official agricultural policies absurd. He had written to his sister in December 1916, 'Most of the agricultural schemes I see mooted are too foolish for words. As if you could sow wheat on commons in that casual way.' He was doing everything he could to keep enough men at Highclere for the farm to continue to function, and was convinced that this would be a more efficient way to maximise output than handing over land to be farmed by strangers on behalf of central government. Carnarvon had asked his long-serving agent, James Rutherford, to write to the authorities to request a dispensation for Blake, the head gardener, removing his obligation to volunteer. 'It is far more important that the Hospital should continue to be supplied with fruit and vegetables than that Blake should be put to some unsuitable form of labour.'

Aubrey and Mary were occasional visitors to Highclere and Eve looked forward especially eagerly to their arrival now that she was a teenager and often starved of company. Aubrey had always been a favourite of both his niece and nephew and they adored him, but his elder brother was troubled by some of the conversations that went on around the dining-room table. Politics could not be kept off the agenda when Aubrey was around and his views were becoming more and more controversial. He was increasingly voting with the Labour Party and the pacifists in the House of Commons. Mary cautioned him that Lord Northcliffe, the newspaper baron who owned both *The Times* and the *Daily Mail*, had a habit of destroying the reputations of men like Aubrey. Look at Lord Lansdowne, who had been vilified for writing that 'the prolongation of the war [would] spell ruin for the civilised world, and an infinite addition to the load of human suffering which already weighs upon it.'

But if ever there was a time for the pacifist position to be taken seriously, it was the second half of 1917. The Allies' prospects were worsening by the day. Field Marshal Haig was insistent that the Germans were on the brink of collapse and that the war of attrition was working, but that simply wasn't borne out by results. In reality the Germans benefited hugely from two developments. Firstly, they managed to knock Italy out of the conflict in just two months through superb logistical management, and thereby prop up the crumbling Austro-Hungarian Empire a little while longer. Then, in December, the demoralised and defeated Russians sued for peace. Ukraine, Georgia and the Baltic states were all turned into a German protectorate and forty German divisions could be transferred from the Eastern to the Western Front. The Central Powers believed the end was in sight. They were to make one last huge effort to break through on the West and defeat the Allies. Morale in England could not have been lower. Eight hundred thousand British soldiers were killed or injured in 1917.

The end of the year saw inches' worth of ground gained and then lost, a depressing back and forth across the bog that had been northern France. The British Army's attack at the Battle of Cambrai utilised tanks as well as a lighter, more mobile artillery, and was planned with the benefit of aerial reconnaissance. Initial gains couldn't be held, though, and the British were fought back by German storm troopers.

At the same time as the deadly dance on the Western Front was claiming more lives, Lord Porchester was rejoicing over the telegram for which he had been waiting almost a year. The 7th Hussars were being sent to fight the Turks. Mesopotamia had claimed the lives of thousands of British and Indian men after the humiliating siege of Kut al-Amara, but the pressing need to defend the oil fields hadn't abated, and since then there had been a change of fortunes. Two hundred thousand men deployed to the region had succeeded in taking Baghdad in March 1917. Porchy was going to join a brigade of reinforcements who were needed to respond to the rumoured counter-attack from the Ottoman Army.

The war in Arabia was the last campaign in which there could still conceivably be a role for the cavalry. Only a few months beforehand, Field Marshal Haig had finally given up on his cherished urge to deploy them against the German trenches, when he had ordered a mounted unit to wait for a breakthrough at Passchendaele and then rush through the lines to attack. The breakthrough never came, the horses churned the ground to even stickier mud and the plan to use the cavalry in France was at last abandoned. But the desert sands of the Middle East were very different: there were no heavily defended trenches to contend with. Porchy's regiment joined a force being shipped from India over to Basra and from there they began the 500-mile march on Baghdad.

The troops' enthusiasm for finally seeing some action evaporated almost instantly in the ferocious heat. Even as they set off, Porchy and his men heard that there had been 360 deaths from heatstroke the previous day. It was blisteringly hot by day, freezing by night, and dysentery, malaria and sand-fly fever were rampant.

Allied High Command were proved right about the usefulness of highly trained men and horses, though. One band of men rode hard into the desert away from the Euphrates to cut off the flank of the Ottoman Army, and Porchy and his men mounted an ambush on the Aleppo road to pick up the Turkish forces as they retreated. It all worked exactly as planned, and the Ottoman 50th Division was defeated. But, even in the midst of this low-casualty success, a boy's own adventure compared to the slaughter in France and Belgium, there was horror. Porchy came upon a cave in the hills of the desert in which an entire Arab village had taken shelter from the conflict. They had been completely cut off by the Ottoman Army and hundreds of people had starved to death. At first he thought there was no one left alive, that the cave was full of emaciated corpses, but then he saw that a few of them were still clinging on to life. The regiment of happy-go-lucky Anglo-Indians, who had been playing polo just two months before, were incredulous at the fate of these civilian men, women and children. When they desperately tried to feed the villagers their rations of condensed milk, it was more than the Arabs' wasted frames could take. The last remaining survivors died in the soldiers' arms.

The war turned up suffering everywhere – there was a never-ending supply of it – but at Bryanston Square there was an enclave where it could at least be alleviated with expertise and patience, and in comfort. The contrast between what the men had seen and what they experienced under Almina's care was almost surreal, like the sickening disconnection between starving villagers and condensed milk.

Sidney Roberts was sent to Lady Carnarvon's hospital from France with a shattered right leg. The orderly who dispatched him said he was sending him to Lady Carnarvon's place 'because they liked good surgical cases there.' Sidney captured the oddness as well as the luxurious ease of life at '48' perfectly when he wrote to thank Almina and told her what he particularly remembered. There was the exquisite breakfast in bed served by Almina's butler, while the footman politely enquired not whether he would like to read a paper, but which paper he required first. Like so many of Almina's correspondents, Sidney was obviously much cheered by the banter of the Irish nurses. Dr Johnnie had also made a great impression. He was undoubtedly an excellent doctor but apparently he never really got the hang of the X-ray machine. At Sidney's first examination he turned various switches on and off in 'an experimental way' before saying brightly, 'Well, the whole place will probably blow up. You don't mind do you?' It's a good thing Sidney Roberts was inclined to laugh, because one can't help thinking that some of Almina's patients might have taken that quip rather hard.

Sidney was out by Christmas 1917 and able to go back to his parents' place in Worthing with his leg in a splint. Not all of Almina's patients survived, though. Sid Baker arrived at Bryanston Square at about the same time as Sidney Roberts, but all Almina's skill and nursing couldn't save him. When he died he left a little daughter and his widow, Ruth, who wrote to thank Lady Carnarvon for not merely sending a beautiful wreath but actually attending his funeral. There is the familiar moving struggle to express limitless gratitude and appreciation. 'I am unable to find words to express my thanks for your sweetness and kindness.'

It was the end of the most terrible year. Battlefields all over the world were still filling up with corpses, and cities were acquiring more widows like Ruth. Whoever officially won the war, it was starting to feel impossible to establish what victory would look like. The moral and mental exhaustion was too great to allow any meaningful assessment.

As the Carnarvons embarked on 1918, they had dramas of their own to focus on. In the middle of January, the Earl spent a morning out shooting with a friend and was just finishing lunch at the Castle when he was taken ill with agonising abdominal pain. Almina received the telegram at Bryanston Square and dropped everything to race down to Highclere, fetch her husband and bring him back to the hospital, where he was immediately operated on for appendicitis. Almina's longstanding colleague, Sir Berkeley Moynihan, who had rushed to help, told Lord and Lady Carnarvon after the operation that with half an hour's delay, the Earl might have died. Lord Carnarvon wrote to his sister Winifred to tell her what had happened and attributed his recovery to 'the skill and devotion of my wife'.

The Earl's lucky escape had to be set against the loss of Alfred de Rothschild just three weeks later. The old man, who had never recovered his *joie de vivre* after the outbreak of war, had been getting frailer and frailer for years. He died on 31 January after a short illness. Almina was already exhausted, and had only just recovered her calm after her husband's close-run thing. Now she was devastated. Lady Evelyn came to London the moment she heard the news and found her mother weeping uncontrollably at Alfred's deathbed in Seamore Place.

Alfred was buried with great ceremony at the Willesden United Synagogue Cemetery in north London the following day. His extraordinary generosity and boundless affection for his family had sustained Almina in the enviable position of being both well loved and also gifted with every material thing she desired. His loss was a terrible blow and was to have profound implications for Almina's future life.

Almina had lost her father, just barely saved her husband and had a son fighting in the Middle East to worry about. Once more she threw herself into her work; it was the best possible distraction. Lord Carnarvon remained in London until March, recovering from his operation and fretting about Porchy. Every time he received a scribbled message from him, he rushed round the corner to Winifred's house to read it to his sister. He was also worried about Aubrey, whose record of voting with Labour had made him so unpopular with his Conservative constituency that he'd left the country for Italy and Albania, leaving Mary to deal with the fallout.

The news from the Continent was all bad. The Central Powers judged that the time to secure a decisive victory was now, before the US troops could arrive in France in big enough numbers to make Allied victory all but inevitable. General Ludendorff planned a spring offensive for the Western Front, and threw every last resource into the battle. Seven hundred and fifty thousand men were made ready and on 21 March, vast quantities of artillery pounded the British positions. The German Army proceeded to advance forty kilometres and the British fell back to Amiens, retreating over the fields of the Somme that they had been inching across for the last three years. It was only when the landscape re-asserted itself and the heavy German artillery became bogged down in the mud, that the offensive slowed. British reinforcements were sent in to Amiens in red double-decker buses and the two armies paused to assess.

It was the biggest movement in any direction since 1914 and, with hindsight, the start of the end of the war, but it was also the end of Field Marshal Haig's dominance. He placed himself under the command of an outstanding French General, Ferdinand Foch, and on 26 March, General Foch was appointed Supreme Commander of the Allied forces.

The Germans were still advancing and on 13 April Haig told his troops it was 'backs against the wall', urging every last man to 'fight on to the end'. Everyone was praying that the US Army under General Pershing would deploy in time to give the Allied forces the boost they so desperately needed. The Germans lost at least 110,000 men at the Battle of the Lys, and the Allies even more. But by the end of April it became clear that the Germans were overextended and undersupplied. The British, for all that they had lost the ground they had spent years defending, had in fact conceded little more than a muddy swamp. By 29 April the extraordinary German advance was again temporarily halted. The outcome of the war was felt to hang in the balance. Both armies gathered their forces, called up more reserves, and then Ludendorff moved emphatically against the French, northeast of Paris at Aisne, catching them completely by surprise. The German Army reached the River Marne and

Paris was within sight. Kaiser Wilhelm was elated – the Germans thought victory was near. Their elation was short-lived.

The Battle of Château-Thierry on 18 July was a day of fighting as ferocious as anything that had been seen earlier in the war. But now, finally, the American Expeditionary Force had arrived: hundreds of thousands of untraumatised, well-rested men. It was a turning point. American machine gunners fought alongside French colonial troops from Senegal and beat the Germans back. At last the Allies had gained the initiative.

Summer 1918 saw a series of strategic wins, but men kept dying and Bryanston Square was still full to the rafters. Major Oliver Hopkinson of the Seaforth Highlanders was wounded for the third time in France in 1918, and to his relief it was serious enough for him to be evacuated back home. He had pleaded to be returned to Lady Carnarvon's hospital. 'If you knew what a difference it made to me the last time I went to France, knowing that if hit again I should have every chance of being under your special care . . .' he wrote to Almina when he was discharged from the hospital for the last time.

Almina became firm friends with some of the returning men and invited them to Highclere to take their convalescence there. Kenneth Harbord was with the Royal Flying Corps and had spent a month at Bryanston Square in 1916. British pilots in the First World War were incredibly lucky to survive being shot down because, unlike their German counterparts, they were not issued with parachutes. If they were hit they had no option but to try to land their plane safely. Many of them suffered horrific burns because the planes caught fire on the way down but they couldn't bail out. Kenneth Harbord survived this ghastly Hobson's Choice not once but twice. He had asked to be passed fit after his first crash landing and recovery, but he got shot down again and was back in Almina's hospital at the end of 1917. He again recovered and Almina, who was deeply impressed by his bravery, invited him to spend the weekend at Highclere with Lord Carnarvon.

Almina was naturally thinking of the good it would do Kenneth Harbord, but she was also worried about her husband. He was having a dreadful few months and needed cheering up in good company. His childhood friend Prince Victor Duleep Singh had died of a heart attack in June in Monte Carlo. Victor had been an immoderate eater all his life and by the end he was clinically obese. Lord Carnarvon was utterly cast low. He was also furious with Aubrey, who had got the Carnarvon name mixed up in a libel trial.

Lord Carnarvon had only met the defendant in the 'Billing Trial' once by chance for ten minutes, but Aubrey, who didn't have a judgemental bone in his body, had been inviting him to Pixton rather indiscriminately. The case revolved around a delusional American eccentric and a libellous poem entitled 'The Cult of the Clitoris'. Conducted by Mr Justice Darling, the trial degenerated into farce, albeit one the newspapers adored. By the time the case came to court that summer, Aubrey was abroad again, heading up the British Adriatic Mission and co-ordinating special intelligence in Rome. It was left to his older brother to handle the fallout as the newspapers raked over the stories of anyone even remotely connected to the defendant. Carnarvon had to instruct Sir Edward Marshall Hall, QC, Aubrey refused to come back, and Carnarvon tried to ignore the whole matter.

Kenneth Harbord proved to be extremely congenial company and was invited to Highclere several times. The Earl of course shared Harbord's passion for flying. He invited another house guest, a longstanding friend of his, to participate in their conversations about planes and aerial reconnaissance. John Moore-Brabazon was the first Englishman to fly, albeit in a French machine, and in August 1914 he had joined the Royal Flying Corps. Lord Carnarvon's knowledge of photographic technique was highly regarded, and he had discussed reconnaissance with Moore-Brabazon throughout the war. By the time the Allies launched their Hundred Days Offensive, which effectively ended the conflict, the Royal Flying Corps had been combined with the Royal Naval Air Service to form the Royal Air Force and was playing a crucial role in intelligence.

The Germans believed that the great losses suffered by the Allies in 1917 would preclude the British and French from undertaking any major offensive in 1918. The Germans knew that they had to strike before American troops arrived in force and the general consensus was that there would not be enough American troops in France until early 1919. Allied activity in 1918, therefore, would have to be restricted to meeting the planned German advance. The Americans did not want to amalgamate their troops into French and British battalions, preferring to wait until an independent American Army could be shipped to French soil, which exasperated the Allies. Events rapidly overtook the disputes as salients were pushed forward or held, and the estimate of early 1919 for the arrival of the American force turned out, crucially, to be wrong.

August 1918 really was, at last, the endgame. By then, 200,000 American troops were arriving every month, and the British Army was reinforced by the return of large numbers of troops from the Middle East and Italy. The British Navy's blockade of Germany had destroyed the German public's spirit and the Central Powers' resolve folded in a series of heavy defeats. In the end, after four decimating years of death, victory came in just three months of sharp, decisive battles that cost the Germans two million men killed, captured or injured. Once the Allied forces had broken the Hindenburg Line of defence, the German Army was in retreat. By October the Allies were claiming victory and the exhausted General Ludendorff, who had been certain that his men were on the brink of capturing Paris just four short months before, had a nervous collapse. Across what had been the Austro-Hungarian Empire, countries were declaring independence; now it was the turn of the politicians to begin the long and painful process of working out the terms on which to end a conflict that had engulfed millions of people.

Kaiser Wilhelm abdicated on 9 November and the guns stopped at the eleventh hour on the eleventh day of the eleventh month, 1918. The war had stuttered to a close, with rearguard actions being fought right up to the very last moment. The Germans sat down to negotiate US President Woodrow Wilson's proposal for peace, with General Foch. The Armistice was signed in a carriage of his private train, stopped in the countryside north of Paris. The news was passed as fast as possible to the armies, and hundreds of thousands of men from dozens of different countries finally dared to hope it was really all over.

The end hadn't come soon enough for everyone in the last little band of Highclere men to go to fight. Fred Bowsher who probably worked in the gardens had joined up with several Sheerman and Maber boys in the gloomy days of 1917. Both the Mabers made it back to Highclere but one of the Sheerman boys, Harry, was drowned when the HMS *Leinster* was sunk by a German submarine in the Irish Sea a month and a day before the Armistice. Fred Bowsher was killed on 21 June, aged twenty-one. His friend Arthur Fifield, whose brother had been killed in Mesopotamia back in 1916, was buried in France in the summer of 1918. The last Fifield boy made it to Armistice Day and went home to his mother.

17

From War to Peace

Of course, after the initial disbelief, there was euphoria everywhere, from the battlefields of Flanders to the servants' hall at Highclere. David Lloyd George issued an official communiqué at 10.20 a.m. on 11 November, announcing the ceasefire, and by the end of the day, Newbury was decked with flags and the local newspaper reported fireworks and 'liveliness' in the streets. Aubrey walked through the crowds in London, which had 'gone wild with delight', according to the *Daily Mirror*, and noted their jubilation. It wasn't until a few days and weeks later that sheer fatigue overtook people, civilians and soldiers alike. Across the Middle East, North Africa and all of Europe, millions of men were crisscrossing countries, trying to get home. Florence, the former housemaid from Highclere, whose husband Tommy's body was never found, had to face a future without the man she loved, like so many other women across the world. Nerves had been stretched almost to breaking point over four years, and now, as the Peace Conference of Versailles got under way, it was time to ask the question: what had it all been for?

On Sunday 17 November 1918, a service of thanksgiving was held at the Newbury Corn Exchange. Lord Carnarvon spoke in his capacity as High Steward and told the crowd of local dignitaries that, although it was very proper to rejoice, the people there that day could never repay the debt they owed to those who had fought. Almina and Eve were both at his side, but Porchy of course was not. He had sent word that his regiment was to stay in Mesopotamia for at least a couple of months before beginning the long trip back. At the end of the gathering, a patriotic note was struck by the singing of the new verse of the national anthem: 'God save our valiant men'.

Almina lost no time in returning to Bryanston Square after the service. The hospital would have to be dismantled, like all the rest of the apparatus of war, but for now it was still home to some twenty or so men, as well as the band of nurses.

Just as Almina got back to London, she went down with the Spanish flu, as did some of her patients. News of this great disaster had been emerging since the summer and now the numbers affected were terrifying an already traumatised population. Broken Europe was swept by an influenza pandemic so deadly that it claimed many more lives than the recently finished war. At least 50 million died all over the world, from the Arctic to the Pacific Islands. The war had not caused the flu, but the fact that men with weakened immune systems had been closely herded together for four years probably helped to incubate it. The sickest flu patients were hospitalised and shipped home with the wounded, spreading the disease across the Continent and then the world. It was an unusual strain in that it afflicted healthy young adults rather than the more usual victims, and it was terrible to nurse, as the sufferer drowned in his own mucus.

Dr Sneyd, the doctor at Bryanston Square, was one of those affected; Almina sent him to Highclere to recover. She had only contracted a mild strain herself, so she stayed on at the hospital and, as soon as she was better, continued to nurse her patients. There was cruel luck for one young man whom she couldn't save: having survived three and a half years at the Front, he died of the flu just weeks after Armistice Day.

At the end of the year, Almina was also preoccupied with resolving the matter of her inheritance. Alfred de Rothschild had left her virtually everything. He gave generously in death as he had done in life. There were sizeable bequests for friends and family and £50,000 for charity, £25,000 of which went to Lord Kitchener's Memorial Fund for the relief of suffering amongst members of the Armed Forces. The National Gallery received a spectacular painting by Sir Joshua Reynolds. Alfred's beloved Halton House went to his nephew Lionel, since he was 'the only Rothschild not to have a great house', but Seamore Place was left in its entirety and with all its contents to Almina. It was an impeccable and enormous house in Mayfair and it was crowded with beautiful things and priceless paintings, some of which Alfred asked that Almina consider as heirlooms and not dispose of. In addition, Almina received a tax-free legacy of £50,000 and Lord Carnarvon, Porchy and Lady Evelyn all received bequests of £25,000. This was wealth on a staggering scale, given that a gardener at Highclere was paid £24 a year in 1918, and the top salary, for the chef, was £150.

From now on the Carnarvon family home in London was Seamore Place; Berkeley Square was sold. Almina, who all her life loved few things more than doing up a house, set about a programme of renovations. The property, for all its museum-quality furnishings, apparently left something to be desired with regards to the drains. In December she was asking her solicitors, Frere and Co, to write to Alfred de Rothschild's solicitors to ask for a substantial contribution to her funds. She explained that she had been obliged to carry out major repairs to Seamore Place and had also incurred very heavy liabilities with regard to her hospital. She therefore intended to sell two of the paintings left to her, tax-free as long as she retained them, and required the executor of Alfred's will to bear the cost of the duties payable.

If there was one sin of which Almina could certainly be guilty, it was a tendency to fecklessness with money. She was unfailingly generous when giving it away and delighted in the spending of it; she was also entirely casual about the getting of it. The fact that Alfred's death meant his money was now by definition finite does not seem to have occurred to Almina. She simply asked for more, as she had done all her life.

The executor of Alfred's will was the distinguished barrister Sir Edward Marshall Hall, who took a stand and refused to bow to Almina's somewhat imperious demand. Almina did sell her paintings, despite Alfred's stipulation that she shouldn't, and she did have to pay the tax on them herself. It was a small adjustment to the new reality of life without her beloved benefactor.

Adjusting to the new reality was the nation's work for January 1919. Elsie, the Dowager Countess of Carnarvon, was sixty-three years old in 1919 but, with typically unflagging energy, determined to do her bit to alleviate the aftershocks in combatants' lives. She became vice-chairman of the Vocal Therapy Society, which was instrumental in developing modern speech therapy. The aim was to restore normal speech to thousands of ex-soldiers who were struggling to cope with disabilities. Many of them had severe shell shock, as well as amnesia and panic attacks; they stammered or simply couldn't speak. Elsie raised funds and awareness, but her big idea was the use of music and singing to help patients breathe more effectively, relax and have fun. She founded King's Services Choirs, which were hugely successful at improving patients' speech so that they could reclaim their social lives and look for work. Some men discovered a passion for singing and had individual lessons; some took up Spanish classes. One man with a stammer recovered so well that Elsie was able to find a place for him as a gardener on an estate not far from Highclere. At a concert in Lancashire, a mill hand was asked about being wounded.

He replied, 'I lost t'leg and t'voice but t'voice is back again, so t'leg doesn't matter!'

Almina was winding up the hospital, but before it was formally closed on 15 February 1919, she, her team of medics and nurses and the last few residents received another visit from Prince Arthur, Duke of Connaught. He had been so impressed and moved by what he'd seen on his previous tour that he came to personally thank the staff for the work they had done.

The hospital's closure was reason to be thankful, of course, but it was poignant as well, to leave the place that had bonded so many people so closely. As Kenneth Witham Wignall, one of the last inmates put it, 'It was simply pathetic leaving 48. I am quite sure that if it had not been for all the magnificent care and skill . . . I should certainly be without my one remaining leg.' Letters continued to pour in from patients and their relatives. Lizzie Hooper wrote in an uneven hand to thank Lady Carnarvon for all she had done for her two boys. 'I am utterly in your debt for all the care and skill they received.'

Almina wrote to thank all the surgeons with whom she had worked over the previous four and a half years. She sent many of them gifts, silver tea caddies with their names and dates of service engraved, mementoes of their time at Highclere and Bryanston Square. Hector Mackenzie wrote by return to thank her for all her support and for the enormous amount of energy she had spent instilling the sense in her colleagues that they were doing everything they possibly could. 'I have seen you as an angel, rejoicing when your efforts have been crowned with success, hoping against hope and fighting for some desperate case and now sorrowing when all your efforts have been in vain.'

A great many people worked, as Almina did, throughout the First World War, to provide a desperately needed medical service. She knew only too well that she could not have done it without her doctors and nurses. It was of course pleasant to be recognised for these efforts, and doubtless Almina appreciated it, but the endless small acts of kindness: the funerals attended personally, the exquisite attention to detail that made every patient feel like a house guest, the willingness to get down and dress a man's gangrenous stump herself were carried out for their own sake and without expectation of anything in return.

Almina's generosity and energy combined, in her hospital work, to produce a significant achievement, one that was noticed by the highest authorities. Sir Robert Jones, the Inspector of Military Hospitals, wrote to her on 28 January to express his personal thanks.

I have always looked upon you as one of the discoveries of the war. You have devoted yourself with such extra-ordinary vitality to helping our wounded soldiers and I am sure the nation should be very grateful to you for it all. I shall always have the pleasantest memories of Highclere, the wonderful times the officers had there, and particularly of the self-sacrificing way in which you ministered to their mental and physical well-being.

Having devoted herself to the health of others for years, Almina was in desperate need of a rest. In February, once the last patient had been sent off to a trusted convalescent home, and the last nurse had found another position, the family left for Egypt for the first time since 1915. Lord

Carnarvon was beside himself with excitement and desperate to join Howard Carter to resume their work. London was bitterly cold that winter, with snow and icy winds, which gave him an added incentive to leave.

They crossed to Boulogne, and from there they caught a train to Paris. France was in the grip of a giant clean-up operation. At Versailles, the political fallout was being picked over in painstaking detail by delegations from every combatant nation. Across northern France and Belgium, the task of burying the dead in war cemeteries was under way.

The Carnarvons made a stop in Paris to visit Aubrey, who had rushed there when he heard news that his great friend, Colonel Sir Mark Sykes, who was part of the British delegation to the peace negotiations, was dying of flu. Sir Mark, who had called on Almina back in the opening days of the war to give her the information that Aubrey had been shot, died on 16 February, aged thirty-nine. He was the creator of the Arab Bureau, which existed to 'harmonise British political activity in the Near East'. Aubrey and T. E. Lawrence both served in the bureau and all three men spent weekends at Highclere and Pixton discussing the future of politics in the Middle East over port and cigars. Sir Mark had been diligently pushing the causes of both Arab nationalism and Zionism up the Versailles agenda when he was struck down. Aubrey was horrified that his friends were still dying, even after the cessation of hostilities. When he too succumbed to the flu, he and his wife Mary decided to go to Italy for the winter so that Aubrey could convalesce.

They spent three months at the house that Aubrey's father,

the 4th Earl, had acquired in 1882 and dubbed 'Alta Chiara', Highclere in Italian. It perched on the cliffs overlooking the harbour of Portofino and commanded spectacular views over the Mediterranean. It must have been the most romantic and peaceful place to calm the spirit and regain strength.

The Carnarvons pushed on to Marseilles and from there sailed via Bizerte in Tunisia to Alexandria. The war had been over for barely four months and travel was still very much affected, with potentially deadly consequences. The Carnarvons' ship had been used to transport sick and wounded men and had not been disinfected properly before it was returned to civilian use. Under pressure from people's desire to see things return to normal, corners were inevitably cut. In this case, conditions were so unsanitary that several passengers died of infections they picked up on board. Almina had only just recovered from flu and the Earl was never in good health, but they made it ashore without problems. For the first time in four years, Lord Carnarvon was again in the dry air and, as they disembarked in Alexandria, he and Almina were surrounded by a familiar cacophony of sounds and confusion. Things were different here too, though. The end of the war had fomented a new vision of nationalism and independence amongst the Egyptian people.

They travelled to Cairo before catching the train down to Luxor, where they were met by Howard Carter. Carter and Carnarvon were desperate to resume their work in the Valley of the Kings. It had been five long, frustrating years since they secured the concession for excavating in the valley just before the outbreak of the war. They were in two minds about whether it was, as they were repeatedly told, exhausted, but they weren't going to give up on the long-cherished dream of digging there without at least one excavation.

Almina and Eve stayed at the Winter Palace Hotel, which had been virtually shut up during the war years but was resurrecting itself as fast as possible to meet the needs of the returning travellers. Lord Carnarvon stayed with Carter out at his house, which was much more convenient for the site of the dig. 'Castle Carter', as it was nicknamed, had been constructed nine years ago from bricks shipped out from England by Lord Carnarvon. It was modelled on a traditional Egyptian design and had a dome in the central courtyard that kept it cool, as well as more modern comforts.

The two men were brimming over with enthusiasm at being reunited and working again. They were both convinced that there were more treasures to be found in the Valley of the Kings; the site they had identified to test their hunch was in front of the tomb of Thutmose I. Every morning, as dawn was breaking, they set off, astride their donkeys, to oversee progress. Most days, Almina and Eve went to join them.

Almina was relieved to have a project to distract herself with, even if it wasn't her own. She wasn't used to relative idleness and, although it was restorative to be in the familiar luxury of the Winter Palace, she felt more ambivalent about life's return to old routines than either her husband or her daughter. Unlike Carnarvon and Eve, Almina had spent the last five years working on an exhausting but hugely rewarding and important task. Now that task was concluded, and Almina missed the sense it brought her of doing some good in the world. In the back of her mind she was pondering plans for her next hospital. Having learned that she had a gift for nursing and hospital administration, and given that the need for good, dedicated care was hardly about to vanish, she wanted to continue with her mission in some form. It would be a continuation of her father's philanthropic legacy. For now, though, she was gathering her strength, and was an enthusiastic participant on site. As it turned out, Almina's life would be irrevocably altered by the events that overtook the Carnarvon family, and it would be another eight years before she could realise her plans.

On 26 February, they discovered a cache of thirteen alabaster vessels at the entrance to the tomb of King Merenptah, the son of Ramesses II. Lady Carnarvon knelt in the sand to help dig them out with her own hands. This was exciting, but it wasn't the breakthrough discovery the men were longing for. They would have to wait another two years for that.

The unsettled political situation in Egypt was getting worse, and Lord Carnarvon began to worry about his wife and daughter's safety. On 9 March 1919 there was an uprising, led by Egyptian nationalist Saad Zaghloul. He had served as a government minister for years, steering a careful course between extreme nationalists and the British ruling powers. But everything changed with President Wilson's famous 'Fourteen Points' speech in January 1918. During the war Britain had declared Egypt a British Protectorate, with scant regard for nascent Egyptian nationalism. The Egyptians, however, were inspired by President Woodrow Wilson's declaration that 'every peace-loving nation which, like our own, wishes to live its own life and determine its own institutions, [should] be assured of justice.' The end of hostilities and the peace conference in France gave them their best shot.

Zaghloul began a campaign to send a delegation to negotiate for Egyptian autonomy at Versailles, but his activities did not endear him to the British ruling forces, who promptly arrested him and sent him into exile. This served only to exacerbate the situation. There were student demonstrations, general strikes and rioting. A few Europeans were killed and several hundred Egyptians died over the course of the next few months.

In the midst of the chaos that followed Zaghloul's arrest, Lord Carnarvon resolved to send Almina and Eve home. He managed to get them passage on a ship from Port Said and was very relieved when he received a telegram from Almina to say they were on board and bound for England.

He stayed on in Cairo. He was deeply involved in local politics and knew many of the key players from both the Egyptian and British sides. He had, after all, been entertaining them at Highclere, often at the same house parties, for years. When General Lord Allenby was dispatched from London on 25 March and told to restore order in Cairo, Lord Carnarvon lent his services as a mediator. He dined with ministers and Sultan Fuad of Egypt, who upset Carnarvon's constitution terribly by serving a lunch of twelve courses within half an hour.

The diplomacy seemed to ease the situation. Zaghloul was freed by the British on 7 April and on 11 April 1919 he achieved his goal when he led a delegation to the Versailles Peace Conference, demanding autonomy for Egypt. The day they arrived was, ironically, the day the US issued a statement recognising Britain's Protectorate over Egypt. Nobody in Paris cared about Zaghloul's cause: extracting reparations from Germany was the main event and everything else was sidelined. That would prove fatal for long-term stability in Germany and the Middle East alike.

18

Another Glittering Season

On a beautiful sunny day in June 1919, Porchy rang the
bell at Seamore Place. He had finally made it home from
Mesopotamia. An astonished Roberts, who had progressed
from being the groom of the bedchamber at Highclere to
the position of butler at Seamore Place, opened the door
to him. Roberts had been an ally since Porchy was a little
boy being sent to bed without his dinner, and was delighted
to see him. Porchy asked whether his mother was in and,
collecting himself sufficiently to shake His Lordship heartily
by the hand, Roberts told him she was. Porchy might have
been forgiven for expecting a hero's welcome, but when
Almina saw him she cried out, 'Oh darling, what a surprise!'

Almina was plainly still in nurse mode because she

proceeded to ask him whether his uniform had been fumi-
gated and he had been deloused. Delousing, which was
supposed to take place on board the ships bringing the men
back from war, was not a trivial matter, since conditions
such as sand-fly infestation could be very unpleasant. Nevertheless, Porchy was somewhat taken aback. They hadn't seen
each other for more than two and a half years and a great
deal had happened in between. Porchy had grown up and
Almina had grown into her role as a respected nurse; it was
no wonder that it took a moment to adjust before there
was a proper welcome. Her son had come home in one
piece when, as Almina knew only too well, so many young
men had not.

The whole family was overjoyed to have him back. There
was a moment of brief anxiety when he developed appendicitis shortly after his return, but Almina leapt into action,
just as she had with her husband's case the previous year.
She ensured that Sir Berkeley Moynihan operated on her
darling son and then supervised his convalescence herself
at home at Seamore Place.

The summer of 1919 saw an uneasy mixture of the
return to what used to be normality and a sense that nothing
could ever be the same again. Almina was looking for new
outlets for her energy but for the moment was happy nursing
Porchy; Lord Carnarvon was overjoyed to be able to excavate.
Elsie had her new speech therapy project and Eve was an
excited eighteen-year-old in the middle of her debutante
season, but for some in the family, as in the country at large,
there was a deep sense of despair.

Aubrey was a bitter man. He was utterly disillusioned by
everything he saw at the peace conference at Versailles.

He felt that England was being 'tied to the tail of all this continental hate'. Aubrey dined most evenings during the Versailles meetings with T. E. Lawrence, who was trying to make the British government honour the various promises they had made during the war. Their colleague, the writer and expert on Middle Eastern politics, Gertrude Bell, wrote that it was all a nightmarish muddle. 'You foresee all the horrible things that are going to happen and can't stretch out your hand to prevent them.'

The peace treaty was concluded on 28 June 1919 in the Hall of Mirrors at Versailles. It had taken months of wrangling, during which the hopes of many nations and aspiring nations dwindled. The Middle East was divided into spheres of influence among the Allies, with disastrous fallout that lingers to this day. The Germans lost various territories, which provoked huge resentment, and above all they were fined billions and billions of gold marks. France was determined to totally dominate its neighbour and Britain wanted to repay its massive war debt. The scale of the reparations demanded by the Allies was considered by many to be excessive, not just in Germany but by such figures as John Maynard Keynes, the Treasury's main representative at the negotiations. It was reduced in 1924 and again in 1929, but by that time Germany was feeling persecuted, and Hitler's election was only four years away.

As Versailles drew to a close, many of the Carnarvons' friends from Egypt came down to Highclere for a weekend of racing. The summer season of parties was cranking up again and, for the first time in years, Highclere readied itself to receive dozens of guests. Streatfield, who was still the house steward, was in charge of seeing that standards hadn't slipped. He had only three more years of service left in him. He was sixty-three years old and was starting to tire. But he was as meticulous as ever and the team of footmen didn't disappoint him.

It was not exactly the same as it used to be, though. How could it be when the pre-war world, a political and social landscape that the 4th Earl would have recognised, had gone for ever? Millions of men had died in the service of the old regimes and the public resentment and grief were enflamed by an austerity drive combined with a recession. Carnarvon noted in the guestbook entry for the party, 'Races' and 'Strike'. There were lots of those in 1919. Nearly half a million workers in the cotton mills walked out in June, the police were out in August, and in September it was the turn of the railway workers. Pay was low and jobs were scarce: disillusioned veterans went begging in the streets.

Even the Earl of Carnarvon was concerned about money, albeit on a vastly different scale. His income from agriculture had been falling since before the war and his tax bill in 1919, after Lloyd George's legislation, was a sizeable £7,500. He had sold some of the furniture from his house at Bretby in May 1918, and now he sold the cream of the Bretby library at Sotheby's. He was well aware that there was no more income for Almina and that budgeting was not exactly her strong suit.

Almina, however, felt totally insulated by the enormous legacy she had been left by Alfred de Rothschild and saw no reason not to carry on spending. While the Earl fretted about his tenants' ability to pay their rent, Almina planned a ball for Eve, who was making her debut in Society that summer. No expense was to be spared. Hundreds of guests wcre invited for dancing until dawn and *The Times* reported that it was crammed with people. Entertaining at Seamore Place was constant. The chef was required to make sure the food matched the opulent surroundings, which, given that the house was a monument to Alfred's love of treasures, meant he had his work cut out. His must have been one of the most coveted cook's jobs in London. He had a free hand to indulge his imagination and the budget to back it up.

There could not have been a more resolute statement of Almina's intention to escalate, not to scale back, the Carnarvons' pre-eminent position in post-war society than her passion for throwing the biggest and best parties. It was typified by an occasion the following year in the Season of 1920. Almina and Eve had been to a ball given by Sir Ernest Cassel, one of the wealthiest financiers of the era, for his daughter Edwina. Almina so enjoyed it that she said to her daughter, 'Let's give a ball of our own tomorrow night.' Eve was horrified and wondered how on earth they could manage it. (Eve was always considerably more grounded than Almina; perhaps she could imagine the chef's reaction in the kitchen at being asked to prepare Seamore House-worthy party food with less than 24 hours' notice.) Almina informed Eve that she had 'already invited everyone here so I'm sure we will have a wonderful time.'

It seems Almina hadn't informed her husband, though. Not that he liked big parties, anyway. The next day was a Friday and Carnarvon left on the 6.00 p.m. train every Friday for Highclere. Eve could tell he knew something was in the air from the way he hovered around. Almina was desperate to get on with preparations and asked Roberts repeatedly whether His Lordship had yet left. Eventually he did, but Roberts had to report to Almina that Carnarvon had walked past the back stairs just as ten dozen lobsters were being brought in by the footmen. The ball was a total success and, when Almina arrived at Highclere the following day, Carnarvon's only reaction was to ask her with a smile whether she was not very tired. A wise man knows how to pick his battles.

Lord Carnarvon was expert at dealing with the whims of his more capricious family members. Aubrey was diverting himself from his anguish by spending more and more time in his beloved Albania. In the late summer of 1920 he was on his way to Constantinople when he discovered that the Prime Minister of Bulgaria was on the train. Stamboliski introduced himself to Aubrey, who later wrote to his brother that 'the fellow looked like a brigand moving through a blackberry bush.' This was clearly not as damning as it sounds, because he also requested that Carnarvon ask Stamboliski to Highclere, which Carnarvon duly did. The Bulgarian premier signed the guestbook on 17 October. Bulgaria had sided with the Central Powers in the Great War and Carnarvon had got nervous about his guest, despite Aubrey's assurances that he was totally pro-British. He decided to invite some of his Orientalist acquaintances along to keep the conversation ticking over; Sir William Garstin and T. E. Lawrence were also staying. In the end, a good time was had by all. Carnarvon showed Stamboliski the stud and the farm and discovered that, unsurprisingly given his guest had been born to peasant farmers, they could talk at length about livestock.

All the family were in London for the Armistice Day

memorial on 11 November 1920. It was a day of national mourning and thanksgiving. Hundreds of thousands of people lined the streets to pay their respects as the gun carriage, drawn by six black horses and bearing the coffin of the Unknown British Warrior, began its journey through London. King George V unveiled the Cenotaph and, after two minutes' silence, the body of the Unknown Warrior, which had been transported from an unmarked grave in France, was carried towards its final resting place. It was accompanied by 100 recipients of the Victoria Cross and buried with great solemnity in the central nave of Westminster Abbey. George V threw a handful of the soil from a Flanders battlefield into the grave. Families of those men whose place of burial was unknown, such as Frederick Fifield and Tommy Hill, could derive comfort from the respect paid to this one unknown comrade. The moment marked a line in the nation's grieving. People up and down the land remained traumatised, but at least now the country had honoured its dead.

The following April Aubrey and Mary had a son, Auberon Mark Henry Yvo Molyneux, who was named for the cousin and friend whom Aubrey still mourned. Aubrey had always been typically eccentric in his attitude to children. He wrote to his brother Mervyn on the subject of Mary's pregnancy, 'It's very provoking. I have never looked on children as anything but a misfortune – like public speaking a duty and a bore – but there it is'. But he and the family needed some positive news. It was good to have a new baby when for years life had felt like one long succession of funerals.

The Carnarvons went as usual to Egypt in January 1921.

They found it almost as unstable as ever. It was becoming clear that the British would have to relinquish their Protectorate. They had exiled Saad Zaghloul for a second time after he had organised demonstrations to protest against Sultan Fuad's appointment of a rival as Prime Minister. The reaction from the public was, as the previous time, to riot. Lord Allenby was leaving Cairo as the Carnarvons arrived, heading back to London to try to persuade the Cabinet to declare Egypt's independence.

There was a sense of wearying familiarity to the excavations as well. Despite attaining the longed-for concession in the Valley of the Kings, Carter and Carnarvon had still not found anything of real note. Money worries were now becoming acute for the Earl, whose expenditure in Egypt was enormous. In July 1921 he sold the furniture from Bretby Hall. He had already sold land to Dulverton Rural Council at £5 an acre for house building.

Lord Carnarvon might sell his land but he would never sell his Egyptian art. He had built up the finest collection in private hands in the world and had turned the Smoking Room at Highclere into the 'Antiques' room in order to exhibit it. The walls were hung with paintings that had been in the family for generations. Over the fireplace was the still life by sixteenth-century Dutch painter Jan Weenix that still hangs there today. But along two sides of the room there were dark wooden cases the height of a tall man, on which were ranged the Earl's exquisite pieces: a faience chalice, jewellery from Queen Tye's tomb, a bronze mirror from the 12th dynasty which was therefore about 4,000 years old, a beautiful electrum statue, several vases, charming pieces with delicately carved animals and a gold statue of the god Amun as the Pharaoh Tuthmosis III.

Howard Carter was at Highclere for the summer with other friends from Egypt such as Leonard Woolley and Percy Newberry. A new guest that year was a young man called Brograve Beauchamp, a very tall and striking gentleman who went on to be Conservative MP for Walthamstow East for fourteen years. He had met Aubrey through his father, who was also a politician, and Aubrey had – in his typically open-handed way – invited him down to Highclere.

One person was particularly glad to make his acquaintance. Eve had been out in Society for three Seasons now and had met Brograve at various balls; she adored dancing with him. Eve was beautiful and charming and of course she was rich, so was never going to be short of admirers. But she was no timorous mouse desperate to find a husband. She had helped her mother to nurse wounded soldiers when the hospital was at Highclere and had been going for years to Egypt to share her father's passion for ancient art. She had a bookish mind as well as a lovely disposition, and she was perfectly conscious of her own worth. So were her parents. Eve had been told she should take her time in choosing a husband, and she did.

Brograve caught her eye at Highclere that summer. How could he not, when at more than six foot tall he towered over her? He was the son of the Liberal politician and former Chairman of Lloyd's of London Sir Edward Beauchamp, and was handsome, thoughtful and excellent company. The two young people flirted gently in the Drawing Room and Eve found she had a decided preference, but she resolved to wait and see what the coming months would do to Brograve's interest. They were sure to see each other in London before too long.

That summer, Lord Carnarvon spent a few days in Paris with his son. It was a city they both loved. Porchy's Army career was prospering and he had been in Gibraltar for most of the year. It was there that he met a girl called Catherine Wendell, an American with no great financial backing but considerable charm and sweetness. Porchy always figured prominently on the social scene wherever he was – he was a great ladies' man; but he was quite clear that Catherine was 'the only one I could even begin to see as a future Lady Porchester.' He, like Eve, was not minded to make sudden moves, and although he had his preference, he bided his time.

At the end of 1921, Howard Carter was helping Lord Carnarvon to organise the catalogue for an exhibition mounted by the Committee of the Egyptian Exploration Society, of which the Earl was a prominent member. Carnarvon lent the society the bulk of his collection for the show, which was held at the Burlington Fine Arts Club and was a roaring success. Then, in January, the two men set off on the annual trip. They spent most of the first three months of 1922 out in Egypt.

Aubrey was also back in one of his favourite stamping grounds – Constantinople; as was Porchy, who had just been sent on secondment from his regiment to the British Embassy there. Aubrey's vocal criticism of the British position in the Middle East had earned him the suspicion of His Majesty's government, so a junior member of embassy staff was to be dispatched to keep an eye on what he was up to. Whoever was in charge of that mission hadn't done his homework properly, because he chose to send Lord Porchester, Aubrey's nephew. The two men were delighted to see each other, and over dinner on the first night, Porchy told his uncle what he was up to. They agreed to cook up a few stories to keep Porchy's superiors entertained.

Porchy was having a fine time, as was his way. He ran into General Baratoff, the White Russian commander to whom he had delivered a shipment of gold on the shore of the Caspian Sea when the British were still trying to prop up the Russian Army back in 1917. Porchy was sent because he spoke French, the common language, and had been under orders to ascertain how much fight the Russians still had in them. The answer was not a great deal: Baratoff was generally depressed, though plainly relieved to receive the gold. Since then the General had lost a leg and been forced to flee the Bolshevik revolution. He was penniless and even gloomier than ever. Porchy also bumped into Miss Catherine Wendell again. She was accompanying her mother on her travels and the three of them dined together several times. It was enough to make up Porchy's mind. He asked Catherine to marry him and, being accepted, invited her to meet his parents when she was in London later in the year.

When the time came, Porchy was very nervous. He knew full well that his father was worried about money and would have hoped for his son to marry an heiress, as he had done. Porchy wrote to Eve begging for her support in the matter. His sister stepped in to play mediator once again. The family assembled in Seamore Place to receive Catherine and her mother. Despite the Earl's disappointment he could see that

Porchy was in love and that the girl was delightful, so he allowed himself to be won round. Almina was enthusiastic, as one might expect, unconcerned about anything except that Porchy be happy and Catherine be welcomed into the family in style. She threw herself into arranging the wedding.

Almina decided to give a little dance for Catherine on 14 July, at Seamore Place: *The Times* reported that 1,000 people were invited. The wedding was held three days later, in St Margaret's, Westminster, the same church at which, twenty-seven years before, Almina Wombwell had married the 5th Earl of Carnarvon. Catherine wore a simple satin gown and a floor-length veil over her fashionable waved bob cut. She had eight attendants who wore large white hats dressed with ostrich plumes and, in the photo of her and Porchy with their pageboy, the couple look relaxed and happy.

Naturally, given that Almina was the driving force, it was a huge event. The church was packed, and among the relations and friends were Prince George the Duke of Kent, the Marquess of Milford Haven, the American Ambassador, the Duke and Duchess of Marlborough, Miss Edwina Ashley and Lord Louis Mountbatten, who were to be married the following day and, of course, Elsie, the redoubtable Dowager Countess of Carnarvon. The guest list must have been overwhelming for the bride, with a host of titled dowagers and aristocrats. Her own friends from America were of necessity a much smaller crowd.

Watching Catherine marry her son, Almina couldn't help but remember standing in the same spot and pledging her life to the Carnarvon cause. The difference was considerable, though. When she married into the Herbert family she might have been a relative unknown, but at least she had a fortune backing her up. Catherine did not, and it was up to Almina to champion her. She assisted Mrs Wendell in finding a house in which to hold the wedding reception, just as Elsie had helped her and Marie all those years ago. Twenty-one Grosvenor Square was lent for the occasion and the couple were given a tremendous send-off. Henry and Catherine Porchester left to spend a few days' honeymoon at Highclere before sailing for India to rejoin Porchy's regiment.

Almina revelled in extending her habitual largesse, but it was a bad moment for Porchy to be marrying without money. The Earl had spent months steeling himself to have a conversation he was dreading, with Howard Carter. He had decided to 'draw stumps' on his concession to excavate in the Valley of the Kings. He simply couldn't afford to continue. It is estimated that by 1922 the Earl had spent some £50,000 (£10 million in today's money) over the course of fourteen years on excavating in Egypt. It was a serious outlay, even for a man of means. He had sold three of the four estates he had inherited and was one of the last private excavators left. Britain had given up its Protectorate and declared Egypt a sovereign state earlier in the year, and the era of British aristocratic archaeologists was fading. Excavation was increasingly the province of museums or government bodies. And, to cap it all, although he had amassed a great collection of art and was renowned for the diligence and scientific method of his expeditions, he had failed to find the great treasure, the tomb that he and Carter had believed in for so long.

He told Carter of his decision at a Highclere house party

during Newbury races. Carter was desperate and, having been unable to move Lord Carnarvon by persuasion, said simply that he would fund one last season himself. Carnarvon knew this would bankrupt his old friend. He considered. Touched by Carter's willingness to risk everything he owned, the Earl agreed to pay for a last season. He was, after all, a gambling man, and it was true that there remained an unexplored area in the vicinity of the tomb of Ramesses VI.

The two men met again in London in October. Lord Carnarvon came straight from the Memorial Service for the war dead at Newbury, where the Bishop of Oxford had presided over a ceremony attended by 8,000 people.

The mood was sombre all round. This was the last chance for Carnarvon and Carter's joint dream of glory. They had decided that they would begin the excavation work earlier than usual this year. By January there were always so many visitors to the tomb of Ramesses VI that it would be quite impossible to investigate what lay under the remains of the workmen's huts in front of it.

Carter arrived in Luxor on Friday 27 October. He began work the following Wednesday. On Monday 6 November, less than a week later, he sent Lord Carnarvon the cable that would change their lives:

At last have made wonderful discovery in the Valley. A magnificent tomb with seals intact. Recovered same for your arrival. Congratulations.

19

'Wonderful Things'

Howard Carter dispatched the telegram and then returned to the Valley of the Kings to refill the stairway down to the entrance to the tomb. He and Carnarvon had been colleagues and friends for fifteen years, and he was not about to press on with what he was convinced was the find of a lifetime without his patron. But what an enormous amount of restraint that must have taken. Carnarvon and Carter's hunch or, better put, their informed guess, closely cherished for years, had paid off. And now Howard Carter was going to have to wait the two or three weeks it took for Lord Carnarvon to arrive. The tomb had to be kept safe from grave robbers in the meantime, so Carter was all discretion, telling as few people as possible about what he believed he had found. He hunkered down to wait.

He left Luxor for Cairo on 18 November, only to discover when he got there that Carnarvon's ship was delayed. Carter made use of this enforced pause to begin to assemble a team of experts to assist at the opening of the tomb. Arthur Callender was a noted chemist and longstanding friend. He had to ask Carter to repeat himself when he heard the news. It sounded too good to be true: the sealed, unplundered tomb of a pharaoh? If Carter was right, then this was a totally unprecedented moment in archaeology. Callender agreed at once to come along and help out.

Lord Carnarvon paced the deck of the ship from Marseilles, willing it to travel faster. Eve was with him but Almina was not. She had gone with her husband on every trip he had made to Egypt since their marriage, but now she was unwell with terrible pain in her jaw and head. On Dr Johnnie's advice she had reluctantly elected to stay at home in case she should need dental treatment. She waved her husband and daughter off, demanding that they call on her if she could be of any use.

The whole family knew what was at stake. They had been discussing 'the undiscovered tomb' for years. Carter's informed guess was based in part on American Egyptologist Herbert Winlock's suggestion that some of the interesting fragments turned up by Theodore Davis, Carnarvon and Carter's predecessor in the Valley of the Kings, might be items used during Tutankhamun's funeral rites. Davis wasn't interested in such minutiae at the time, but Winlock, who had been a guest at Highclere, was. And so were Carnarvon and Carter.

On Friday 24 November, Lord Carnarvon and Lady Evelyn arrived at Luxor. The mood was of tense excitement; everyone was on edge. Eve was very fond of Howard Carter but she also found him a bit difficult to deal with because of his absolutely single-minded obsession and tendency to sarcasm; now she braced herself for the increase in pressure. Carter and Callender lost no time in clearing the rubble away from the staircase once more. It wasn't until the afternoon of Sunday 26 November that the party of four found themselves standing in front of the doorway. Lord Carnarvon wrote, 'We wondered if we should find another staircase, probably blocked, behind this wall or whether we should get into a chamber. I asked Mr Carter to take out a few stones and have a look in.'

Carter made a small hole through which he could insert a candle into the space beyond. He would describe the moment of discovery for the newspapers over and over. 'Presently, as my eyes grew accustomed to the light, details of the room within emerged slowly from the mist, strange animals, statues, and gold – everywhere the glint of gold. For the moment – an eternity . . . I was struck dumb with amazement, and when Lord Carnarvon . . . inquired anxiously, "Can you see anything?" it was all I could do to get out the words, "Yes, wonderful things."'

Carter's three companions exploded into relieved delight. His heart pounding, Carter widened the hole and made way for Eve, who took her turn to peer through into the chamber. 'On getting a little more accustomed to the light, it became apparent that there were colossal gilt couches with extraordinary heads, boxes here, boxes there . . .' Carter could contain himself no longer. He pulled at the wall, scrabbling to enlarge the hole sufficiently to let himself down to the chamber. He scrambled in and started to tread, softly, reverently, as he held the candle above his head to cast its light as far as possible into the corners of the space. The others followed and stood still in amazement at what they saw by flickering candlelight. 'We knew we had found something absolutely unique and unprecedented.' Carnarvon wrote that there was a throne of 'surpassing beauty . . . the delicacy and grace indescribable . . . from a period when Egyptian art reached one of its culminating points.' Here, finally, after fifteen years of searching, were the treasures of the Pharaohs. And, as their eyes adjusted and their minds raced to catch up with what they were seeing, the group realised that just as significant, if not more so, was what *wasn't* there. There was no sarcophagus. Which meant that there had to be more chambers, perhaps a whole series of them.

Then they spied something, 'between two life-size statues, a wall covered in seals and low down . . . traces of a break large enough to admit a small man.' Perhaps thieves of early millennia had robbed the inner chamber. Overwhelmed, Carnarvon called a halt. Carter agreed: there were procedures that needed to be followed.

The group clambered back out and stood staring at one another in the fading daylight. Everyone was elated. Carnarvon and Carter clapped each other on the back in mutual congratulation. Carter looked as if he might burst with excitement. Arthur Callender had the expression of a man who couldn't believe his luck, and Eve, overjoyed for her beloved father, thought wistfully of how much Almina would long to be there when they told her.

There were drinks on the terrace of the Winter Palace Hotel and then Lord Carnarvon placed a call to his wife, during which he, like Carter with Callender, had to repeat himself several times before Almina could take in what he was saying. Who could sleep after what they had seen? A small party secretly returned later that night to explore the other, partly closed room. It was not difficult to knock out the wall through which the robbers had gained access 3,000 years earlier. Carter, Lady Evelyn and Carnarvon simply had to enlarge it again and slip through.

The little party left unable to speak about what they had seen. They carefully placed some old rush baskets against the lower part of the false door. Attention from visitors would be taken by the pair of life-size gold-kilted statues. They had found it: the burial chamber of Tutankhamun.

The following morning, Carter sent a note to Engelbach, the local Chief Inspector of the Antiquities Department, informing him of the developments. Engelbach had been told about Carter's initial discovery of the steps and was present when Callender and Carter began to clear the debris away again. But he, like almost everyone else, believed that the Valley of the Kings was exhausted, and didn't consider Carter's staircase worth hanging around for on a Friday afternoon.

Now he sent a representative of the Department to accompany Carnarvon's group as they returned to the tomb. They had arranged to connect to the mains electricity in the valley, so this time, when they stepped into the chamber, they could see everything in crisp detail. Carter later wrote in his book, *The Tomb of Tutankhamun*, 'Three thousand, four thousand years maybe, have passed and gone since human feet last trod the floor on which you stand, and yet . . . the blackened lamp, the finger-mark upon the freshly painted surface, the farewell garland dropped upon the threshold – you feel it might have been but yesterday . . . Time is annihilated by little intimate details such as these . . .'

Carnarvon and Carter stood in wonder, beginning to assess the scale of the glorious task that lay ahead of them. They were going to need an army of expert help to remove, catalogue and preserve every single object, each one at least 3,200 years old. They were also going to have to make the tomb secure, immediately. Any find that included gold was a magnet for every tomb robber in the area. That night an armed guard was placed at the top of the steps leading down to the first chamber and the following day, Carnarvon hired military policeman Richard Adamson to oversee security. Carnarvon built him a police hut to provide some shelter from the blistering sun, and Adamson virtually took up residence there.

The first viewing for visitors took place on Wednesday 29 November. There was to be a tour with Howard Carter followed by lunch. It was a low-key affair. Lady Allenby deputised for her husband the British High Commissioner; also invited were Monsieur Lacau, the Chief Inspector of Antiquities; the local chief of police and, crucially for subsequent events, the correspondent of The Times, Arthur Merton.

There had been a series of murders of British citizens since the declaration of independence and the imposition of martial law, so there were anxieties over drawing too much attention to what was taking place. But even more than that, nobody in officialdom had yet woken up to the enormity of what had just been found on their doorstep. M. Lacau and his assistant missed the official unveiling entirely: they were too busy to turn up until the following day.

By the time they did, *The Times* had published the first article in what became the longest-running news item ever. There has still never been a story that took more column inches than Carnarvon, Carter and Tutankhamun. Merton, like a good newspaperman, had immediately seen the significance of what he was being shown. Instantly the world's press descended upon Luxor in force, camping in hotel gardens when the rooms ran out. *The Times* approached Almina and asked her to write an exclusive article about accompanying her husband on his trips to excavate in Egypt, which she duly did.

There was a siege around the site, and it immediately created problems for the men who were simply trying to carry out their painstaking work. Carnarvon and Carter took the decision to reseal the tomb while they dealt with the publicity and assembled a full team of expert help.

Still, alongside the desire to get on with the job was a huge urge to celebrate. Carnarvon threw a party that was open to everyone at the Winter Palace Hotel. Telegrams of congratulation poured in from all over the world. One of the first was from King Fuad, who thanked the two men warmly for their work. M. Lacau, who had evidently put right his previous indifference, wrote to commend them for their disinterested attitude and scholarly investigations.

The scale of the interest from the world's public, not to mention the unprecedented historical and cultural significance of the find, had knocked its discoverers sideways.

Carnarvon decided to return home with Eve to plan how they should proceed. He left with a growing sense of unease about the vested interests, tension and rivalries they had unleashed.

Carnarvon and his daughter arrived back in Britain as celebrities. On 22 December he visited Buckingham Palace at the King's request to regale Their Majesties with the story of the discovery. The King and Queen requested more and more details, and Carnarvon listed the priceless objects and exquisite workmanship on display in the first chamber. He assured the King that further searches would yield the actual tomb of the Pharaoh.

The family spent Christmas at Highclere in a state of mild shock. They all wrote to Carter on Christmas Eve. Carnarvon's letter was a long summary of the current issues, to be dispatched with their old friend Dr Gardiner, who was sailing for Egypt in early January and whom he had asked to join the team. Carnarvon told Carter he had arranged for them to have the use of a Ford motor car, which would make life easier. A plum pudding was enclosed in the package.

Eve wrote to say how thrilled she was for Howard, and that he thoroughly deserved his success after all the years of hard work. 'Of course one is pestered morning noon and night . . . there [is] no hour or place that one [is] not met by a reporter.' She remarked that her father was really tired by all the attention, but that if she needed to perk him up she simply referred to the imminent discovery of the sarcophagus and this reference to 'the Holy of Holies always acts like a magnum of champagne.' Eve is sweetly swept away by the splendour of being the first woman to step inside the burial chambers. 'I can never thank you sufficiently for allowing me to enter its precincts, it was the best moment of my life.'

Almina sent her love, blessings and congratulations for his success after all his long-suffering perseverance. She had been discussing how to manage the newspapers with her husband and had various typically practical thoughts on the subject. She also told Carter that she was still too unwell to come out to join them. It looked as if she would have to have an operation on her jaw.

After Christmas, Carter resumed work. He had been busy sifting through the numerous offers of help and deciding which to accept. Mr Lythgoe of the Metropolitan Museum in New York cabled his congratulations and was duly taken up on his offer. Four more American Egyptologists joined him, including the distinguished Chicago University professor, James Breasted. Harry Burton joined as official photographer and Mr Lucas, a chemical specialist with the Egyptian government, also signed up. The team headed to Cairo to purchase supplies of wadding, rope, packing materials and a steel gate, which was placed at the entrance to the tomb.

Carter was irascible at the best of times, and he loathed the constant interruptions from the press. All he wanted was to get on with the complex job in hand. On 27 December the team had begun to remove the first objects and transfer them to the Tomb of Seti II, where further work could be done before they were transported to Cairo. Carter was completely focused on clearing the antechamber in a methodical way, and it drove him mad to have to deal with the endless stream of journalists and supposed VIP visitors who were invariably in possession of a 'special pass'.

The work was hard and stressful: space was cramped and hot and the objects were extremely delicate. Each one presented difficulties: how to stop it disintegrating, how to restring beads or stop wood from shrinking as it was exposed to the dry air. As far as Carter was concerned, all of that was far more important than talking to the media or to tourists.

Meanwhile, back in London, Carnarvon was concentrating on precisely that. He had been talking to Pathé-Cinéma about filming, to the directors of the British Museum and the Metropolitan in New York – and at length to *The Times*. He discovered that the newspaper had just paid £1,000 for fifteen exclusive cables from the Mount Everest Expedition. After a lot of discussion with Howard Carter (he sent him the summary of terms in cypher), Lord Carnarvon decided to sign an agreement giving the paper sole rights to interviews and black-and-white photographs. He was to be paid £5,000, and he retained all rights to any book, lecture or film. Carnarvon stipulated that *The Times* had to pass on articles, without charge, to the Egyptian press and the *Newbury Weekly News* but could charge a fee to other newspapers.

It was a money-making scheme, of course, a desperately needed one given the expense of the operation, but it was also intended to make working conditions on site more manageable. The theory went that this way they would only have to deal with one set of journalists. The plan backfired spectacularly when the rest of the press, furious at being cut out of the biggest story in history, stepped up their hounding and began to spread all sorts of scurrilous reports about Carnarvon and Carter's plans. They were painted as arrogant adventurers who intended to close the Valley of the Kings to tourists.

Carnarvon summoned his resolve as he prepared to return to Egypt. In his mind the issue of the press was settled, whatever the ludicrous headlines in the papers. He said goodbye to 'poor Almina', who, as he wrote to Carter, had been 'doing various things, all of them very well', but was still too poorly to travel. He encouraged her to go for treatment in Paris, where she would be less visible to the press, and to join them whenever she could. Then he took his leave of his son and daughter-in-law. He was relieved to catch them before they sailed for India again with Porchy's regiment. They left him Susie, the little three-legged terrier that had belonged to Porchy when he was a boy but had been adopted by Lord Carnarvon and slept on his bed when he was at Highclere.

Susie stayed at the Castle when Lord Carnarvon and Eve set off once again from Highclere, even more burdened with hopes and expectations than the last time they had made this trip, just weeks previously. The 5th Earl's attention was all focused on his destination, not his point of departure. He paid no particular mind to the last view of the house as he and his daughter were driven through the park to the waiting train that would take them to Southampton. Why should he? He assumed he would be back soon enough, and with plenty of new pieces for his 'Antiques' Room. In fact he would never see his lifelong home again.

20

Lights Out

There was an enthusiastic welcoming committee to meet Lord Carnarvon and Lady Evelyn as they stepped on to the red carpet that had been laid on the platform of the little train station in Luxor on 25 January 1923. In his excitement, the Earl, who was always absentminded, had left his two false teeth in the railway carriage; they were returned to him on a crimson cushion. Eve was presented with a bouquet and the cameras of the world's press flashed as she, her father and Carter edged their way through the crowds. Carter went straight to the site; Eve got her father settled comfortably at the Winter Palace and spoke to the chef about the menus for various lunches and dinners that she was helping her father with. There was going to be a great deal of entertaining and Eve was delighted to act as her father's hostess. *The Times* had assigned Arthur Merton to cover the story round the clock. He wrote that it was 'impossible not to be impressed with the extremely friendly, even affectionate attitude of the Egyptians towards Lord Carnarvon. He likes them and he likes Egypt.'

The same positivity could not be said to characterise relations with the rest of the press. The Valley was full of people, journalists and tourists alike, hanging around to catch a glimpse of the latest precious artwork as it was removed to the field laboratory. When they got frustrated, as they invariably did, tempers frayed. The criticism in the newspapers was getting more vitriolic and looked likely to affect crucial relations with the Egyptian Department of Antiquities. Carnarvon decided to leave Carter and the team to their work and go to Cairo to settle matters diplomatic-ally and make preparations for the grand opening of the burial chamber.

The day chosen to break through was Friday 16 February. The antechambers had been completely emptied by then and only the two black and gold-kilted guardian statues were left, staring at each other across the sealed entrance to Tutankhamun's burial chamber. There were about twenty people assembled at the entrance to the tomb: Lord Carnarvon, Lady Evelyn, the Hon. Mervyn Herbert (Carnarvon's half-brother), the Hon. Richard Bethell, (Carnarvon's private secretary, recently hired to assist him with his now vast correspondence), Howard Carter, Arthur Mace, Arthur Callender, Professor Breasted, Harry Burton with his camera, Dr Alan Gardiner, Mr Lythgoe and Mr Winlock from the Metropolitan Museum, Sir William

Garstin, Sir Charles Cust, equerry to King George V and M. Lacau from the Department of Antiquities, Mr Engelbach with three local inspectors, and H. E. Abd el Halim Pasha Suleman, representing King Fuad's government.

Carter began to remove the stones from the blocked entrance, working from the top down. He had built a little platform to cover the gap through which the three of them had entered the previous time. After half an hour his audience could see what appeared to be a sheet of solid gold appearing, just a few feet beyond the entrance. Carter dropped a mattress through to protect the object and laboured on, assisted by Lacau and Callender, for another two hours of infinitely careful work. When it was done they had revealed a large golden shrine, as big as the antechamber they were standing in but some four feet lower.

Carter, Carnarvon and Lacau lowered themselves into the narrow passage, paying out the electric cable to give themselves some light. The walls of the chamber were brightly painted with scenes from the Book of the Dead featuring larger-than-life-size figures. In one corner were propped the seven oars needed by the dead Pharaoh to ferry himself across the Underworld. The two golden shrine doors were covered in cartouches and hieroglyphs and were held shut by a bar and ropes. Gently extricating the bar and loosening the ropes, they drew back the outer doors to find another golden shrine nestled within, seals intact.

The rest of the party was following them. Eve came next. Carter had turned his attention to a further chamber, a treasury, containing a canopic shrine of creamy alabaster that he later described as one of the most awe-inspiring works of beauty he had ever seen. The burial chamber was now filled with people, all of them struck dumb by an enormous sense of privileged amazement. They were in the presence of the Holy of Holies, staring at the spectacular remains of a vanished world.

That was enough for one day. To go any further meant handling the sarcophagus itself and Carnarvon and Carter were both quite clear that it should be treated with the strictest reverence and ultimately left in its resting place in the Valley of the Kings. The group retreated, utterly staggered by what they had seen. The two men directing the enterprise were exhausted and stressed already, torn between jubilation and worry.

From 19 to 25 February the tomb was opened to the press and public. Carter and Carnarvon hoped in this way to take the edge off the press's rancour. It didn't work. The American journalists, furious that US expertise was being used while they were being denied complete access to the story, began to report the entirely erroneous line that Carnarvon wanted to remove Tutankhamun's mummy to England. He was angry and hurt. Carter was at breaking point, ground down by the endless interruptions. His diary tersely records, 'Visitors to tomb, Given up to visitors' for eight consecutive days.

Relations were strained between the two men. On 21 February, Carnarvon visited Castle Carter to try to smooth things over. They had a heated argument and Carnarvon stomped back to the hotel. Eve was a practised mediator and she helped to soothe her father and placate Carter. She knew how much the friendship meant to both men. With her encouragement, Lord Carnarvon wrote a letter to Carter on the 23rd, to make peace, and five days later they took the joint decision to close the tomb and have a week of rest. Carter stayed at home and spent a few quiet days seeing no one except old friends General Sir John and Lady Maxwell. Carnarvon hired a *dahabiyah* (a sailing Nile house-boat) and cruised to Aswan in the company of his daughter Eve, Charles Mace and Sir Charles Cust. He was completely exhausted but the river breezes and gentle pace were very restorative. The only irritation was the mosquitoes at night. Annoyingly he was bitten on the left cheek. By the time he arrived back at Luxor he had nicked the bite while shaving with his favourite old ivory-handled razor.

Lord Carnarvon arrived back in Luxor on 6 March; tempers had cooled and he and Carter were friends again. A few days later they were discussing their plans for the next phase of the work in Lord Carnarvon's hotel room. He was still feeling tired and slightly unwell, and he complained to Carter that he felt rather poorly.

Doctors advised more rest, so he took to his bed as Eve hurried off to Cairo to see her maid Marcelle, a casualty of the Egyptian heat who was returning to England, onto the ship to Marseilles. Carter visited Carnarvon every day and he seemed to be stronger, so he followed Lady Evelyn to Cairo on 14 March and settled in to the Continental Hotel. He still wasn't right, though, and had to leave one social engagement because he was feeling 'very seedy'.

Eve nursed him constantly and tried to suppress her rising anxiety. Her father was never in the greatest of health, but Egypt usually made him better, not worse. She wrote to Carter a few days later to tell him that Pierre Lacau was laid up with flu but added, 'what is much more important is that the old man is very, very seedy himself . . . all the glands in his neck started swelling . . . and he had a high temperature.' Given the hounding that they had already received at the hands of the press, Eve was anxious to keep her father's worsening illness a secret. She ended her letter, 'I wish, Dear, you were here.'

Dr Alan Gardiner was also staying and wrote to his wife, 'our great sorrow during the last few days has been Carnarvon's serious illness . . . Evelyn has been splendid, really, a magnificent little girl full of pluck and common sense and devoted to her father. I really am extremely fond of her.'

News reached Carter from Mr Lythgoe that Carnarvon had gone down with blood poisoning and was gravely ill. By the time Richard Bethell, Lord Carnarvon's secretary, wrote to him to say that he was moving into the hotel to be of assistance, Carter had already received a telegram from Eve asking him to come to Cairo and was about to set off. Panic was rising. Eve telegraphed Almina, and General Sir John Maxwell cabled Porchy's commanding officer in India. He was to grant him three months' compassionate leave and expedite his immediate passage to Egypt. Porchester left that afternoon, leaving his wife Catherine to pack up their house and return to England.

Almina was at Seamore Place when she received Eve's telegram. She had been ill for weeks now, and seeing virtually nobody apart from Dr Johnnie. She loved to talk on the telephone, though, and had been in regular touch with Eve and her husband, so she knew that tensions had been getting the better of him and the work was on hold until everyone had had a rest. She was still totally unprepared for this escalation in the seriousness of Eve's communication.

Carnarvon was grievously ill, two thousand miles away, and their daughter was clearly terrified.

It was the sort of situation Almina possessed all the right qualities to handle. Immediately she phoned De Havilland and enquired about chartering a plane and a pilot. Then she threw some clothes in a bag, informed Dr Johnnie that they were leaving for Egypt immediately, and set off for Croydon aerodrome. They flew in a three-seater plane to Paris, took the train to Lyons and picked up a second plane to take them all the way to Cairo. A journey that could still take up to three weeks by boat and train took them three days. Almina rushed to her husband's bedside and, pausing long enough only to embrace Eve and resume her nurse's air of patient calm, set about nursing him back to health. She had done it many times before and would not countenance anything less than a complete recovery. Her beloved husband was in the hour of his triumph; he simply must get better.

On 27 March *The Times* reported that Lord Carnarvon had rallied. The King sent a message of encouragement. On the 28th it informed its readers that the Earl of Carnarvon had relapsed. There was a press bulletin from Seamore Place on the 30th: 'patient slightly better; temperature 102; condition still very serious.' By 3 April the press were reporting every few hours on Lord Carnarvon's progress. His illness was now the story: on the state of his health depended the next chapter in the Tutankhamun saga that had gripped the entire world.

On 1 April Alan Gardiner went in to see Carnarvon. 'He had a terrible crisis just before 6 o'clock . . . I was quite miserable about it . . . why am I so fond of him . . . and that poor little girl, it nearly breaks my heart with her devotion, there she sits day and night tired out and waits. Yesterday he was given up for hopeless but Evelyn and Lady Carnarvon insisted he would pull through. This morning he insisted on being shaved and has been much better.'

By the time Lord Porchester arrived, Carnarvon had developed pneumonia and was delirious. Almina was losing hope. Henry stared down at the feverish man; the father he hardly knew, who he had only lately begun to realise loved him dearly. The war had separated them at the time when they might have become friends, and now it seemed it was too late to catch up.

In the early hours of Thursday 5 April, Carnarvon appeared to rally briefly. 'I have heard the call, I am preparing.' He died shortly after.

Almina was kneeling at his side, weeping softly. Gently, she closed his eyes. One of the nurses rushed to fetch Porchester and Lady Evelyn. As they made their way to their father's rooms, the hotel corridor was plunged into darkness. The lights went out all over Cairo. Back at Highclere, Lord Carnarvon's beloved terrier Susie howled once, waking the housekeeper in whose room she was sleeping, and died.

Eve was inconsolable and, having kissed her father's hands, her brother helped her out of the room. Howard Carter, Alan Gardiner, Dr Johnnie, the Bethells and the Maxwells were all gathered in the sitting room and, as Porchy comforted his sister, Dr Johnnie went in to help Almina.

Nobody slept much that night. The following morning, the new Earl of Carnarvon found Carter, eyes dull from exhaustion, reading the obituaries of his dear friend and patron. All the Egyptian newspapers were edged in black as a mark of respect. There was a second wave of cables from all around the world, except this time they were of condolence, not congratulation.

Almina was distraught. Her children worried about her but she reassured them: they should get on and leave Egypt, she would make arrangements to bring Lord Carnarvon's body home. So Evelyn and Porchester set off for Port Said, where they met Catherine en route from India and made their way back to England. Porchy, who had always disliked Egypt, couldn't wait to get away. Eve had adored the place; she never went back.

As Almina arranged for her husband's body to be embalmed, the press unleashed lavish speculation about the Curse of the Pharaohs. The biggest story in the world just kept growing. *The Times* reported more soberly, 'Millions who do not ordinarily take much thought . . . of antiquities have watched the progress of [Lord Carnarvon's] great adventure with deep and growing interest.' The question was, what would happen next?

Howard Carter remained in Cairo with Almina until she departed with Lord Carnarvon's body for England on the P&O steamship *Malova*, on Saturday 14 April. Carter returned to Luxor the following day, very low in spirit. There are no entries in his diary for the next week. He was an intensely private person with few close friends and was lost without the one he had worked alongside for fifteen years, with whom he had made the greatest archaeological discovery of all time. They should have been planning the opening of Tutankhamun's sarcophagus together. But Carnarvon would not, after all, ever lay eyes on the innermost secrets of the tomb. It was for Howard Carter to come face to face with Tutankhamun's extraordinary funeral mask, without the man who had made that possible by his side.

Almina and Dr Johnnie made the long, slow voyage back. Lord Carnarvon had stipulated in his will that he wished to be buried in a simple grave at the top of Beacon Hill, alongside the remains of the Iron Age fort and looking out over the Highclere estate. They would land at Plymouth, to be met by Lady Evelyn, and take Lord Carnarvon's body on a special train to Highclere. All the fight had gone out of Almina; this homecoming was an agonising crawl compared to their hope-fuelled dash just weeks ago.

It was a lovely fresh morning on 30 April two days after their return when the mourners gathered in the family chapel. The tall doors to the vaulted flint and brick building stood wide open. The green and cream tiled floor and beautifully carved pews could be glimpsed through the entrance as black-coated undertakers carefully carried the coffin out and loaded it into an Army field ambulance. A young soldier watched them and then climbed up to accompany the casket. Two undertakers climbed up after him and secured the coffin for the final leg of its journey.

The family had asked to be left in peace at this event, but it didn't seem likely, given the enormous amount of coverage they had received ever since the discovery of Tutankhamun's tomb.

The ambulance pulled away up the hill, past the dairy yard, the greenhouses and tenants' cottages. Passing in front of the Castle, it was joined by three long black cars bearing Evelyn, Catherine, Lord Carnarvon's three beloved sisters: Winifred, Margaret and Vera, and his brother Mervyn. Lord Burghclere was there but Aubrey had been staying at his villa in Portofino and was too ill to make the journey, plagued by more problems with his failing sight. Dr Johnnie was there, as was Major Rutherford, the agent. Almina had set off alone in a car fifteen minutes earlier. The procession wound its way down Lime Avenue, a magnificent parade of pale-leaved trees, with rolling parkland stretching away on both sides, passed under the arch at Winchester Lodge and stopped by the golf course that Lord Carnarvon had laid out twenty years earlier along the lower stretches of Beacon Hill.

The new Earl of Carnarvon climbed down from the ambulance; Major Rutherford and Dr Johnnie got down from the cars. They were joined by a group of loyal servants already waiting at the foot of the hill including Mr Streatfield, Mr Fearnside, Mr Blake, Mr Storie and Mr Maber. Accompanied by the rectors of Highclere and Burghclere, the men began the climb to the grave, which had been dug and consecrated the previous day. It was a steep scramble between ancient juniper and thorn bushes.

The ambulance and cars continued to the edge of the golf course where the slope was gentlest and they could just about struggle up the shoulder of the hill. The cars stood out against the skyline as they arrived at the windswept summit, 900 feet above sea level, a grey lookout over the lush wooded landscape below. The ambulance followed behind, attached to a tractor for the last few feet of its journey.

Almina stood, all in black, at the graveside, and greeted the mourners as they arrived. They paused to survey the spectacular view. The whole of the late Earl's adored Highclere was laid out before them, from the stud to the farm, the lakes to the drives and woods. Nestled at the heart of it all was the Victorian Castle, the parkland around it dotted with follies built by his forebears. It provided such a contrast to the dust and deserts of Egypt. The 5th Earl had chosen a majestic, isolated burial site, awe-inspiring in a very different way to that of the barren sand mountains and jagged cliffs of the Egyptian Pharaoh Tutankhamun.

Eight men from the estate bore the coffin from the ambulance and laid it on the wooden bearers over the grave. The casket had been made from an oak tree in the park and was draped in the late Earl's purple, ermine-trimmed coronation robe; his coronet lay on top. At 11.00 a.m., Rev. Mr Jephson and Rev. Mr Best led the simple burial service that Lord Carnarvon had requested. Once it was concluded, the robe and coronet were handed to George Fearnside, the late Earl's faithful valet. The plaque on the coffin was inscribed 'George Edward Stanhope Molyneux Herbert, 5th Earl of Carnarvon, born 26 June 1866, died 5 April 1923'.

As the mourners peeled away, clutching handkerchiefs to their eyes, they left Almina kneeling by her husband's grave. A bi-plane hired by the *Daily Express* buzzed overhead; from within a photographer snapped shots of the widow that appeared the following day. Then, as now, the press could not resist pursuing every story to its limit.

The rumours continued to swirl around the Earl's death. It was said that the ground on Beacon Hill was so difficult to dig that the coffin had to be laid vertically, and then that his faithful terrier was buried alongside him. Over the years the rumours and the fascination with the 'Curse of the Pharaohs' grew to support wild theories. Much was made of some coincidences that linked the Earl to Tutankhamun:

Lord Carnarvon had suffered from a troublesome knee and CT scans suggest one of Tutankhamun's was fractured. A mosquito bite probably contributed to the death of each man: when Lord Carnarvon nicked the bite on his face it became infected, eventually killing him as the consequent blood poisoning overcame him. Experts later discovered that Tutankhamun had probably contracted malaria, which is transmitted by mosquitoes. Even the shape of Lord Carnarvon's head proved of interest to the theorists. He often joked that he never lost his hats to anyone because they would only fit him: his head was slightly domed. Later on, experts would spend much time assessing the shape of Tutankhamun's head, because there seemed to be a congenital domed shape to his skull. The idea that he had been struck on the head has now been dismissed – the indentation marks were probably due to carelessness in carrying out the mummification procedure rather than any skulduggery.

But for the 5th Earl's family, the significance of his death was much more visceral, though it was not exactly simple. Aubrey wrote of his brother's death, 'One never knows how much one cares for a person until it is too late.' The two men had always been close, but nonetheless this truism haunted Aubrey. Evelyn was bereft without her adored father; Almina likewise was devastated. And then there was Porchy, who had perhaps the heaviest burden. He had never been close to his father and now he had to succeed him. As he walked down the hill and surveyed the estate that was now his to uphold, he contemplated the great change that was coming to his life.

Almina felt it too, but for now she concentrated on ensuring that her husband was given the send-off appropriate to a man whose discovery of the Pharaoh's tomb had turned him into a national hero. He had received the intimate funeral he wanted, but now it was time to mark the passing of a celebrity. Almina arranged a memorial service at Highclere church for personal friends and estate employees and tenantry two days later. A further service was held by the Mayor and Corporation of Newbury at St Nicholas's Church. Then she travelled back to London and held a larger memorial service, open to all, at St Margaret's, Westminster, where her son had married the year before and she had married the Earl in 1895. The service was attended by hundreds of people, including Elsie, Lord Carnarvon's loyal stepmother, and Mr Brograve Beauchamp, who had become a friend of Lady Evelyn's and wanted to lend his support.

On the same day a further service of commemoration was held at All Saints' Cathedral in Cairo. The Egyptian papers had reported every detail of the Earl's illness and his funeral on Beacon Hill. Now there were many friends and colleagues who wanted to pay their respects to the big-hearted English gentleman who loved Egypt and whose discovery brought the country incalculable recognition and prestige. Abbas Hilmy el-Masri, a distinguished Egyptian poet, paid a beautifully worded tribute to Lord Carnarvon, saying he had contributed to Egypt's glory in a manner which 'Sahban the greatest Arabic orator, could not have equalled.'

Lord Carnarvon was just fifty-seven when he died, but the old way of doing things, in the Valley of the Kings and at Highclere, died with him. From now on the Egyptian government would lay first claim to the Pharaoh's legacy and, back at Highclere, the family was dealing with the first succession to the title and estate of the twentieth century. The modern world, with its dismantling of privilege for some and extension of freedom for others, had overtaken everyone.

21

Inheritance

Everything changed for Almina when her husband died in May 1923. All her life she had been supported by men who had loved and spoilt her. Firstly through her beloved father, Alfred de Rothschild, and then her husband, she had effortless access to beautiful houses and distinguished people, the finest lifestyle that Imperial Britain had to offer. She could throw parties, create hospitals, shower everyone around her with presents, and be gifted a sense of community, and her exalted position within it, in return.

During the war she had used her position and her personal attributes and gifts at Highclere and in Bryanston Square in an extraordinarily positive way. Now she was on her own, widowed at forty-seven. On some days she felt exhausted and quite overwhelmed by grief and loneliness. For the first time in her life, she was unsure of herself. And there was a great deal to think about and to resolve.

Almina started with a few crucial details. What was she going to be called now that she was no longer the Countess of Carnarvon? There was already a Dowager Countess, the indefatigable Elsie, who – though now in her sixties – was definitely not slowing down. She lived mostly at her house in London so that she could be busy with her work for the Vocal Therapy Association and numerous other societies and charities. With that option closed to her, Almina announced in *The Times* that she would like to be known as Almina, Countess of Carnarvon.

Then there was the matter of moving out of Highclere. Tradition dictated that when a new incumbent succeeded, the former holders of the title and inhabitants of the estate retired gracefully from the scene. Naturally the older generations were not exactly put out on the street and, in any case, Almina had her own house at Seamore Place, but even so, she was facing the definitive moment of displacement. Highclere was now the new Earl and Countess of Carnarvon's home, not hers.

Porchy was utterly devoted to the welfare of Highclere, but he was also just twenty-four years old and had never lived there in his adult life. He had had no opportunity to observe how it functioned in detail, and his wife, who had grown up in a very different environment in the States, was going to have to learn alongside him.

In addition to all the adjustments at home, there was also the international dimension to consider. The man to whom Almina had been devoted had died at the pinnacle of his efforts and fame. There was an enormous unfinished task currently stalled in Egypt that needed her input to resume, and its repercussions in terms of negotiations with the Egyptian State, various museums and the media had barely begun.

Almina had some significant problems. The 5th Earl had died without mentioning the Valley of the Kings concession in his will. Almina knew she wanted to carry on the work in Tutankhamun's tomb in her husband's memory. As far as she was concerned, that meant extending financial help to Howard Carter so that he could press on with the project. She told Carter that she would continue to fund the excavation and that he should make plans for the forthcoming season. On 12 July she also signed an agreement with Monsieur Lacau of the Department of Antiquities that granted her the right to spend a further year clearing the tomb, from November. The rest of the Valley of the Kings no longer formed part of the concession.

Howard Carter was in England for most of the summer and made several visits to Highclere, where he helped Almina to pack the Earl's priceless collection of antiquities safely. It was utterly unique, with many items worth more than £20,000 each. Lord Carnarvon had made various bequests to the British Museum and the Metropolitan Museum of New York, but both Carter and Almina hoped that, if the collection were to be absorbed into a museum, the bulk of it would remain a single unit.

Carter was of course hugely relieved that his work was not in jeopardy, and very grateful to Almina, but he missed his old friend's company and collaboration terribly. He was incapable of idleness and he spent most of his time preparing a book. *The Tomb of Tutankhamun* was published later that year. Carter dedicated it to his 'beloved friend and colleague Lord Carnarvon, who died in the hour of his triumph. But for his untiring generosity and constant encouragement our labours would never have been crowned with success. His judgement in art has rarely been equalled. His efforts, which have done so much to extend our knowledge of Egyptology, will forever be honoured in history and, by me, his memory will always be cherished.'

Poor Carter was permanently downcast after Lord Carnarvon's death. His dedication never wavered and he eventually completed his task, but it was a struggle. He and Almina ended up in a dispute with the Department of Antiquities that ran until the end of the following year. It began when Carter resumed work in the November of 1923. He couldn't cope with the constant interruptions and eventually closed the tomb completely. The Egyptian government promptly banned him from both the site and his laboratory. For a nation exploring its new-found independence, it was an ideal opportunity to try to bring the excavation back under an Egyptian aegis. Exhausting wrangles with Egyptian officialdom, legal arguments over rights and obligations and much petty squabbling caused Carter to sink further into depression.

The outcome of the legal case in the Egyptian courts was disappointing for Almina and Carter. Mistakes were made, all of which would probably have been avoided if Lord Carnarvon were still alive. She did, however, succeed in persuading the Egyptian administration to allow Carter to complete the excavation and recording of the tomb. For a man who had only ever wanted to be left alone to do his work, that was enough.

Meanwhile, there was more paperwork to contend with at home. The 5th Earl had left Highclere entailed to his son and his heirs, but almost everything else, from horses to other houses, was left to Almina. There was a knotty tax situation that was absorbing a lot of time and looked set to absorb a great deal of money as well. This was the scenario that Carnarvon had been quietly dreading for years, ever since Lloyd George's super tax became law in 1910 and his annual tax bill started to climb from something negligible to, by 1919, more than 60 per cent of his income. The nation naturally needed to rebuild itself after the war, pay for pensions for the war wounded and the widows, and build the thousands of homes 'fit for heroes' called for by Lloyd George, but it was a very sudden change in the amount of money that the old class of landowners had to find.

Lord Carnarvon was permanently worried about the overdraft at Lloyd's and how to plan for the future. The Earl, like so many of the aristocracy, was much richer in assets than cash, and spent money on a lifestyle more as a matter of custom than on the basis of carefully calculated net income. He had written to Rutherford only months before he died to ask him to ensure all expenses were trimmed as much as possible, but that proved to be too little too late: now Porchy, his heir, and Almina, his widow, were facing a very substantial death-duties bill.

The issue of death duties, payable when a large estate passed from one generation to another, was the other tax nightmare that haunted the landed classes, especially after 1920 when they were massively increased. Cash had to be raised fast to pay the tax owed on these enormous assets, and often that meant that the house had to be sold, or at least emptied of contents. The situation with Highclere was alleviated, as always, by the Rothschild money. Almina was stoical – as far as she was concerned, it was simply a question of deciding which paintings to part with, but the bill was certain to be huge and the whole process complicated. It meant that none of the bequests to George Fearnside, Albert Streatfield and other longstanding friends and staff could be carried out until the matter was resolved. In the meantime, Almina wanted to stay busy. It had always been her tactic when under pressure, and now she swirled out to dinner from Seamore Place, visited Porchy and Catherine at Highclere, was looked after by friends and went to Paris to shop. She also began to spend more time with Lieutenant Colonel Ian Dennistoun, whom she had met through his ex-wife, who was a friend of hers.

Almina met Dorothy Dennistoun when their mutual friend, General Sir John Cowans, was dying in 1921; the women immediately became very close and Dorothy came constantly to Highclere. Sir John was the brilliant quartermaster who had played a crucial role in the Great War, but his reputation was overshadowed by revelations that he had had a number of affairs. One of them was with Dorothy, who had been separated from her husband for some time. After the Dennistouns divorced, Ian was often alone. He used a wheelchair, as he had broken his hip very badly, and he had terrible money worries too, but he was kind, charming and a good friend to Almina after her husband's death. Almina had never in her life been alone, and now she found herself drawn to Ian. She looked after him and they began to spend more and more time together.

There was a great piece of good news for the Carnarvon family in the midst of all their difficulties: Eve was getting married. She and Mr Beauchamp had been meeting for several Seasons now, and Eve's fondness and respect for him had been growing steadily. He was a lot of fun and they loved to dance together. When her father died, Eve was completely bereft. Brograve offered her his support and that summer he became a constant visitor to Highclere.

He had spent the previous year attempting to follow in his father's footsteps as an MP, with no success. He was the National Liberals' candidate in Lowestoft after his father resigned the seat, but lost heavily. That general election was a drubbing for the divided Liberal Party, but Brograve fought hard, despite the fact that his heart lay more with a career in business. He decided not to follow his own inclinations, though, chiefly to please his mother, Lady Beauchamp. Brograve was always very protective of both his parents after his older brother Edward was killed in France in 1914.

He was by nature cheerful and relaxed, and got on very well with Almina as well as Porchy and Catherine. He played golf badly, bridge well and enjoyed racing only because Eve loved it so much. Aside from all his personal qualities, she appreciated the fact that her father had liked him. They shared a passion for cars and had been known to go out for a spin together in Lord Carnarvon's Bugatti. Brograve had been wonderful at cheering Eve and making her laugh again. If ever she was down she used to ask him to sing 'God Save the King'. He was completely unmusical and it was so flat that everyone would fall about laughing. In truth he was the only man Eve had ever seriously contemplated marrying, and the wedding was set for October, much to everyone's delight.

The other joyous announcement that summer was that Catherine, the Countess of Carnarvon, was pregnant with her first child. The baby was due just after Christmas. Highclere would be a home to children again, and there was a sense of renewal in the air, despite the family's sadness.

The relief at the good news was short lived. Aubrey had been feeling very low in spirit due to his worsening health for most of the spring and hadn't been able to face battling back from Italy for his brother's memorial service earlier in the year. But by summer he was feeling a bit better and he and Mary returned to England and went to stay at Highclere in July. It was to be his last visit. He went on to Pixton and consulted various doctors. He had always been slim but now he was looking gaunt; he was nearly totally blind and was running out of energy to battle his lifelong health problems and cope with the loss of his sight.

One of the doctors, clearly a total quack, gave him an extraordinary piece of advice: that having all his teeth removed would restore his sight. Poor Aubrey must have been desperate because he went ahead and had it done. It turned out that he had a duodenal ulcer and the poison spread throughout his weakened body, developing into septicaemia, as had happened to his brother. Elsie rushed to her son's bedside and she and Mary worked in shifts to bring his temperature down, but in an age before the discovery of penicillin, even their nursing couldn't save him. His fine mind became increasingly lost in delirium and he died on 26 September.

Aubrey was just forty-three years old; he left four young

children. His obituaries paid tribute to his irrepressible spirit, and to the amount of life he had managed to pack into such a short span. He was a great linguist and traveller, he fought and negotiated in the Great War, was a maverick MP, championed small nations, especially Albania, wrote poetry and gathered devoted friends from all over the world, thanks to his remarkable charm. His wife, mother, younger brother Mervyn and half-sisters, Winifred, Margaret and Vera, buried him at Brushford Church on Exmoor. The memorial service in Piccadilly overflowed with friends.

His mother, Elsie, had now buried both her husband and her oldest child, but she carried on, brave and stoical, throughout the 1920s. She had lived her life with dignity and purpose and encouraged everyone around her to do likewise. After her beloved son died, she established hospitals, schools and anti-malaria clinics in Albania, as well as a village for refugees called Herbert, after her son.

There had been two deaths in one year and now everyone wanted to focus on Eve's wedding. Mary, Aubrey's widow, and Almina combined their forces to organise it. Mary's help was invaluable, as Almina was also in the process of buying a new house. She and Ian were planning to marry and move to Scotland.

On 8 October 1923, Lady Evelyn Herbert married Mr Brograve Beauchamp in St Margaret's, Westminster. She was followed down the aisle by ten little bridesmaids and given away by her brother, the Earl of Carnarvon. There is a beautiful photo of the couple leaving the church, which almost overflows with happy energy. Brograve, almost a foot taller than Eve, smiles straight at the camera, supremely pleased with his good fortune in marrying the woman he loves. Eve is wearing a highly embellished drop-waisted dress and a fashionable full-length lace veil thrown back over her hair, and is laughing, bending to speak to a well-wisher. She looks uncannily like a younger Almina.

The end of 1923 brought a small announcement in *The Times*: the marriage of Almina, Lady Carnarvon and Lieutenant Colonel Ian Dennistoun had taken place at a register office in London. Eve and Brograve were the only people present. Almina and her new husband spent Christmas alone at the house they had just bought in Scotland, while Eve and Brograve travelled to Highclere to spend the holiday with Catherine and Porchy. Dr Johnnie was there, too. There was an atmosphere of excited anticipation about the baby's birth, but there was to be a departure as well as a new arrival. It was Streatfield's last Christmas serving the family. He had decided to retire and George Fearnside would be stepping up to his place as house steward. Streatfield had nearly forty years of service and, as he had always known he might, he had outlasted Almina, whose arrival he had witnessed back in 1895. Countesses come and Countesses go, but a good house steward stays for life.

The new Lord Carnarvon had a smaller staff than at any time in the house's history. Major Rutherford had been succeeded by one of his sons, but he had insisted on the cuts in expenditure that the 5th Earl had requested just before his death. They were relatively straitened times. But even so, and despite the shudders that went through the social system in the wake of the war, Highclere was still a mutually dependent community of people who lived and worked together, mostly in harmony. Some commentators had predicted after the war that it was the end for the great

English country house. In fact, that proved not to be so. Despite the economic and political upheavals of the Twenties and Thirties, Highclere continued to be the setting for glamorous house parties. Standards were maintained, and indeed, Evelyn Waugh used to say that something was 'very Highclere' to mean 'superbly carried out'. The novelist was an occasional guest: he first married the 5th Earl's niece, Evelyn, Winifred's daughter, and secondly Laura, again Carnarvon's niece, but Aubrey Herbert's daughter.

By 1939 the 6th Earl employed less people at Highclere than his father but the Castle still functioned in much the same way (twenty-three inside servants as well as all the estate workers). It was the Second World War, not the First, that altered British society irrevocably. But for now, Highclere continued much as it ever had.

Almina became a grandmother on 17 January 1924. Catherine gave birth to a healthy baby boy, the next heir to the title and the estate, who was named Henry George Reginald Molyneux Herbert. Laid in the cradle that Almina had used for both his father and his aunt, the new Lord Porchester began his life at Highclere adored by his parents and all the family. Eve and Brograve were down nearly every weekend and Eve and Catherine became very close. New friends began to fill the drawing rooms and stay in the bedrooms. Instead of the old waltzes and polkas, jazz and the Charleston wafted out through the open windows on a summer's evening.

The new Lord Porchester was christened in April 1924. He was taken down to Highclere Church in a smart pony phaeton that his late grandfather had used to drive around the park. Local people from Highclere Newtown and even

Newbury had congregated to cheer on the christening party and fill the church. The bonny baby would grow up much loved and come to adore his grandmother Almina as she grew older.

A year later Eve gave birth to a daughter, Patricia Evelyn, a cousin nearly the same age for the second child of Lord and Lady Carnarvon, who was named Penelope.

Almina delighted in her expanding brood of grand-children, and the gaiety that once again filled her beloved Highclere. When she visited she was proud and nostalgic in equal measure, but her life lay elsewhere now. Her husband was often unwell and Almina devoted herself to nursing him. It was the reminder she needed that nursing was her great purpose in life.

There had been so many things to divert her attention since the end of the Great War: her late husband's worsening health, then his discovery of Tutankhamun's tomb, which catapulted the family into the limelight; and, of course, his dramatic, devastating death. Almina and Ian Dennistoun were to spend much of the next year caught up in a long and damaging court case brought by Ian's ex-wife Dorothy, but Almina never stopped thinking about her vision for another hospital. It took until 1927, but when it was finally opened she named it Alfred House, in honour of her beloved father, the man who had made her whole extraordinary life possible.

Epilogue: Almina's Legacy

One hundred years after the nineteen-year-old girl arrived at Highclere with trunks and travelling cases piled high with dresses, silks, hats, muffs, and dainty shoes, Highclere Castle is still home to the Carnarvons. Built in a glorious flight of fancy by the 3rd Earl, Highclere Castle represented an outstandingly confident tribute to the times.

Almina attended the funerals of both Queen Victoria and her son, Edward VII, as well as two Coronations. She was a generous host, frequently entertaining her family and friends, amongst whom were politicians, adventurers, generals, surgeons, Egyptologists, racehorse trainers, bankers and aviators.

She had no qualms about spending prodigious amounts

of money to get things done. Most of us come up against the frustration of having ideas and aims with insufficient resources to fulfil them. By virtue of her doting and incredibly generous father, a lack of funds was never an obstacle so she 'thought big' in life and, whilst her first husband was alive, certainly succeeded.

During the First World War, Almina devoted an extraordinary amount of energy to helping others, with no thought for the cost in terms of time or money, just a straightforward focus on doing in every moment what was required for each person. She helped to save countless lives, and neither the men she nursed nor their families ever forgot it. Today the only traces of the hospital at Highclere are the stories. Visitors still arrive hoping to share their memories or find out a little more about their relatives.

Almina's support and nursing of her husband saved his life on several occasions, and their long and happy marriage gave him the opportunity to continue working out in Egypt to pursue his passion and obsession. Carnarvon and Carter were a unique team, both mavericks but both focused and persistent. The tomb of Tutankhamun is still the only Ancient Egyptian royal burial site ever found intact, a holy grail revealing untold treasure. Its discovery culminated, like so many good stories, in tragedy at the moment of triumph, but the history of the boy-king has fascinated people from schoolchildren to eminent academics around the world ever since.

Even today, Egyptologists are grateful to Almina for her unstinting support of Howard Carter after the 5th Earl died. She continued to maintain him, his team and the laboratory until he had finished the detailed excavation and recording of every single object. In recognition of her support, the Egyptian government repaid Almina £36,000 in 1936, which reimbursed her expenses for that period. It also transferred some of the investment and the ownership of the discovery into Egyptian hands.

The Rothschild influence is still visible at Highclere in the green silk damask wall hangings in the Drawing Room, which is also where Almina's beautiful piano sits. Stanhope bedroom has retained its red silk wall coverings, part of the redecoration in honour of the Prince of Wales's visit in 1895.

Almina's love of comfort based on the latest in practical technology ensured that Highclere was one of the first houses to enjoy a fully plumbed hot- and cold-water system. The same structure is still used today, even if pipes have been replaced. She also ensured that the installation of electricity and electric light was undertaken early. That meant vastly fewer candles and oil lamps were used, cutting the risk of fire – a hazard which claimed other large houses similar to Highclere.

Almina obviously loved a good party and was as energetic in organising the big weekends at Highclere as any Edwardian hostess. Her passion for the best in rich French cooking still permeates the food eaten here. Highclere's chef offers some of her dishes, such as crab *au gratin* with a generous amount of butter and cream, herb-crusted roast lamb and very rich cold chocolate pots.

The enormous marriage settlement bestowed on Almina by Alfred de Rothschild was a turning point in the Carnarvon family's fortunes, as debts were cleared and the estate put on a much sounder footing. Although many of her husband's properties were sold to pay death duties or debts, Almina's cash and chattels from her father, and the sharp deal she eventually did with the Metropolitan Museum for Lord Carnarvon's collection of Egyptian antiquities, may well have saved Highclere for future generations of her family.

Perhaps it was in the field of medicine that Almina left the greatest legacy. She realised that post-operative and trauma care were as much a part of the healing process as the best surgical techniques and the latest equipment. Almina's understanding of the word 'care' was sincere. She realised that the nursing and physical environment at her Highclere hospital was going to make all the difference to the lives of the patients arriving from the horrors of the Western Front. Almina treated them as if they were country-house guests; nothing but the best food was served, with pastimes and recreation in the Castle State Rooms and park for those that were fit enough. She was a stickler for hygiene: perfect cleanliness in terms of nurses' uniforms and every household surface were the order of the day, with attention paid to the smallest detail. Almina knew that nurses had to deal with psychological as well as physical suffering and her approach was to offer kindness, comfort and an ordered environment. She used all the wonders of Highclere to succeed in this goal, and the many letters from patients and their families are a tribute to her determination to get things right.

She championed the view that poorly trained or loosely managed nurses might take their eyes off the 'care' ball, resulting in poor hygiene and patient morale and a consequent increase in the mortality rate. Her patients were always at the centre of her thoughts and actions. A great believer in new surgical techniques, Almina enjoyed the company of some of the leading practitioners of her time but, even so, she believed that their work should never take precedence over good nursing practice. Severe bacterial infections may have been a major problem in the trenches, but they would not be tolerated at Highclere.

Almina felt a real duty to help and care for the wounded and sick of the war. Her generous spirit and Christian view of the world inspired her to spread her wealth and share its benefits. Small in stature, she glowed with charisma as a powerhouse of energy and willpower.

She lived a long life, as did her son. Consequently the Castle was not subject to further rounds of death duties; it survived intact into the age of a different way of thinking about the old country houses. The welcome and well-timed establishment of English Heritage was a critical development in the preservation of many of the UK's historic houses and their contents.

Highclere Castle, like its alter ego, Downton Abbey, remains an ensemble cast of characters today, just as it was in Almina's time. I have felt so much affection for the 'real' characters such as Aubrey, and his mother Elsie, as I researched their stories. Meeting relatives of the staff from those times has also thrown invaluable shards of light on to life 'downstairs'.

Today, the Castle and estate still house families who have worked and lived here for generations. They pass down stories of predecessors. Retirement is possible but not mandatory. The new generation learns from the old. 'Newcomers' have worked here for fifteen or twenty years and 'proper Castle people' may stay for up to fifty years. Some people think they are coming to work for a short time and find it hard to leave.

The challenge for Highclere is to ensure that the Castle and its estate businesses remain strong enough to preserve their rich heritage. It is the same need to balance business and conservation that confronted Almina. We hope that, if she were here today, she would recognise things and feel a sense of pride that much of what she loved had been preserved and that the spirit of her work was continuing through her great-grandson and his family.

Acknowledgements

I must say thanks and love to my patient husband Geordie, for his help with research and editing. Thanks as well for repeated encouragement from my sisters; Sarah in particular has consistently clarified my thoughts and language. I cannot thank Patricia Leatham enough for her hilarious stories.

Hodder & Stoughton have been enthusiastic partners in this enterprise and also assigned Helen Coyle to support me as a more than able editor who retained a sense of humour during the midnight hours.

Thank you to Kevin Morgan and Mike Blair from ITV who introduced me to Hodder & Stoughton and thereby helped me undertake the book in record time. Part of the research for this whole project was also for the ITV *Countrywise* programme who have sought to visually share Highclere and its Estate with ITV viewers – the real *Downton Abbey*.

The staff at Highclere have been wonderful, supporting me in so many different ways. David Rymill, our archivist, has been unfailingly detailed and knowledgeable, Candice Bauval has organised me and aided my research and Duncan Macdougall has been invaluable and helped me find images and files. Paul and Rob the chefs made sure I ate, and the household staff such as Diana Moyse and Luis Coelho have quietly worked around me trying to tidy and giving me endless cups of tea. Thank you to so many others who have forgiven me for forgetting to do things and to John Gundill who has encouraged my progress whilst he interrupted me, which was always most welcome.

Outside the Castle, the staff at the Bodleian archives were very helpful and expedited my research; thank you to Dr Verena Lepper (Staatliche Museen zu Berlin) who introduced me firstly to Dr Malek, Keeper of the Archive, (Oriental Institute, Oxford) who allowed me to peruse Howard Carter's diaries and secondly to the Metropolitan Museum of New York who allowed me to spend time reading through their archives. Peter Starling at the Royal Army Medical Corp Museum was very helpful suggesting books to read and aiding the research into First World War records.

I am also grateful that Julian Fellowes was inspired to write a series *Downton Abbey* based around Highclere Castle which Carnival Films produced and Peter Fincham (ITV Chief Executive) took the bold decision to back. It has been an extraordinary journey. So many people have come to love Highclere and be enthralled by its television alter ego.

Transcript of Letters

p. 189 – Letter from Charles Clout to Lady Almina, written on the night of his wedding in 1918, from the Lake House on the Highclere Estate where he and Mary Weekes, Almina's secretary, honeymooned).

The Lake House
July 2nd

My Dear Lady Carnarvon

My Dear Fairy Godmother I should like to call you, as it is as such that I should always think of you, I am trying in this little note to express some of my thanks to you for all you have done, and are doing, for Mary and me. I cannot attempt to convey to you all I feel in a letter, but I will always try to live life to the great trust you have placed in me and will do my best to repay you, by every means in my power, for the great help that you have given me in my start in life.

May I thank you again for the splendid presents you have given me. I am delighted with the links and studs which are charming, and with the plate, I think I shall never want to dine out with such beautiful things to use at home, and also for the care and trouble you have given in arranging the details of the wedding for me and for your very kind loan of this house.

You will see from the few things I have mentioned for which I am indebted to you, how impossible it would be for me to attempt to thank you for everything in this note, but I hope you will believe me when I repeat that my life shall be an attempt to prove worthy of your help and trust.

With very best wishes and love from
Yours Sincerely
Charles W Clout.

p.190 – Letter from Mary Weekes to Lady Almina, written the day after her wedding to Charles Clout

July 3rd
Lake House
Wednesday

(note to top left side – "you must forgive this odd paper but the white note paper has not arrived")

My dearest Little Lady

Thank you so much for your sweet letter which I was so pleased to get this morning.

How can I even try to thank you for all you have done for me. I just long to tell you what I feel about your wonderful love and affection, but alas! No words of mine could adequately express what I really feel. Had I been Eve you could not have done more. What a wonderful memory

I have to carry into the future and if I can only be half as good and kind as you are I shall be pleased. I hope I shall always be a credit to the kindest little lady I know, who has indeed been a mother to me for the last 7 years and I know will go on being so in the future.

I think Charles wrote you last evening after tea. I was rather tired so had a bath and went and lay down.

It is glorious down here and there is nothing one could want for. The food, care and attention are all perfect.

I am going to write to Lord Carnarvon, he was so sweet to me on Tuesday and made one long to know him better. What a wonderful father and mother Eve and Porchy have got and it made me wonder on Tuesday if they realized it.

Well my darling little lady a thousand thanks for all you have and are doing for me.

With love from us both

Yours affectionately
Mary (C)

Picture Acknowledgements

Most of the photographs: © Highclere Castle Archive.

Additional sources:
© Alamy: 4 (top right), 26 (bottom left). By kind permission of the Clout Family: 20. © Corbis: 29 (top). © Country Life Picture Library: 14. With special thanks to Country Life Magazine who kindly donated these photographs to the Highclere Castle Archive: 16 (bottom), 30 (top right), 32 (top). © Getty Images: 7 (top), 27, 28. © Mary Evans Picture Library: 2 (top), 5 (top left), 29 (bottom left & right), 31 (top). © National Portrait Gallery, London: 4 (left), 7 (bottom). © TopFoto.co.uk: 5 (top right), 26 (top), 30 (top left & bottom left), 31 (bottom), 32 (bottom). © V&A Images: 1/ photo LaFayette.

Bibliography

This is not an exclusive list but the following may interest those who wish to pursue areas of historical interest further:

Asher, Michael, *Lawrence: The Uncrowned King of Arabia*, Viking: London, 1998

Blunden, Edmund, *Undertones of War*, Penguin: London, 1972

Borden, Mary, *Forbidden Zone: A Nurse's Impression of the First World War*, Hesperus: London, 2008

Budge, Wallis, *Tutankhamen: Amenism, Atenism and Egyptian Montheism*, Revised edition, Dover: Egypt, 2003

Campbell, Captain David, MC., *Forward the Rifles: The War Diary of an Irish Soldier, 1914–1918*, The History Press: Gloucestershire, 2009

Carter, Howard, *Tutankhamen: The Politics of Discovery*, Revised edition, Libri: Oxford, 2001

Carter, Howard and Mace, Arthur, *The Discovery of the Tomb of Tutankhamen*, Revised edition, Dover: Egypt, 1985

Cushin, Harvey, *From a Surgeon's Journal*, Little, Brown: London, 1936

Davenport-Hines, Richard, *Ettie: The Intimate Life and Dauntless Spirit of Lady Desborough*, Weidenfeld & Nicolson: London, 2008

Edwards, Amelia, *A Thousand Miles Up the Nile*, Routledge: London, 1889

Eksteins, Modris, *Rites of Spring: The Great War and the Birth of the Modern Age*, Houghton Mifflin: Chicago, 1999

FitzHerbert, Margaret, *The Man Who Was Greenmantle: Biography of Aubrey Herbert*, John Murray: London, 1983

Hattersley, Roy, *Borrowed Time: The Story of Britain Between the Wars*, Little, Brown: London, 2007

Havilland, Geoffrey de, *Sky Fever: The Autobiography of Sir Geoffrey de Havilland*, Airlife Publications: Shrewsbury, 1979

James, T. G. H., *Howard Carter: The Path to the Discovery*, Revised edition, Tauris Parke: London, 2003

Jarrett, Derek, *Pirton – A Village in Anguish: The Story of the 30 Men from a Hertfordshire Village in World War One*, Pirton Local History Group: Pirton, 2009

Leatham, Patricia E., *The Short Story of a Long Life*, Wilton: Connecticut, 2009

Lewis, Bernard, *The Middle East: 2000 Years of History from the Rise of Christianity to the Present Day*, Revised edition, Phoenix: London, 2001

Macdonald, Lyn, *They Called it Passchendaele: Story of the Third Battle of Ypres and of the Men Who Fought in it*, Penguin: London, 1993

Maclaughlin, Redmond, *The Royal Army Medical Corps*, Leo Cooper: Yorkshire, 1972

Mansfield, Peter, *A History of the Middle East*, Viking: London, 1991

Melotte, Edward, Ed., originally by an anonymous MP, *Mons Anzac and Kut: By an MP*, Pen & Sword Books: Chicago, Revised edition, 2009

Messenger, Charles, *A Call to Arms: The British Army 1914–1918*, Weidenfeld & Nicolson, 2005

Morton, Frederic, *The Rothschilds: A Family Portrait*, Readers Union: London, 1963

Owen, H. and Bell, John, *Wilfred Owen: Collected Letters*, Oxford University Press: Oxford, 1967

Reeves, John, *The Rothschilds: The Financial Rulers of Nations*, Gordon Press: Surrey, 1975

Reeves, Nicholas, *The Complete Tutankhamun: The King, The Tomb, The Royal Treasure*, Thames & Hudson: London, 1995

Roberts, Sydney C., *Adventures with Authors*, Cambridge University Press: Cambridge, 1966

Shephard, Ben, *A War of Nerves: Soldiers and Psychiatrists, 1914–1994*, Jonathan Cape: London, 2000

Stone, Norman, *World War One: A Short History*, Penguin: London, 2008

Taylor, A. J. P., *The Struggle for Mastery in Europe: 1848–1918*, Oxford University Press: Oxford, 1973

Weintraub, Stanley, *Edward the Caresser: The Playboy Prince who Became Edward VII*, Simon & Schuster: London, 2001

Whitehead, Ian, *Doctors in the Great War*, Pen & Sword Books: Chicago, 1999

Winstone, H. V. F., *Howard Carter and the Discovery of the Tomb of Tutankhamun*, Constable: London, 1991

I have been lucky to have had help from kind experts at the following archives:

The British Museum Archives
The Bodleian Archives
The Metropolitan Museum Archives
Griffiths Institute
Winchester Archives
Rothschild Archives
The Times Archives
Highclere Castle Archives

Index